Employment Relations in Britain:

25 Years of the Advisory, Conciliation and Arbitration Service

Employment Relations in Britain:

25 Years of the Advisory, Conciliation and Arbitration Service

Edited by

BRIAN TOWERS *and* WILLIAM BROWN

ISBN: 0-631-22326-6

First published 2000

Blackwell Publishers Ltd
108 Cowley Road
Oxford OX4 1JF, UK

Blackwell Publishers Inc
350 Main Street
Malden, Massachusetts 02148, USA

British Library Cataloguing in Publication Data has been applied for

Library of Congress Cataloging in Publication Data has been applied for

Typeset by Downdell, Oxford

Contents

Preface   vii

Introduction
ACAS's first quarter century
William Brown and Brian Towers   ix

1
Setting the pace or running alongside? ACAS and the changing
employment relationship
W. R. Hawes   1

2
Building bridges and settling differences: collective conciliation
and arbitration under ACAS
John Goodman   31

3
Doing more with less: ACAS and individual conciliation
Linda Dickens   67

4
Operating with style: the work of the ACAS conciliator in
individual employment rights cases
Gill Dix   93

5
Learning through ACAS: the case of union recognition
Stephen Wood   123

6
Supporting collective bargaining: some comparative reflections
Bob Hepple   153

7
After collective bargaining? ACAS in the age of human
resource management
John Purcell   163

Conclusions
The best and the worst of times: ACAS's survival and progress,
1974–2000 and beyond
Brian Towers   181

Contributors   197

Index   199

Preface

The past quarter of a century has seen dramatic change in the landscape of the world of work, particularly in employment relations. ACAS has been, and remains, a key player in the development of employment relations through its preventative and advisory role and involvement in the resolution of both collective and individual employment rights issues.

The twenty fifth anniversary of ACAS and the new millennium provides a fitting context in which to reflect on the past and comment on the future of work, and it is with pleasure that we welcome the collection of papers in this volume.

The contributors were invited by ACAS to reflect on this period of employment relations and consider our role. The authors have provided in depth and critical analyses of work and ACAS's role within it. This historical reflection is of considerable value, but even more valuable are the insights and reflections about the future. ACAS looks forward to meeting the challenges posed by the forthcoming decades of employment relations in an ever changing environment.

ACAS very much appreciates the contributions to this anniversary book and the considerable time all the contributors have given in producing their careful analyses and interpretations. We particularly appreciate the work of the editors—Professor Brian Towers and Professor Willy Brown—for the skilful way in which they have knitted together the volume, and for their personal commentaries in the opening and concluding sections.

Cecilia Wells OBE
Acting Chairwoman

Derek Evans
ACAS Chief Conciliator

ACAS Council:

Brendan Barber, Deputy General Secretary, Trades Union Congress
Professor William Brown, Montague Burton Professor of Industrial Relations, Cambridge University
John Cridland, Deputy Director General, Confederation of British Industry
John Edmonds, General Secretary, GMB
Janet Gaymer, Head of Employment Law, Simmons & Simmons
Bill Knox, Partner, A F McPherson and Co Builders
Bill Morris, General Secretary, Transport and General Workers Union
Professor Tony Pointon, Case Consultant, Association of University Teachers
Bruce Warman, Director of Personnel, Vauxhall Motors
Jan Williams, Chief Executive, Bro Taf Health Authority

Introduction
ACAS's first quarter century

William Brown and Brian Towers

The last quarter of the last century of the second millennium has witnessed profoundly destabilising sociopolitical, economic and technological changes. Closely associated with these changes has been a transformation in the employment relationship. This has been a quieter transformation but a transformation for all that and crucially important, in its consequences, for most people for the larger part of their lives. This is not the place to add to the vast literature on the changing employment relationship.[1] It has, however, been closely linked to a weakening of the influence of employees and their representative institutions and the growing influence of global corporations as well as that of the regional and international extensions of national political authority.

This internationalism and globalisation has created powerful, or at least influential, agencies in the fields of economic, social and employment regulation. These agencies have survived many crises and some remain at the centre of fierce controversies over their purposes and consequences. But they have, for the most part, survived, and for long periods.

At national level, state agencies involved in the formulation and implementation of labour and employment policies have, in many countries, faced the consequences of change in different ways. Some have led, others have coped, and far from all have survived changes in government and ideology. In Britain, the Advisory, Conciliation and Arbitration Service (ACAS) remains as one of the more notable survivors. Yet a casual observer could be forgiven for thinking that much of the justification for ACAS's creation in 1974 has now gone.[2] Since it was first established, strike incidence

---

[1] For Britain, the last twenty years has been exhaustively monitored, initially in the three Workplace Industrial Relations Surveys in 1980, 1984 and 1990. These were followed by the 1998 Workplace Employee Relations Survey, recently published (and analysed in the context of the entire period from 1980 to 1998) in two volumes (Cully *et al.* 1999; Millward *et al.* 2000). The findings of these surveys are discussed throughout this volume but especially in Chapter 1 and the Conclusions. Other countries have carried out, or are considering, similar surveys, notably Australia and Ireland.

[2] It was initially founded as the Conciliation and Arbitration Service (CAS) in 1974, and after its conversion to ACAS in 1975, was established as an independent, tripartite, statutory body under the Employment Protection Act of the same year. Northern Ireland has a separate body, the Labour Relations Agency, with functions very similar to those of ACAS.

has tumbled from the highest to the lowest levels since British records began. The coverage of collective bargaining has halved. Trade-union membership has fallen by over a third.

Despite this apparent collapse of collectivism, the demand for ACAS's services is greater than ever. In part this is because, so far as collective bargaining is concerned, ACAS's energies are now more committed to anticipating industrial disputes at an earlier stage than before. Arbitrations may be at a historically low level, but conciliation in collective disputes has not fallen in step with strikes and ACAS staff are busier than ever in propagating good practice. More significant in terms of its workload has been the rapid recent growth in cases concerning individual employees. The number of complaints going to ACAS as part of the Employment Tribunal process has passed through 100,000 a year and is still growing. Contributing to this has been the rapid rise in the number of statutory rights available to employees in recent years, which has increased ten-fold since ACAS was first established. But ACAS has also seen an acceleration in demand for its less formal individual services, by means of telephone advice via its regional Public Enquiry Points. By the end of 1999 the number of calls dealt with per year had passed 700,000, and had increased by a third over the previous year.

One way of putting what has happened would be to say that the recent growth in demand for ACAS services has not been *despite* the decline of collectivism in employment, but *because of* that decline. It has been the retreat in the coverage of collective bargaining and of both trade unions and employers' associations, with their established channels of representation and grievance settlement, which has forced so many individual employees and small employers to turn to ACAS for conciliation and advice. Adding to this, there has also been an important shift in the legislative emphasis on the part of successive governments, of both parties, since the late 1970s. They have increased or retained the legal constraints on collective bargaining, but have widened the range of individual statutory rights of employees, in whose administration ACAS plays so active a part.

These developments were very evident when an invited group of academics, arbitrators, practitioners and officials met at Templeton College, Oxford in September 1999, to discuss ACAS's first 25 years. The main issue was not how ACAS survived through often politically difficult times. It was, much more positively, how ACAS's role had changed and grown. The papers presented at that conference form the major part of this book. They are brought together and augmented here to review past experience, and to take stock of where ACAS stands now, and where it might be heading.

We begin, in Chapter 1, with an insider's review, by Bill Hawes, of the economic, political and industrial relations changes since the 1960s and their impact upon the formation, development and policy responses of ACAS. Understandably, perhaps, the agency's policy response to political change has, for the most part, been pragmatic, even cautious. But, as Hawes concludes, there are now some signs that ACAS may now be responding to government initiatives in a more proactive, reforming style. In any case, ACAS will be required, even under budgetary constraints, to develop to meet two new, probably exacting, demands. Under the 1999 Employment Relations Act's (ERA) trade union recognition procedure it will be involved, with the Central Arbitration Committee (CAC) in encouraging voluntary rather than imposed agreements. It will also have the responsibility for the operation of the arbitration alternative to taking unfair dismissal claims to the increasingly hard-pressed employment tribunals.

Hawes reminds us that ACAS did not invent its most newsworthy activity, that of dealing with collective disputes. John Goodman, in Chapter 2, describes how ACAS was born of a long tradition of state sponsored conciliation stretching back into the last quarter of the nineteenth century. This shaped its constitution in a way that defended both independence of government and impartiality between employers and unions. The chapter describes the development of collective conciliation over the period, years in which the relative bargaining power of the protagonists, and government sympathy towards collective bargaining, have changed substantially. It then analyses the development and practice of voluntary arbitration, with the author able to bring the insights of considerable personal experience.

It is appropriate to turn next to the dominant part of ACAS's activity in terms of resources, the provision of conciliation in individual employment rights disputes. In Chapter 3 Linda Dickens discusses this growing area of activity. Drawing on a wide range of research, she is able to explore the nature of ACAS settlements, how they have developed, and how they are achieved. Financial pressures to increase the caseload per conciliator may be distorting the quality of the justice delivered. She suggests that the imminent introduction of a less formal, arbitrated procedure, in part inspired by her own research, may be motivated and impaired by similar pressures. Budgetary restrictions may thus be reducing the practical value of the many new statutory individual rights that Parliament has provided.

What lies behind the conciliation process? What do conciliators do? In Chapter 4 Gill Dix draws on a series of extended interviews with conciliators across ACAS regional offices to develop a picture of the roles that they play and the way they play them. As her vividly illustrated account makes clear, conciliators adopt very different styles in pursuing their delicate task as impartial broker in an often highly emotional power relationship. ACAS conciliation has dealt with over a million cases in its first 25 years, and this chapter provides rich insights into the nature and value of this work.

The early years of ACAS's history were made extremely difficult by the part it was required to play in the statutory trade union recognition procedure that was introduced in 1975 and repealed five years later. Will the recognition procedures of the 1999 Employment Relations Act once again compromise ACAS's independence? In Chapter 5 Stephen Wood draws lessons from that early experience and argues that they have mostly been applied in the shaping of its future role under the new legislation. Indeed, he suggests that the 1999 Act may enhance the potential for ACAS to assist in building the partnership relationships at the workplace to which the present government is committed.

The implications of the 1999 legislation for ACAS are discussed in greater legal detail in Chapter 6 by Bob Hepple. By standing back, as it were, and discussing how emerging British procedures fit into a comparative international perspective, he is able to suggest how ACAS's role might develop as the 1999 Act takes effect. The government remains unwilling to return collective bargaining to the centre of labour relations policy and reluctant to respond to European pressures to provide consultation rights. The legislation itself is weakened by its unnecessarily legalistic method of enforcing compliance on employers who refuse to abide by the new procedures. The role of ACAS in promoting voluntary recognition agreements will, he concludes, be more important than ever.

The 'Advisory' part of ACAS's title was a somewhat later addition, but it has come to be a central part of its mission. In Chapter 7, John Purcell, who has studied this aspect of ACAS work for some years, describes how the advisory role has changed and developed. He discusses how far the initial collective bargaining orientation of ACAS's advisory mediation role has adapted to a world increasingly concerned with the more individualistic approach of human resource management. It may also be that ACAS's future in disseminating good practice lies increasingly in smaller firms where trade unions are unheard of.

Finally, in the concluding editorial there is a return to some of the themes discussed earlier by Bill Hawes, placing ACAS's 25 years in the context of the accompanying, far-reaching changes that have occurred in industrial relations. Drawing together the ways in which its role has changed Brian Towers speculates on how ACAS's functions and policies could shift in response to further developments. These developments, as other authors have discussed in earlier chapters, include ACAS's new statutory duties. The progress of the European Union's (EU) social dimension also continues to influence British employment law and practice. European Works Councils have already imported the concept of social partnership into British employment relations. This concept could yet be strengthened by the EU-wide extension of national works councils. This highly speculative, indeed controversial, note may be a fitting way to conclude a volume published at the beginning of a new millennium.

ACKNOWLEDGEMENTS

The Editors acknowledge with gratitude those who have made it possible to adapt and extend the original papers to form a published volume which we hope will inform present and future discussion and debate on the role of ACAS both outside and within its doors. First and foremost we are grateful to Peter Syson and his successor Andrew Wareing who, as ACAS's Director of Strategy, conceived and implemented the idea of a 25th Anniversary appraisal of ACAS's contribution to public policy. In this they were much helped by Roger Undy in organising the conference at Templeton College, Oxford. The Conference was expertly presided over by John Hougham, the then Chairman of ACAS whom we wish well in what promises to be an active retirement. We were also greatly assisted in the co-ordinating, reading and revision processes by Gill Dix, Head of Research and Evaluation at ACAS who also managed to contribute a chapter. Thanks are of course specially due to the authors who rose to the occasion with chapters of originality and insight with the added bonus of ranking them expertly, and in good time. Bill Hawes here needs a special mention. His contribution was not commissioned until January yet he managed to catch up with the rest of the team. We must also acknowledge the role of Blackwell's editing and production staff—notably Jane Croft and Mark O'Hare—who maintained their usual high standards, and courtesy, within the tightest of schedules.

Finally, it is of some note that this is the first time that the two leading British academic industrial relations journals—the Industrial Relations Journal and the British Journal of Industrial Relations—have come together in the editing of a joint publication. We hope it will not be the last and that the outcome is a book which will be both interesting and useful to those concerned with the role of public agencies in the development of industrial and employment relationships which combine fairness with effectiveness.

REFERENCES

Cully, Mark, Stephen Woodland, Andrew O'Reilly and Gill Dix, (1999), *Britain at Work: As depicted by the 1998 Workplace Employee Relations Survey*. London and New York: Routledge.

Millward, Neil, Alex Bryson and John Forth (2000), *All Change at Work: British employment relations 1980–1998, as portrayed by the Workplace Industrial Relations Survey series*. London and New York: Routledge.

1

Setting the pace or running alongside? ACAS and the changing employment relationship

W. R. Hawes

INTRODUCTION

ACAS was created out of earlier government industrial relations services in the 1970s, a time of great complaint about the condition of British industrial relations, and its consequences for the economy and for social cohesion. The 1970s also saw the creation of the British Workplace Industrial Relations (WIRS) series, arguably one of the main success stories of postwar employment research in the English-speaking world.

Both the WIRS series, through its published reports and academic secondary analyses, and ACAS, through its annual reports, have chronicled what has on many accounts been a remarkable and unexpected transformation of many aspects of British industrial relations since 1980. Indeed the changes have been so marked that many of the policy and intellectual underpinnings to ACAS operations—and to the initial WIRS design—have been called into question. This chapter reports on and reflects on some of these changes and the puzzles they bring. Parts draw also on the author's experiences and memories of working in the Ministry of Labour and its successors in the 1960s and 1970s, and with ACAS between 1982 and 1998.[1]

THE BRITISH 'SYSTEM' OF INDUSTRIAL RELATIONS BEFORE THE 1970s

Origins and principles

There was never in any simple way a 'system' of industrial relations in Britain. While the word appeared in the academic literature about industrial relations which

---

[1] Memories are, of course, notoriously untrustworthy. Others might offer different accounts.

appeared before and immediately after the Second World War, few of its authors bothered to say precisely what they meant by it, or offered any brief or tidy account of how the term might be applied.[2] Nonetheless, underlying the immense variety and muddle of reality to be observed, one kind of model came to be widely accepted (albeit cautiously and often implicitly) as providing both intellectual underpinning and a guide to good practice and future policy. This began in the view that conflict at work was inevitable, permanent and incorrigible. Although its form, volume and consequences varied at different times, conflict did, and would in the future, arise habitually between workers, between workers and managers, managers and managers, managers and owners and, in modern economies with high degrees of interdependence, between all these and consumers and other interest groups. Quite why this inevitability arose was debated.

Some saw the cause in particular historical developments; some in much broader general and inescapable conflicts between capital and labour in the processes of economic development. Yet others saw the answer in sociobiology: human beings were essentially competitive, in working relationships as elsewhere. Whatever the reason, disagreements on a sufficient scale to inconvenience not only those directly involved, but also wider groups up to and including the whole of society was assumed.

A second element in the model was that although force and the exercise of power would necessarily underpin conflict, they would also play a part in discouraging and controlling its most dramatic manifestations, as they did in other areas of social and economic life. But by themselves they were not enough. If social breakdown was to be avoided, acceptable and accessible mechanisms and procedures were needed through which disagreements could be mediated and perhaps resolved.

Thus far the implicit model was no different from that underpinning industrial relations arrangements in many other countries. The third aspect, however, was more idiosyncratic. In Britain, except on a small range of issues, particularly health and safety, private rather than public systems of negotiation and adjudication rapidly came to be seen as much the most effective way of resolving industrial disputes. Through the nineteenth century and into the first years of the twentieth, trade union activities, although undertaken with increasing vigour and covering a growing part of a greatly expanded urban population, generally fell outside the ambit allowed by common law and statute law. Political and judicial agreement on whether and how the law should be reformed, and how it should be applied, proved difficult to achieve. The passage of the Trade Disputes Act of 1906, after substantial Parliamentary confusion and fudge, clarified matters to the extent that trade union calls for industrial action generally remained unlawful, but allowed that those

---

[2] The most notable examples were Flanders and Clegg (1954), a text in widespread use for teaching purposes until the late 1960s, and Clegg's revision (Clegg, 1970), neither of which included definitions or index references for the idea of a 'system' although the term was used in the titles of both books.

responsible would, in certain circumstances, be given immunity from civil actions brought by employers and, perhaps, other interested parties. Even so the courts remained difficult places in which to argue a trade-union case.

Partly as a result, collective bargaining between employers and trade unions was developed as the main way of mediating conflict at work. Employers and their organisations reached written procedural agreements with trade unions and their federations which defined their relationships with each other, their respective functions, arrangements for agreeing terms and conditions, and methods of resolving disputes. With exceptions in very large companies, most major agreements were reached at industry or regional level, rather than within enterprises and workplaces. Many lasted essentially unchanged for decades. Although often long and detailed, very few agreements were designed to be legally binding. Many allowed the parties wide options and freedoms in choosing whether or not to go to successive stages. Indeed many, for what the parties considered good reason, incorporated elisions and contradictions which would have made them void for uncertainty in any legal forum. These procedure agreements, the heart of the British 'system', were supplemented by agreements on substantive terms and conditions which changed at frequent but irregular intervals.

The growth and spread of these arrangements was such that, by the mid-1930s, the Ministry of Labour could proclaim, in the most self confident way, that:

> collective bargaining between employers and workpeople has, for many years, been recognised in this country as the method best adapted to the needs of industry and to the demands of the national character, for the settlement of the conditions of employment of the workpeople in industry ... collective bargaining ... has discharged its important functions, on the whole, so smoothly and efficiently and withal so unobtrusively, that the extent of its influence is apt to be, if not altogether overlooked, at least underestimated. It has produced a highly coordinated system of agreed working arrangements, affecting in the aggregate large numbers of workpeople and defining, often with great precision, almost every aspect of industrial relations (Ministry of Labour, 1934).[3]

Along with this emphasis on collective bargaining went a fourth aspect of the model: a particular view of the functions of trade unions. Unions were seen as essentially protective, *reactive* entities.[4] So far as change at the workplace was concerned the assumption was that employers would initiate, and that trade unions would, as necessary, react to protect their members. Employers would not offer, and trade unions would not want, or accept, joint responsibility for management decisions and actions. Trade unions came to be seen as a sometimes inconvenient but a still

---

[3] These words were repeated, almost verbatim, in the Ministry's *Industrial Relations Handbook* in 1944 (Ministry of Labour and National Service, 1944). See also the Conclusions in this volume, p. 183.

[4] Other approaches to trade unionism were widely discussed. Some proponents of workers' control argued for the extension of collective bargaining into the boardroom as well as the workplace. Guild socialism had its supporters. But in Britain these ideas attracted relatively little support. Most unions and employers recognised, of course, that there were issues and areas on which conflict did not, and generally would not arise. Joint consultative and like machinery was often devised to deal with these; but again in nearly every case it was management which decided on action.

legitimate and permanent opposition, rather than as a prospective partner in a management coalition. Collective bargaining was thus not expected, and certainly not designed, to lead to and extend to, any significant union action and involvement in management control.

These two aspects lead, implicitly, to a fifth characteristic. Success in industry and commerce was regarded as being in the hands of the managers and owners of business, not in the hands of labour. Trade unions could complain about management inadequacy but would take no responsibility for correcting it. The test of successful industrial relations arrangements was not therefore whether businesses prospered, or were efficient, innovative and inventive. In the eyes of most commentators 'successful' industrial relations meant little more than an absence of industrial action. At a time when much, perhaps most, employment involved routinised physical labour, under closely controlled conditions, this was an understandable view.

The success of this 'system' gave further reinforcement to a widespread view, particularly among trade union officials but increasingly shared by employers and governments, that recourse to the law and the courts on employment matters could only add uncertainty to what should be predictability arising from frequent contacts and shared understandings. At most, relying on legal advice and the courts in resolving employment problems was a second best: usually it was found to be positively unhelpful. Where laws were needed—for example to create Wages Councils to set minimum wages in sectors where collective bargaining had not yet developed— their preferred aim was not just to provide minimum protection but to encourage the parties to move beyond what was hoped would be temporary statutory arrangements towards creating their own private bargaining arrangements. Although other industrial relations models were sometimes argued, both to describe and understand practice and policy, these found few prominent adherents. The British 'system' came to be seen as founded on industry-wide collective bargaining, reactive trade unionism and avoidance, so far as possible, of the law and courts. The object was the containment and control of conflict.

Support mechanisms: conciliation, mediation and arbitration

Government conciliation and mediation services existed to support this developing system from the end of the nineteenth century. Ministerial powers to offer conciliation were set out in the Conciliation Act of 1896, and later in the Industrial Courts Act, 1919.[5] The essence of the arrangements set out there remains, in re-enacted form, the basis of state conciliation arrangements today. The 1896 Act

---

[5]   Initially operated within the Board of Trade. The Ministry of Labour was created in 1917, replaced by the Department of Employment and Productivity in 1968, renamed the Department of Employment in 1970 and abolished in 1995, when its industrial relations responsibilities reverted to the Department of Trade and Industry.

provided that where 'a difference exists or is apprehended between an employer, or any class of employers, and workmen, or between different classes of workmen' the Minister could:

> ... take such steps as may be seen expedient [to him] for the purpose of enabling the parties ... to meet together ... under the presidency of a chairman mutually agreed upon or nominated by the [minister] or by some other person or body, with a view to the amicable settlement of the difference; or ... on application of employers and workmen interested, and after taking into consideration the existence and adequacy of means available for conciliation in the district or trade and the circumstances of the case, appoint a person or persons to act as conciliator or as a board of conciliation. (Conciliation Act, 1896: s2).

The policy of successive governments, through the 1920s into the 1970s, was clear: these conciliation powers should be used to foster, promote and facilitate the growth and smooth operation of voluntary collective bargaining, not to provide alternative or substitute arrangements. Conciliation was generally offered only when 'the agreed procedure in the industry had been exhausted' or, if there was no agreed procedure, after the parties had attempted to resolve their difficulties. Crucially, where conciliation took place, 'it was in effect a continuation of the process of collective bargaining with outside assistance'. To ensure that formal agreements were supported, conciliators were generally reluctant to become involved in unofficial and unconstitutional disputes. 'The intention of conciliation [was] to help the parties concerned to find a mutually acceptable basis for the settlement of the difference'. Another essential feature was the 'independence and impartiality' of the conciliator. 'In their position of neutrality the Ministry's conciliators cannot be identified with either one side or the other. The aim is to help both sides reach a settlement for which the parties are then responsible'. Partly to ensure this, services were provided free to the parties at the point of delivery and all costs were met by general taxation. Conciliation took no set form, varying in formality and method according to circumstances, the judgement of the conciliator and the preferences of the parties. Further, in line with the overall ethos of collective bargaining arrangements, the minister had no powers to compel the parties to a dispute to take part in conciliation. Conciliation was 'in essence a voluntary process' (Ministry of Labour, 1965, pp. 94–96).

The 1896 and 1919 Acts also empowered the minister to appoint arbitrators and to conduct inquiries into industrial disputes. Both powers were again operated with a view to reinforcing rather than replacing the parties' own arrangements. Outside special arrangements created during and shortly after the two world wars, the minister had no power to proceed without the agreement of all parties: 'the consent of the parties is thus essential both for the reference of the matter for settlement and to the form of arbitration to which the matter is to be referred'. Further, the minister could not make a reference unless he was clear that the existing voluntary arrangements had failed to bring a settlement. 'The purpose of this provision [was, once again] to ensure that existing negotiating arrangements in organised industry are properly used' (Ministry of Labour, 1965, p. 101).

The minister was also empowered to inquire into industrial disputes, by setting up 'courts of inquiry' as 'a means of informing Parliament and the public of the facts and underlying causes of [a major] dispute', or, in cases of more local interest, 'committees of inquiry'. In these cases, the court or committee, while not acting as conciliator or arbitrator, would generally make recommendations about how the dispute might be settled for consideration by the parties. Again, participation of the parties in the inquiry, and their acceptance of its recommendations, was voluntary.[6]

To undertake conciliation and to advise ministers on when and where to initiate broader inquiries, the Ministry of Labour operated a conciliation service staffed by civil servants. It was provided through a small regional network which dealt with local and regional problems, backed up by a headquarters branch which involved itself in national, high profile disputes. Conciliation staff were supplemented by a small personnel management advisory service, originally created in the Ministry of Aircraft Production during the Second World War and transferred to the Ministry of Labour on the former's abolition. This had broader advisory and consultative functions relating to the efficiency of work organisation at factory and establishment level and was staffed by people who had been recruited direct from industry. The two services long co-existed as separate, complementary operations. Integration of the two, which shared a belief in the promotion of joint management–union decision-making machinery, but whose priorities appear otherwise to have been somewhat different, began only in the 1960s and has only recently been fully achieved.[7]

By the 1950s, then, the state's industrial relations services, together with such law as was thought necessary to define the broad boundaries within which employer and trade unions might operate, offered discretion in use, diversity in form and variety in procedure and method. The possibilities for state involvement ranged over a wide continuum, from what has sometimes been called 'tactical' conciliation or mediation, in which the third party operates entirely within a bargaining context and procedures defined and agreed by the parties, through to 'strategic' conciliation and mediation in which the third party seeks to structure or restructure the situation of management and unions with the aim of creating a more positive environment in which they can relate to each other (Kerr, 1964). Within the constraints set by an overall policy in which smoothly-operating collective bargaining was the aim, conciliation and arbitration services offered both 'maintenance' services to existing arrangements and at least the possibility of more creative, inventive help to parties who wished to introduce reforms.

---

[6] There were other powers. For example ministers could and sometimes did, set up inquiries into long-standing industrial relations issues under their own general ministerial powers. Once again the participation of the parties and their acceptance of any recommendations was voluntary.

[7] A number of now elderly accounts of the conciliation arrangements are available, notably Sharp, (1950) and Wedderburn and Davies (1969). No history of the Personnel Management Advisory Service appears yet to have been published.

THE SYSTEM UNDER THREAT

The system and its critics

During and after the Second World War this 'system' of industrial relations was greatly extended beyond its coverage in the 1930s, with government encouragement to trade union recognition and a growing incorporation of trade union officials into the processes of central government. Officially recorded disputes remained low, to the point where academic commentators began to talk of the 'withering of the strike' (Ross and Hartman, 1960). The future of the system was widely seen as secure.

From the mid-1950s onwards, however, major criticisms began to surface. Pre-war governments had had only very limited ambitions when it came to managing the economy. They had had neither the necessary economic ideas, nor the necessary economic data to attempt more than the broadest economic management. Post-war governments, with new economic tools, took a much more interventionist course with publicly stated aims of developing and maintaining full employment and positive economic growth while ensuring low inflation. While initially real incomes, money incomes and inflation rose at a moderate rate, by the mid-1950s there were signs of growing inflation and alarming indications, too, that Britain's record of economic growth and innovation was beginning to fall behind those of her competitors. The response of successive governments was the creation of a succession of initiatives on incomes and prices and economic growth generally, some under the wing of a range of new tripartite bodies and committees, most notably the National Economic Development Council set up in 1962. Industry-wide bargaining continued as the mainstay of the system, although in some sectors, notably engineering, there began to be growing concern about tensions between local negotiating arrangements in companies and establishments and the broad frameworks of rules and agreements set by industry negotiators and central bargaining arrangements.

Through the 1960s, more vigorous criticisms emerged. The numbers of disputes began to rise, and public concern about the consequences of some of these, particularly unofficial and unconstitutional stoppages in the docks and car industry, began to grow. The suspicion grew, among economists inside and outside government, that collective bargaining arrangements were leading directly to growing inflation, via the increasing use of comparisons between sectors in pay negotiations. All this, together with a number of judicial decisions which called into question the extent of immunities given to union officials, when initiating and leading industrial action,[8] lead all the main political parties to argue that reforms were needed.

The second half of the 1960s saw a further extension of prices and incomes policies, including the creation of the tripartite National Board for Prices and Incomes

---

[8] Wedderburn (1971) remains a lively guide to events as they were seen at the time.

(NBPI) and a Royal Commission on Trade Unions and Employers' Associations (the Donovan Commission). The NBPI is widely credited with developing what were then new methods of inquiry in British industrial relations research, based on systematic survey and case study methods,[9] as well as increasing official and public awareness of the need for new, reliable nationally representative data on earnings.[10] Some of its general reports, for example on payment systems, produced important new evidence which became standard references for some years. But the nature of the Board's work meant that it never produced a general statement assessing the whole of British industrial relations.

The Donovan Commission did propose such a broader analysis, including criticism of existing arrangements which came in due course to assume greater prominence in the political world than some of its members probably wanted. It argued strongly that collective bargaining arrangements should continue to be the bedrock of the British approach and that the role of law should continue to be limited. The practicalities were, however, in need of major reform. By degrees there had grown up not one but two 'systems' whose relationship was dysfunctional. Traditional industry-wide bargaining arrangements were now in conflict with, and being subverted by, a second informal system based in the activities of managers, shop stewards and work groups at the workplace. Partly in consequence wage drift, the difference between earnings and locally and nationally agreed pay rates, was growing apace and increases in informal workplace bargaining had ceased to be matched with disputes procedures, so putting strain on conflict resolution processes. The Commission proposed that industry-wide agreements be retained, but confined to matters which only they could determine, and that below them new formal agreements should be created at plant and company level to be operated by local managers and lay union representatives. To facilitate the process the Commission recommended that agreements in larger employers should be registered with the Department of Employment and Productivity and a new permanent tripartite body should be established to offer assistance and report on progress. Except in one area, the Commission rejected more interventionist legal proposals. That exception, however, was to prove of great importance. While collective bargaining and trade union protection covered a majority of the workforce, there were still areas where, as Wedderburn had famously put it, practice followed the legal position in which a worker could be dismissed 'for any reason or none' (Wedderburn, 1971). The Commission argued for the introduction, for the first time in Britain, of wide-ranging statutory protections for workers against unfair dismissal, with disputes about dismissal and the terms of contracts of employment to be decided by new specialist labour tribunals.

---

[9] See generally Kessler and Bayliss (1995) who provide a most useful overview of the Board and its context, and Mitchell (1972) for a more official discussion of the Board's achievements.
[10] Subsequently provided, for the first time in 1968, by the New Earnings Survey.

This last proposal attracted support on all sides of the political spectrum.[11] On other issues government and opposition reacted sceptically, although in different ways the maintenance and improvement of voluntary collective bargaining remained at the heart of their positions. Thereafter matters moved fast. The then Labour government introduced a White Paper, with the ringing title *In Place of Strife*, proposing new legal powers for ministers to enforce conciliation pauses in unconstitutional strikes, compulsory ballots before major stoppages and measures for dealing with troublesome inter-union disputes. All of these ideas provoked trade union protest and were eventually withdrawn. A Commission on Industrial Relations (CIR) began operations in 1969 with employer-union support, proclaiming itself a 'fire prevention' agency, unlike the official conciliation services which concentrated on 'fire fighting'.

In 1970, with the return of a Conservative government, much more dramatic legal reforms were introduced. Government concern over pay and prices control became the more urgent and a new Industrial Relations Act created a new branch of the High Court to deal with employment disputes arising from a new civil offence of 'unfair industrial practice'; provided that collective agreements would be treated as legally binding unless the parties explicitly declared otherwise; and limited trade union immunities to trade unions registered under the Act. The CIR was given statutory power to deal with union recognition disputes. A Code of Practice was issued giving advice on good industrial relations practice, which although not formally binding, could be used in evidence before industrial tribunals and the new court.

Most significantly for present purposes, the right not to be unfairly dismissed recommended by the Donovan Commission was introduced, providing for cases to be determined by industrial tribunals.[12] A new individual conciliation service was created in the Department to assist the parties towards voluntary settlement of cases, staffed at more junior grades than the collective conciliation and advisory services and managed separately from them. The justification for this new service was partly in traditional ministry thinking: it was assumed that voluntary settlements between the parties were likely to be more satisfactory to them than any decision by a third party. It was also expected that many applications would come from workers who were not in trade unions and could not afford legal representation, and from smaller employers, to both of whom the jurisdictions would seem challenging. Conciliation was expected to help through informing the parties of their rights and obligations and the way tribunals were likely to consider their disagreement. But just as, and probably more, important, was a financial consideration. No sound basis existed for

---

[11] Although some parts of the trade union movement were unhappy with it, arguing that it might subvert the extension of collective representation and the protections provided by collective bargaining.

[12] The tribunals already existed, dealing mainly with claims for statutory redundancy payments, which had been introduced in 1965.

forecasting likely unfair dismissal caseloads but it was guessed that they would quickly run into thousands each year, requiring large-scale public expenditure on tribunals.[13] Conciliation was seen as an essential first, though voluntary, port of call for the parties. It was conceived as a cheap alternative to tribunal adjudication.

The Act was fiercely opposed by the labour movement. Employers largely ignored its provisions. All but a very few collective agreements were given disclaimers. Even the government declined to use its provisions in the major dispute in coal mining in 1974, which led to electricity cuts across the country, and the imposition in industry of a three-day working week. The impartiality of the new court was challenged (Weekes et al, 1975).

Looking back it seems clear that 1969–1971 marks the point where long-lasting agreements between the main political parties that the functions of statute law in regulating employment relationships should be limited, and that recourse to the law should be exceptional rather than normal, were abandoned. Henceforth, in different ways, governments set out to use law as a tool of social engineering, with the deliberate aim of changing employer, trade union and worker behaviour.

Problems with conciliation

Through this period of legislative turmoil the Department of Employment's conciliation services had come in for criticism. Three main strands emerged. First, successive government incomes policies had increasingly required officials to undertake a policing role in relation to pay increases in collective bargaining by employers and trade unions. Under several of the policies operating during the 1960s and 1970s, application to the Department was required, evidence about productivity and cost consequences of proposed increases had to be provided by the parties, and officials cleared or rejected the proposal. Although different officials dealt with incomes policy applications from those who provided conciliation services, the freedom of conciliators to operate, both in tactical and more strategic ways, was—or was seen to be—increasingly compromised.

A second criticism arose from the fact that the government was directly and indirectly the employer of a growing part of the working population. During the 1960s and 1970s, what had been systems of management–staff consultation in central and local government, health and education services and so on were transformed into fully-fledged collective bargaining arrangements. Civil-service staff and professional associations turned themselves into trade unions. Adversarial relationships replaced quieter, paternalistic ones. The result was greater conflict but also a greater reluctance among ministers and officials from other departments to seek assistance

---

[13] Forecasting tribunal caseloads, required each time new jurisdictions are proposed in Parliamentary Bills, and generally for assessing ACAS resource requirements, remains a problem today, despite several attempts at multivariate model building and the occasional application of common sense.

from officials in another ministry which competed with them in government for resource and influence.

A third, perhaps more serious criticism was also voiced. If, as increasing numbers of commentators thought, current industry-wide and establishment collective-bargaining arrangements were not coping adequately with industrial conflict, perhaps even encouraging unofficial and unconstitutional industrial action and contributing to high inflation levels, then what was needed was a more proactive policy of reform. The Department's collective conciliation services had observable limitations in this context. As two well-placed observers argued:

> the conciliation service was designed to cope with the exigencies of the formal system and still bears its imprint. It also continues to operate on a scale that assumes that there is nothing really wrong with the system ... it assumes [absurdly] that the parties ought to be more or less convinced of the need for strategic mediation before it is even suggested to them ... (McCarthy and Ellis, 1973, p. 118).

Related to this were proposals from some quarters that the extension and improvement of collective bargaining could only be achieved if the state offered more explicit, statutory, backing for trade union recognition, if necessary against employers' wishes.[14] On this view, what was needed, if reforms were to be introduced on any large scale, was a new, more vigorous interventionist level of state mediation, conciliation and inquiry to supplement existing arrangements. Given the long-standing and inevitably inbred nature of official policy, a new institution should be created which included new people and ideas.

The emergence of ACAS

A new Labour government was elected in 1974 which, through the Trade Union and Labour Relations Acts, 1974 and 1976, repealed all the major provisions of the 1971 Act save those dealing with unfair dismissal, and essentially restored trade union immunities to the position under the 1906 Act. The Commission on Industrial Relations was abolished, along with the Court and the Registration machinery for trade unions. A new Conciliation and Arbitration Service, later rechristened ACAS, was created, with an explicit brief to be a proactive change agent as well as provide more traditional reactive industrial relations services. Its tasks were wide-ranging, but as with its predecessors, focused primarily on the extension and improvement of collective bargaining, an objective explicitly laid down in statute. It was to examine and make recommendations on applications for trade union recognition under a new statutory trade union recognition procedure; to inquire into and make recommendations on industrial relations reform in different sectors; to report on the need for and operation of statutory wage bodies; and to issue Codes of Practice. It was also to provide the conciliation, mediation, arbitration and inquiry services formerly offered

---

[14] The conciliation service had long voiced reservations about the workability of such suggestions and the difficulties they would pose for impartial intervention (Ministry of Labour, 1965, p. 99).

by the Department of Employment together with its free personnel management advisory service, and it was to provide conciliation in unfair dismissal and other cases brought before the industrial tribunals. As before, services were to be free at the point of delivery.

To perform these tasks the Service took over the management and staffs of the collective conciliation, advisory and individual conciliation branches of the Department, along with a number of enquiry staff from industry and academia formerly employed by the CIR (ACAS, 1975). Parts of ACAS were thus given clear reforming objectives aimed at extending the role and effectiveness of collective bargaining. Parts retained the ethos of the 1896 Act and the former official collective conciliation service, aimed at helping parties cope with conflict through existing voluntary machinery. And parts were aimed at assisting parties going through the judicial processes provided through industrial tribunals. Collisions between these aims were perhaps inevitable.

Between 1974 and 1980, ACAS activity was intense and innovative. Growing controversy over how to deal with recognition claims by trade unions became a major preoccupation of the ACAS Council. Major investigations about the state of industrial relations were conducted in several sectors[15] and attempts were made to help the parties there towards bargaining reforms. Several inquiries were conducted into the need for and organisation of wages councils, leading to recommendations for their extension and reform and, in one case, that collective bargaining machinery should be established.[16] As the 1974 Act required, three Codes of Practice were submitted to the Secretary of State and approved by Parliament. Two, designed to assist smoother collective bargaining, related respectively to time off for trade union duties and activities and disclosure of information to trade unions by employers, and the third set out good practice in disciplinary and dismissal procedures. Work began on others, for example on worker participation. There was a further growth in collective conciliation, related particularly to pressures on pay negotiators arising in part from high and increasing levels of inflation. The Personnel Management Advisory Service continued its relatively quiet work and, more visibly, began publishing a series of basic advisory guides to good personnel practice and administration. Plans were made for a national network of telephone enquiry points to deal with questions from workers and employers about law and good practice. Discussion papers were issued on moves to harmonise the terms and conditions of blue and white-collar workers, and on developments in collective bargaining. There was substantial growth in applications to industrial tribunals, particularly relating to dismissal.

---

[15] Electricity supply, national newspapers, provincial newspapers, the fire service, bus and coach transport.

[16] Road haulage, the retail trades, button manufacturing, toy manufacturing, the fur trade, the licensed residential and restaurant trades, laundries, contract cleaning (where the creation of industry-wide collective bargaining was recommended), aerated water and hairdressing were all covered.

Throughout this period the traditional model, modified to take account of work-place level bargaining, and with additional statutory support, still formed the basis of understanding and public policy on industrial relations. But storm clouds were growing thicker. As the 1970s ended, the Labour government, like its Conservative predecessor, found itself deeply embroiled in conflict with the trade union movement over pay and earnings restraint. Although trade union membership and recognition increased, to its highest level ever, no doubt in part because of the clear public-policy line set out in statute, there were increasing indications of public concern over union decision-making and democracy. Public disorder had arisen in a number of trade-union recognition disputes leading to widespread debate about the merits of the statutory procedure.[17] There was a growing public perception that industrial action, especially in the public sector, caused such inconvenience and economic dislocation that greater public control might become necessary, a feeling encouraged by the media presentation of events in late 1978 as the 'winter of discontent'. The general election of 1979, which is now seen as having turned on the vote of trade union members (Kessler and Bayliss, 1995, p. 37) brought in a radical Conservative government with very different ideas about the management of the economy and the proper conduct of employment relations.

POLICY-MAKING AND CHANGE AFTER 1980
IDENTIFYING CHANGE AND THE ROLE OF RESEARCH

The traditional model not only had implications for policy. It had implications for information gathering and research. Industry-wide collective bargaining was in practice conducted by a relatively small number of employer and trade union representatives. The agreements which resulted were written down. It followed that for many years, within the Ministry of Labour, officials could rely heavily on direct contacts with small numbers of key informants in employers' associations, large employers and trade unions for such information as they needed.[18] The *Industrial Relations Handbooks* published in 1944, 1953 and 1961, which described main institutions and practices, were produced through contacts of this kind and, together with statistics of trade union membership and limited data on pay rates, larger stoppages of work and employment changes, provided most of the information that officials considered necessary for policy oversight and development.[19]

---

[17] ACAS experience of the operations of the recognition procedures was described in detail in its report for 1980 and is considered by Wood in this volume. In fact ACAS officials were by no means united on how to approach the jurisdiction and how it might have been improved. See Beaumont, Harris and Phayre (1995).

[18] Indeed officials had standing invitations to observe and assist the deliberations of many national joint industrial councils.

[19] A further official edition of the *Handbook* was published by ACAS in 1980, but updating was then abandoned. A final edition was prepared and published commercially by Industrial Relations Services in 1988.

After the 1950s, however, the limitations of this approach began to be noticed. As governments came to take on more interventionist roles, and as more industrial relations issues came to be settled below industry level, the need for more extensive and detailed information became evident. Pay policies could not be monitored without much more precise indicators of earnings levels and movements in pay than had been available. Much more detailed data on employment, skills and training was needed. A revolution in the coverage and depth of the Department's statistics followed. Not only was subject coverage, depth and detail greatly extended, but major changes in methods were introduced. Ad hoc returns from employers were replaced by more proactive inquiries. The former reliance on administrative data sources and on informal surveys whose methods were not always fully describable began to be supplanted by specially created surveys using formal sampling techniques and professional question design. Alongside these developments, in 1971 the Department created a new specialist research branch with industrial relations as well as broader interests. It was there that discussion began about extending earlier exploratory surveys of industrial relations practices.[20]

The discussions proved long and difficult. Some senior officials, brought up in a policy world where national figures in industry and the trade unions had provided the bulk of any evidence they needed, thought survey work unnecessary and overly expensive. Others thought that, although costly, it might provide crucial indicators on the current situation and how things might change under different policy regimes. Eventually it was agreed to conduct an experimental one-off nationally representative survey of workplace industrial relations across Britain. To help fund it the officials charged with its design arranged a partnership with the Economic and Social Research Council, the main funder of academic social science research in Britain, and the Policy Studies Institute (PSI), a well respected independent research institute with a strong background in employment research. ACAS joined the consortium in 1982. A joint steering committee was set up to take overall responsibility for design and management of the survey, supported by a research team staffed from the Department and PSI.

The survey was designed to provide a baseline description of workplace organisation and industrial relations which could be repeated if all went well. It covered establishments with more than 25 employees across the whole civilian economy except for agriculture and coal mining.[21] Personal interviews were conducted with some 4,500 managers and trade union representatives in a nationally representative sample of just over 2,000 establishments across the whole of Great Britain, and

---

[20] The history of survey work in industrial relations is reviewed at length in Marginson (1998).

[21] Agriculture was excluded because it had few establishments with 25 or more employees. Coal mining was omitted in 1980 because the National Coal Board's management–union machinery took too long to agree to co-operate for fieldwork to be possible, in 1984 because of the strike then under way, and in 1990 because by then deep coal-mining had all but disappeared in Britain.

across all industries. The choice of subject coverage was strongly influenced by the traditional model. A repeatable core of question modules was designed covering the role of personnel managers; trade union recognition and membership; compulsory trade unionism; the coverage, depth and scope of collective bargaining; union representative structures and functions; manager–worker consultation and communications; pay determination; payment systems and earnings levels; industrial action including action short of strikes; recruitment; dismissal and redundancy procedures and practice; labour flexibility and managements' freedom to organise work. After several years' preparation, the first survey was conducted in 1980 and main findings published in an overview Sourcebook in 1983 (Daniel and Millward, 1983).

The survey was widely judged a technical success, achieving very high response rates and producing a very wide range of new nationally representative information. However, difficulties had arisen within the Department in agreeing the text of parts of the Sourcebook: senior officials as well as ministers continued to debate the best directions for future policy, and some saw the survey evidence as complicating their position unhelpfully.[22] There was both strong support and strong opposition to a repeat survey.

After much argument a second survey was conducted in 1984, with an additional module on technical and organisational change, producing a second Sourcebook and a separate report on management and worker approaches to new technology (Millward and Stevens, 1986; Daniel, 1987). Contrary to the expectation of some observers, this showed a picture of broad stability in industrial relations arrangements over the four-year period. The third survey was carried out in 1990, with fewer reservations within the Department (Millward et al., 1992; Millward, 1994) and suggested that major changes were now under way across a wide range of industrial relations institutions and behaviours. The fourth survey was carried out in 1998, this time positively demanded by policy officials and the social partners. It was significantly redesigned to take account of these changes, and extended to cover workplaces with ten or more workers. For the first time it also gathered information directly from workers as well as from their representatives and managers (Cully et al., 1998, 1999; Millward, Bryson and Forth, 2000).[23]

Taken together, the four surveys offer unparalleled evidence about changes over time in the structures and practices of British workplace employment arrangements. Indicators of change come from comparisons of results from each separate cross-section survey, where on many topics questions were used unchanged from one survey to the next. And for 1990–1998, and less securely 1984, change is also measurable through an additional panel element in the survey, in which interviews were conducted in the same workplaces as had been contacted in previous years.

---

[22] One official went so far as to announce publicly that he would never use data from the survey in briefing ministers and colleagues. He was promoted soon after.

[23] WIRS was renamed the Workplace Employee Relations Survey (WERS) in 1998 at DTI insistence.

Survey methods have well-known limitations and these affect WIRS like all other surveys (Marsh, 1982; McCarthy, 1994; Millward and Hawes, 1995; Hakim, 2000; Hawes, 2000). Taken together, however, the picture presented by the series is sufficiently consistent to be incontrovertible. Indeed, so great are the changes it has recorded that they would have struck most observers in 1980 as not only dramatic but astonishing. The increasingly beleaguered, but in many respects still pervasive, system observable 20 years ago became, on all counts, a shadow of what it was. Over the last two decades managers' enthusiasm for involving trade unions in workplace decision-making activity fell markedly, collective industrial action all but disappeared, and the role of law in resolving employment disputes became pervasive.

Dimensions of change 1980–1998: trade union recognition and collective bargaining[24]

Between 1980 and 1998 there was a dramatic fall in trade union recognition across all sectors. In 1980, two-thirds of all establishments had offered recognition to one or more unions. By 1998, the figure was two-fifths. In private manufacturing, formerly the heartland of the union movement, recognition fell by more than one-half. In private services, by the end of the decade, under one-quarter of establishments recognised a union, and those that did were heavily concentrated in the privatised former public utilities.

Recognition is a necessary precursor to collective bargaining. In 1984, the pay of at least some workers was determined by collective bargaining in some three-fifths of establishments. By 1998, that figure had halved to 29%. To put it another way, establishments without any collective bargaining made up only two-fifths of the total in 1984 but almost three-quarters by 1998. In 1980, seven out of ten workers in establishments with more than 25 employees had their pay at least partly determined through collective bargaining. By 1990, that figure had fallen to just over half, and by 1998 it was down to two-fifths. In private manufacturing and the public sector, the fall was in the order of one-third. In private services the figure halved, to no more than 21%, with surviving bargaining again predominantly in the privatised public utilities. Only in the public sector was a substantial majority of workers still covered by collective bargaining and even here the proportion was falling (Millward, Bryson and Forth 2000, Table 6.5).

There were changes, too, in the way bargaining was organised. Multi-employer, industry-wide bargaining, long in decline but still a major feature of the British scene in 1980, all but disappeared. In 1984, about two-fifths of establishments had been involved in or affected by multi-employer bargaining; by 1998 that share had fallen to no more than one in eight, many of whom were again in the public sector.

---

[24] This section is based heavily on the WIRS main reports, especially Cully *et al.* (1999) and Millward, Bryson and Forth (2000).

Changes in the scope and depth of bargaining also occurred. ACAS was clear by 1982 that where collective arrangements persisted private-sector managers were often taking more vigorous lines in pay negotiations than before, arguing that intensifying competition in product markets constrained their freedom in making offers. In situations where companies were hard pressed to survive, trade unions generally accepted shorter, less intensive negotiations (ACAS *Annual Report*, 1982, pp. 6–18). Outside the pay area, the survey evidence also suggests a decrease in the scope of bargaining in private manufacturing (Millward, Bryson and Forth, 2000, p. 261).

The explanation for these remarkable changes has been debated, but in most sectors seems certain to have been mainly a consequence of deaths among older establishments with long-standing recognition, and a strong disinclination among managers of new establishments to recognise any union at all.[25] Old-established manufacturing sectors which had been at the heart of the old system, where strong traditions of trade unionism and collective bargaining had existed for decades, were hit hard by the recessions of the early 1980s and 1990s. In 1980 a quarter of all workplaces with over 25 workers were in private sector manufacturing, two-fifths in private-sector services. Manufacturing workplaces employed two-fifths of workers and private services one-quarter. In the late 1990s, these positions had been reversed.

The 1998 survey showed clearly that average workplace age had declined substantially since the survey started. Workplaces which had been at their current address for less than ten years, for example, made up as much as one third of all establishments in 1998, compared with a little over a quarter in 1990. Older establishments, which had existed for 20 years, declined significantly as a proportion of the total. Throughout the 1980s and 1990s, newer workplaces were much less likely to recognise trade unions than their older counterparts.

Changes in ownership patterns also affected approaches to employee relations. From 1984, the government's programme of privatisation had involved transfers to the private sector of the public utilities and a range of government services, bringing new management challenges, substantial cost-cutting and job loss. Around one-fifth of public-sector workplaces also reported some change in ownership during 1990–1998, mainly arising from the reorganisation of local government, state education and the National Health Service. Between 1990 and 1998 some two-fifths of private manufacturing establishments experienced a change of ownership, via takeovers, mergers or demergers, while for private services the figure was one-quarter. Foreign ownership has also long been known to be associated with particular approaches to staff management, including higher use of professional personnel managers, and clearly thought-out approaches to trade union recognition and collective bargaining.

---

[25] Several prominent employers actively abandoned long-standing recognition arrangements and more contemplated such moves, profoundly shocking the trade union movement. But overall such vigorous de-recognition remained rare.

Between 1980 and 1998 the proportion of private-sector workplaces covered by WIRS that was wholly or partly controlled by non-UK organisations more than doubled from around 6% to 13%. Across private-sector manufacturing the incidence of foreign ownership almost trebled, to around one in five workplaces. The explanation lay partly in investment in new workplaces, but also, significantly, in the considerably higher survival rates achieved by foreign-owned businesses compared to their indigenous counterparts.

Technology developed remarkably, bringing with it the rapid death or transformation of many older occupations in which trade unionism had flourished. The gender composition of the workforce changed. Linked to the decline in manufacturing and the growth of the service sector was a decline in male employment and a substantial rise in women's employment. Most of the jobs lost from manufacturing had been relatively well-paid and held by men working full-time. Growth in service-sector jobs was in contrast heavily oriented towards part-time jobs, often relatively low paid, with heavy recruitment of married women, many of whom regard themselves as secondary earners rather than main breadwinners (Hakim, 1996, pp. 65–75). There was a substantial growth in self-employment, especially among men, and particularly solo self-employment, where individuals work without any other employees (Hakim, 1998, pp. 200–220). Other forms of 'flexible' or 'non-standard' working also increased. Among men the combination of part-time, self-employment and various types of temporary work grew from about one in seven of the workforce in the mid-1980s to around one-quarter in the mid-1990s. For women the figure rose to over half in the same period (Dex, 1999). Workplaces with no or low proportions of women workers declined substantially as a proportion of the total, while the proportion with high concentrations of women grew (Millward, Bryson and Forth, 2000, Chapter 2).

Industrial conflict

Few in 1980 would have dreamed of the dramatic fall in industrial action which occurred in the following two decades.[26] Table 1 shows indicators of officially-recorded disputes between employers and trade unions. In 1974, nearly 3,000 stoppages of work were recorded by the Employment Department, involving 1.6 million people and 15 million working days lost. By the early 1990s, large-scale industrial action of this kind had largely disappeared. Numbers of recorded stoppages of work fell in the early 1990s to their lowest level since 1897 when the official series began, and stayed low thereafter. The WIRS series seeks data on all forms of industrial action, including small stoppages which fall outside the official net and non-strike

---

[26] Similar falls in the incidence and intensity of strike action occurred in most western European and many other countries over the period. Britain was not unique.

TABLE 1
Stoppages and employment tribunal applications 1980–1999

Year	Stoppages in progress	Total Number of ET applications registered
1980	1,348	41,424
1981	1,344	44,852
1982	1,538	43,660
1983	1,364	39,959
1984[a]	1,221	39,191
1985	903	38,593
1986	1,074	38,385
1987	1,016	30,543
1988	781	29,304
1989	701	34,697
1990	630	43,243
1991	369	67,448
1992	253	71,821
1993	211	71,661
1994	205	88,061
1995	235	108,827[b]
1996	244	88,910
1997	216	80,435
1998	166	91,913

Sources: Official Disputes: Employment Gazette, 1980–1995 and Labour Market Trends, 1995–1999; Employment tribunal applications data from the Employment Tribunal Service

[a] The counting year for ET claims changed from calendar to financial year in April 1984. Figures for this and subsequent years run from April to March of the following year (e.g. 1st April 1984 to 31st March 1985).

[b] Figure includes 27,000 cases received in 1995, registered by part-time employees claiming membership of their employer's pension schemes, following the European Court of Justice decisions in the case of Vroege and Fisscher.

action such as overtime bans and work to rule. In the early 1980s, as many as one in four of all establishments reported experiencing some form of industrial action during the past year. By 1998 that figure had fallen to one in fifty (Millward *et al.*, 1992, Table 8.1; Cully *et al.*, 1999, figure 6.4).

Indicators of industrial action are, of course, only one expression of the extent of conflict at work. In the 1990s another, the incidence of claims to industrial tribunals, also shown in Table 1, showed an equally remarkable increase. Part of the explanation no doubt lies in the growing number of jurisdictions under which employees could apply for redress, the increasing levels of compensation which tribunals could award, and a growing awareness of rights. But it is hard to avoid the conclusion that where collective protections against unreasonable employer behaviour had been weakened or had never existed, workers were turning increasingly to the public forum of the tribunals. In 1998, one in eight of all workplaces were involved in tribunal litigation on at least one occasion. The aggregate number of cases per thousand employees doubled from 1.1 in 1984 to 2.0 by 1998

(Millward *et al.*, 1992, Table 6.7 and Cully *et al.*, 1999, p. 245). A public forum for redress increasingly replaced the private forums formerly provided through collective bargaining.

CHANGE AND THE LAW

The 1970s had seen all British governments moving to the position that more law and regulation was needed to underpin and regulate voluntary bargaining agreements. The period of Conservative government which began in 1979 under Mrs Thatcher introduced not only a massive increase in the volume of statute law regulating industrial relations but, as time went on, law essentially hostile to trade unions. Far from being essential partners in the political and industrial worlds, trade unions were now deemed destructive, conflict-inducing agents which created unfortunate labour-market imperfections and inefficiencies. Instead of introducing a single major enactment, designed, like the Labour government's proposals of 1969 and the Conservative government's 1971 Industrial Relations Act, to achieve major change at a single stroke, a step-by-step approach was adopted. The result was the outlawing of compulsory unionism, restrictions on the immunities available to union officials when calling secondary action, restrictions on other industrial action in some sectors, complex requirements on strike ballots, restrictions on picketing, and changes to check-off arrangements. The programme posed serious practical difficulties for many unions and led some employers to challenge the legitimacy of union voting arrangements in the courts. The effect of these changes on the incidence and conduct of industrial disputes is debated, but there can be little doubt that at the least union officials found it necessary to be better acquainted with law and its consequences than before.

Arguably more significant in the day-to-day employment relationship, however, was the introduction of a growing body of individual rights law regulating unfair dismissal, redundancy, breach of contract of employment, sex and race discrimination and a wide range of other issues. The Conservative government's position on much of this was equivocal. Minimum rights were needed in certain areas but at the same time excessive employee rights and excessive duties for employers meant unreasonable burdens on business. A major complication for them was the growing — and to many eyes unexpected—role after 1980 of European Union judicial institutions in testing the validity of member states' laws against European law, particularly in relation to gender and other forms of discrimination in employment. The result for Britain was a constant flow of new statute and case law, much of which had major implications for payment, recruitment and other processes.

Among the consequences were developments in personnel management. Specialist personnel managers became more common. WIRS evidence suggests that during the 1980s, some one sixth of managers with overall responsibility for employee relations had been personnel specialists. By 1998, this figure had risen to more than a quarter. A fast growing proportion of all managers had professional personnel management qualifications. Many more were women. The increases were particularly large in new and foreign-owned workplaces. Personnel managers also spent their time differently from before. Far fewer spent much time on dealing with collective disputes, while many more were concerned with ensuring that recruitment and other management processes fell within the limits set by individual rights law and dealing with complaints about alleged breaches. More time was taken up in dealing with industrial tribunal cases (Millward, Bryson and Forth, 2000, Chapter 3). Linked with this was a marked increase in managers' use of external advisors. In 1980, only 1% of establishments had sought advice about employment issues in the last year from a lawyer; by 1998 one-third of managers said they had done so. Use of management consultants had quadrupled. In 1980, 10% of establishments had sought advice from ACAS in the previous year. In 1998, that figure was nearly one-quarter (Millward, Bryson and Forth, 2000, Table 3.10).

By the end of the 1990s, then, few could argue that the model of industrial relations which had guided both policy and academic thinking now provided either a secure guide to understanding or to action. The model's assumption of inevitable, enduring conflict remained untouched, though disputes now took new forms. Collective bargaining remained a significant feature in the public sector and larger enterprises, but was otherwise very much reduced in coverage and depth. Industry-wide bargaining had almost disappeared. There was growing questioning both within and outside the trade union movement about whether the 'reactive' model of trade unionism should continue to underpin trade union strategies, or whether more constructive 'partnership' approaches, or even mainstream European ideas of trade unionism should be adopted. Law had been brought four-square into the day-to-day management of the employment relationship.

CONCLUSIONS: ACAS AND CHANGE

These changes, now obvious, occurred by degrees. While its *Annual Reports* make clear that ACAS was aware early on that major developments were under way, their extent and permanence could not initially be assumed. The Service's initial responses were understandably cautious. The 1970s had seen major swings in government policy and legislation and the political parties remained strongly divided about the best way forward. The sensible assumption was that further changes in government would lead to yet further rounds of Parliamentary disagreement and continuing instability in the legal framework. The view was strongly expressed, by employer members of the ACAS Council and employers' organisations, that the Service's reputation for impartiality in its conciliation work had been damaged by publicity associated with the union recognition jurisdiction. Further, with the arrival of the new government in 1979, substantial financial cuts were imposed. The full range of ACAS activity begun in 1974 was felt to be no longer affordable, either politically or financially.

With the arrival of a new chairman in 1980, much of the reforming agenda of the first five years was quietly forgotten.[27] The abolition of the statutory recognition provisions in 1980 encouraged a reversion to a much less pushful voluntarist approach in this area. Following budget cuts, plus doubts about its practical effectiveness, large-scale enquiry work was abandoned and never resumed [see Purcell and other contributions in this volume]. Henceforth effort was to be concentrated on the more traditional functions of collective conciliation, arbitration, smaller-scale advisory work and individual conciliation. ACAS staff numbers were reduced, with the loss of nearly all the contract staff who had been employed alongside permanent officials.[28]

Table 2 shows caseloads for the main ACAS activities over 1974–1999. Initially the cutback in ACAS ambitions was concealed by continuing high demand for collective conciliation, including many cases in both the private sector and nationalised industries which attracted national media attention. Conciliation in high-profile disputes was offered, among others, to employers and trade unions in water supply, fire services, prison service, health service and, perhaps most prominently—although ultimately unsuccessfully—in the coal dispute of 1974–1975 which preceded the closure of much deep-mining capacity in Britain. All told, between 1980 and 1990 ACAS conciliated in 17,093 collective disputes and maintained contacts (in ACAS terminology 'ran alongside') in 3,731 others where the parties were in, or were close to, a dispute. 'Progress towards a settlement' was claimed in over 90% of these (Goodman, this volume). Collective conciliation was, for a time, restored to the place it had enjoyed when at the Ministry of Labour, as the flagship among state industrial relations services.

Alongside this emphasis on collective conciliation went a steady development of less newsworthy advisory work. Initially larger projects, mainly for private-sector companies, involved short consultancy-style investigations at the end of which a report was drafted for consideration by the parties. Topics ranged widely, covering problems with recruitment, retention, payment systems, procedures and so on.

---

[27] The first chairman had been Jim Mortimer who, with Jack Jones, General Secretary of the TGWU, and a member of the ACAS Council, had been a leading campaigner for a reforming ACAS (see generally Stone, 1993; Mortimer, 1998). The second was Pat Lowry, formerly of the Engineering Employers' Federation and British Leyland (Lowry, 1990). The third was Douglas Smith, a former Employment Department official who had been the Department's last Chief Conciliation Officer. The fourth was John Hougham, formerly of the Ford Motor Company.

[28] In 1974 the ACAS Council had concluded that its staff should be drawn from a wider pool of talent than the Department provided and that they should no longer be civil servants. However the bulk of the staff, permanent officials who had been taken over from the Department, strongly objected and the change was not carried through. In the 1975 Act ACAS was turned into a remarkable constitutional anomaly, a 'crown' non-departmental public body, staffed by civil servants who do not answer directly to a minister.

TABLE 2
ACAS Activities: Trends 1974–1998

Year	Request for collective conciliation	Arbitration/ mediation	Public enquiry point[a]	Cases received individual conciliation[b]	Completed advisory mediation projects	Advisory visits
1974[c]	656	75	not available	4,976	65	1,938
1975	2,564	306	not available	29,100	240	7,277
1976	3,460[d]	323	390,000	41,930	208	8,910
1977	3,299[d]	327	not available	43,899	259	8,792
1978	3,338[d]	421	400,000	44,713	365	10,390
1979	2,667[d]	395	449,000	43,406	457	12,602
1980	2,091[d]	322	390,500	46,447	476	15,222
1981	1,958	257	300,000	47,040	468	12,484
1982	1,865	251	284,000	46,996	515	10,841
1983	1,789	207	279,100	42,943	717	10,892
1984	1,569	202	280,000	42,723	842	9,578
1985	1,475	162	275,910	42,887	946	9,160
1986	1,457	184	267,066	51,431	924	8,940
1987	1,302	145	303,819	40,817	956	8,302
1988	1,163	138	320,000	44,443	985	7,628
1989	1,164	167	350,000	48,817	1,144	7,255
1990	1,260	200	418,000	52,071	964	6,980
1991	1,386	157	467,000	60,605	947	6,266
1992	1,207	162	488,000	72,166	787	4,964
1993	1,211	163	481,392	75,181	529	3,918
1994	1,313	156	526,189	79,332	487	3,586
1995	1,321	136	538,394	91,568	539	3,458
1996	1,306	117	446,718	100,399	540	2,820
1997	1,281	71	442,062	106,912	467	2,849
1998	1,301	51	507,896	113,636	530	3,318

Source: ACAS Annual Reports

[a] From January 1996 the method of recording changed from counting the number of enquiries received to the total number of calls (many calls involve more than one enquiry).

[b] Figures include all cases of involved alleged infringement of individual employment rights—both formal applications to employment tribunals ('IT1s') and so-called 'non-IT1s' in which no formal application had been made; data is counted by jurisdiction, rather than application. Many applications include more than one jurisdiction.

[c] September to December 1974.

[d] Excludes figures for recognition raised under Section 11 of the Employment Protection Act 1975.

Although the work attracted little public notice, independent investigators found that it was generally valued by those who used it (Armstrong and Lucas, 1985; Purcell, this volume). Later in the decade, attempts were made to recast much of this work away from the conventional consultancy model in which advisers made formal recommendations for change, towards approaches based on 'joint problem' identification and solving, in which the parties carried out their own investigations and produced their own conclusions, with the adviser operating in a facilitating role. The activity was re-christened 'advisory mediation' (Purcell, this volume.) The process was assisted to some degree by the transfer of the Employment Department's Work Research Unit to ACAS in 1985.[29]

Other advisory work involving short visits to employers, often to offer advice on procedures, also flourished. The series of advisory booklets which had been introduced in 1975 was extended, so that by 1990 12 titles and two larger handbooks had been published, providing introductions to job evaluation, payment systems, personnel records, labour turnover, absence, recruitment and selection, induction of new employees, workplace communications, employment policy-making, employee appraisal and redundancy handling. Although no new codes of practice were proposed,[30] a major revision of the 1976 Code on Disciplinary and Dismissal Procedures in Employment was attempted in 1985–1986, with a view to reflecting changing law and practice in this fast developing area. Ministers rejected the draft on the grounds that it was too long and complicated,[31] whereupon it was turned into an advisory handbook. 170,000 copies were distributed in its first year of publication and it became widely regarded in the industrial tribunals and among personnel practitioners as a key source of helpful guidance.

While these developments were occurring individual conciliation caseloads were rising still further. In 1980 there had been 16 industrial tribunal jurisdictions in which ACAS was obliged to offer conciliation. By 1989 that figure had risen to 22. Growing numbers of tribunal applications meant that earlier conciliation methods which had relied heavily on personal meetings with the parties, had to be replaced more and more by contacts on the telephone. Cases became more complex, with increasing numbers of applications involving two or more jurisdictions (Dickens, this volume). Nonetheless settlement rates remained steady, with about one-third of cases resolved by agreement and another third ending in withdrawal of the complaint. There were special complications in the equal opportunities area as the need for equal opportunities policies and practices came gradually to figure more strongly in the positions of managers and in the aspirations of employees, bringing challenges

---

[29] This was not an entirely happy story. The WRU had been created in the Department in 1974 in response to a perceived need for government encouragement of improved practice in work organisation and the quality of working life. It was overseen by a committee chaired by a minister with employer and trade union representation. By the mid 1980s the Department no longer offered other practical industrial-relations services and did not know what to do with it. Senior ACAS officials did not want it either, fearing that its more reformist objectives would sit inconveniently with the more limited ambitions of their own advisory service. The marriage proved difficult, not least because the Unit's staff found it difficult to agree what their main purposes should be. It was abolished in 1993. It lives on only through the continuing publication of the ACAS QWL (Quality of Working Life) *News and Abstracts*.

[30] The Government's codes on picketing and industrial action balloting were prepared directly by the Department, which knew that ACAS would not have approved their content. ACAS made strongly critical comments on the latter (ACAS, 1990, p.12) but these did not convince ministers.

[31] This happened just at the time of Pat Lowry's retirement from the Chair and Douglas Smith's arrival. One of Smith's last tasks at the Employment Department had been to oversee the drafting of the ministerial letter rejecting the draft Code. One of his first tasks at ACAS was to lead a Council delegation to the minister to tell him he had been poorly advised.

for ACAS operational staff among whom women were then under-represented and ethnic minorities non-existent.[32] There were complications, too, in ACAS's relations with the Equal Opportunities Commission and the Commission for Racial Equality, bodies charged with the active promotion of gender and racial equality who sometimes saw the Service's task of facilitating settlements whose terms were kept confidential to the parties as conflicting with their aim of promoting change through the public identification and shaming of prominent employers (McCrudden, Smith and Brown, 1991, pp. 181–203). Closely related to increased individual conciliation caseloads were growing demands on the new system of public telephone enquiry points which had been set up in regional offices in the early 1980s. By 1990 more than 8,000 enquiries were received each week, about three-fifths from workers concerned about their legal and other entitlement, two-fifths from employers asking about good practice and their statutory obligations.

The 1980s, then, saw an initially lively collective conciliation scene, a redesign and re-orientation of advisory project work, and an ever-growing emphasis on providing advice and conciliation in individual rights disputes. Slowly, however, as the economy changed, and government dislike of trade unionism increased, the former emphasis on supporting collective bargaining came to play a smaller role in ACAS operations, while assisting individual workers and employers who did not recognise trade unions came more to the fore. Proposals were put forward on several occasions during the 1980s that the Service's statutory terms of reference should be amended to delete its key reference to the promotion and extension of collective bargaining. The view within the organisation was that such a move would be unwelcome, but that given the quiet reorientation of its activities it would be unlikely to make much practical difference to the services then actually provided in the field.

Gradually, however, moves in the practical world away from the traditional system began to pose puzzles for the purposes of the organisation. Both practical experience and survey evidence emphasised the difficulties in helping managers and workforces develop communications and joint problem-solving arrangements in the absence of union recognition (ACAS, 1991; Purcell, this volume). The aim of improving collective bargaining had provided a touchstone against which many of its activities could be judged. What ACAS was for was no longer as clear as it had been. After 1990, such reforming zeal as remained in the organisation receded further. Like all non-departmental public bodies ACAS was—and is—subject to five-yearly government reviews which consider whether it continues to provide a necessary public service and whether its funding, staffing and work methods are appropriate to the task. Early reviews had been based on a shared understanding between government and the Service of its underlying aims and purposes which

---

[32] By the mid-1990s the gender mix among ACAS staff was much more equal, except at the most senior level. The under-representation of non-white staff was also beginning to be tackled.

rested heavily on providing support for voluntary collective bargaining machinery. Later reviews were conducted without that certainty, in what from ACAS's perspective was a much more hostile political and financial climate. When in 1993, against the wishes of the Council, ACAS's terms of reference were amended, the changes were more troublesome than expected. The original statutory duty had been:

> to promote the improvement of industrial relations and in particular to encourage the extension of collective bargaining and the development and where necessary, reform of collective bargaining machinery.

The revision, enacted in the Trade Union Reform and Employment Rights Act, 1993, read

> to promote the improvement of industrial relations in particular by exercising its functions in relation to the settlement of trade disputes.

This was a form of words providing a much less secure basis for preventative, advisory work. Charging was introduced for the first time although, at the Council's insistence, it was restricted to short courses for employers and to publications. The Secretary of State took reserve powers to require charging in some other areas. Budgets were also cut substantially, leading in 1991–1992 to large reductions in advisory work. All this, and the imposition by central government of new approaches to the more active management of public bodies, led to an emphasis on survival and internal control systems, rather than providing innovative services to users.

With the decline in collective bargaining coverage and the disappearance of strikes during the 1990s, demands for collective conciliation, formerly the flagship activity, fell to the point of invisibility across most of Britain.[33] ACAS no longer figured much in the media. By 1998 only 7% of the ACAS budget was devoted to it. Arbitration in collective disputes, never strongly recommended by ACAS in recent years, fell into almost complete disuse. When the advisory service had been created, it faced few private-sector competitors. Now, commercial consultants offered apparently similar services on a large scale, raising questions about why in-depth advice should continue to be publicly funded. ACAS responded in two ways. First, it re-emphasised that advisory projects would be undertaken only where managements agreed to the direct involvement of worker representatives in joint management–worker problem-solving groups; and second, it decided that advisory projects would go ahead only when the parties were 'near' dispute. Neither criterion proved easy to operationalise (see Purcell, this volume). Expenditure on advisory services was reduced to around 20% of the total budget. The production of new advisory publications flagged further: during the decade only one was issued, on teamworking. At the same time, growth in demands on telephone enquiry points by employers

---

[33] There were exceptions in Scotland and northern England, which currently provide the bulk of the collective conciliation workload.

and workers increased by leaps and bounds, bringing pressure on staff resource. In 1998, this activity consumed as much as 11% of the ACAS budget. Perhaps most dramatic were the increases in industrial tribunal caseloads which threatened throughout the 1990s to overwhelm individual conciliation staff and management and which required nearly two-thirds of ACAS's total resource in 1998. By then no fewer than 50 jurisdictions provided for ACAS involvement. From playing a supporting role in the Service's early attempts to promote voluntary employer–trade union regulation, individual conciliation moved to centre stage in its own right, with growing demands from government that its principal purpose be redefined as the production of an inexpensive alternative to employment tribunal hearings.

There were benefits to this difficult regime. New forms of self-funding advisory workshop and seminars were devised, aimed especially at smaller employers. Considerable effort was devoted to finding new ways of delivering individual conciliation, via a series of experiments in placing conciliators in tribunal offices and through streamlined 'paperless' conciliation (Lewis, Thomas and Ward, 1997). Investigations were carried out into different conciliation styles and their appropriateness and effectiveness in different circumstances (Dix, this volume). With staff support, schemes were tried in which conciliators were based at their homes rather than in expensive central-office accommodation (Huws, O'Regan and Honey, 2000). The need to demonstrate more clearly the value of its activities to the public and the exchequer led to a substantial expansion of ACAS-funded and supported evaluation research, much of it described elsewhere in this volume (Hiltrop, 1985a, b; McCrudden, Smith and Brown, 1991; Dix et al., 1995; Kessler and Purcell, 1995; Lewis, Thomas and Ward, 1997; Lewis and Legard, 1998; Fox and Dix, 2000; Hines and Dix, 2000; Ford, 1994; Taylor and Woods, 1994; and Tailby, Pearson and Sinclair, 1997). Overall, however, it is difficult to avoid the conclusion that during the 1990s ACAS was more often coping with, or 'running alongside' changes in the employment world, than expanding its range and depth of services and helping to transform industrial relations behaviour in clearly thought out ways.

With the election of a new government in 1997 with different priorities and a clear commitment to the future of ACAS, there are indications that this period may now be over. While financial constraints will undoubtedly continue, a new form of ACAS arbitration to operate as an alternative to the employment tribunals is being developed. A further attempt to revise the Code on Disciplinary and Dismissal procedures is currently at the consultation stage. There are signs of innovative thinking in ACAS involvement in new national and international forums on the future of work and the quality of working life.

ACAS does therefore seem to have come through recent political upheavals and the long decline of collective bargaining intact as with a future both assured and useful. But the employment and employment relations background to ACAS's activities remains far from stable. Though collective bargaining has not disappeared— and may even be set for an early, partial recovery—it no longer offers the dominant, unifying paradigm of an industrial relations 'system'. Some alternatives have over the years come forward to offer themselves as replacements. These include 'human resource management theory' (Legge, 1995), labour flexibility (Atkinson, 1984; ACAS, 1988), the 'psychological contract' (Guest et al., 1996), the 'representation gap' (Towers, 1997) and 'partnership' (Guest and Peccei, 1998; Knell, 1999). These may have some promise and partnership has the benefit of strong government and social-partner support. But none of them, as yet, offers a sufficiently coherent and comprehensive way towards a widely-accepted rationale to guide employment policy-makers, government agencies, employment practitioners and employment researchers. The old 'system' may have been more imaginary than real but it undoubtedly had its uses and now needs adequate replacement or, perhaps, repair. Here it is of some note that in the past industrial relations researchers contributed to imaginative debate and positive reforms. Their successors now need to make a similar contribution. 'Running alongside', as with ACAS, is not a satisfactory option. The current lack of broad-based models which help integrate and focus thought and debate raises questions about the coherence and viability of industrial relations as a field of study and about the role and design of survey and other research as a backcloth to policy and practice (Kochan, 1998; Whitfield and Strauss, 1998).

REFERENCES

ACAS (1975–1998), *Annual Reports*. London: ACAS.
ACAS (1988), *Labour Flexibility in Britain*. Occasional paper 41. London: ACAS.
ACAS (1991), *Consultation and Communication: the ACAS survey*. Occasional Paper 49. London: ACAS.
Atkinson, J. (1984), *Manning for Uncertainty: Some Emerging UK Work Patterns*. Brighton: Institute of Manpower Studies.
Armstrong, E. and R. Lucas (1985), Improving Industrial Relations: the Advisory Role of ACAS. London: Croom Helm.
Beaumont, P., R. Harris and R. Phayre (1995), 'Large multiestablishment companies and opposition to unions in Britain.' *Review of Employment Topics*, 3, pp. 103–125.
Clegg, H. A. (1970), *The System of Industrial Relations in Great Britain*. Oxford: Blackwell.
Cully, M. *et al.* (1998), *The 1998 Workplace Employee Relations Survey: First Findings*. London: DTI, ESRC, ACAS, PSI.
Cully, M., S. Woodland, A. O'Reilly and G. Dix (1999), *Britain at Work, as Depicted by the 1998 Workplace Employee Relations Survey*. London: Routledge.
Daniel, W. W. (1987), *Workplace Industrial Relations and Technical Change*. London: Pinter.
Daniel, W. W. and N. Millward (1983), *Workplace Industrial Relations in Britain: the DE/PSI/SSRC Survey*. London: Heinemann.
Dex, S. (ed) (1999), *Families and the Labour Market: Trends, Pressures and Policies*. London: Joseph Rowntree Foundation.
Dix, G., W. R. Hawes and S. Pinkstone (1995), *Asking ACAS: An Evaluation of the ACAS Public Enquiry Point Service*, Occasional Paper No. 56. London: ACAS.
Flanders, A. and H. A. Clegg (1954), *The System of Industrial Relations in Great Britain*. Oxford: Blackwell.
Ford, C. (1994), *Teamworking: key issues and developments*, Occasional paper 54. London: ACAS.
Fox, M. and G. Dix (2000), *ACAS Individual Conciliation: Processes and Outcomes*, Research Paper 4. London: ACAS.

Guest, D., N. Conway, R. Briner and M. Dickman (1996), *The state of the psychological contract in employment*. London: Institute of Personnel Management.

Guest, D. and R. Peccei (1998), *The Partnership Company: Benchmarks for the Future*. London, Involvement and Participation Association.

Hakim, C. (1996), *Key Issues in Women's Work: Female Heterogeneity and the Polarisation of Women's Employment*. London: Athlone.

Hakim, C. (1998), *Social Change and Innovation in the Labour Market*. Oxford: Oxford University Press.

Hakim, C. (2000), *Research Design: Successful Designs for Social and Economic Research*. London: Routledge.

Hawes, W. R. (2000), *Enterprise Surveys in Labour Market Policy Analysis: A Brief guide to Methods And Uses*. Geneva, ILO.

Hiltrop, J. (1985a), 'Mediator behaviour and the settlement of collective bargaining disputes in Britain', *Journal of Social Issues*, **41**, pp. 83–99.

Hiltrop, J. (1985b). 'Dispute settlement and mediation: Data from Britain', *Industrial Relations*, **24**, pp. 139–146.

Hines, I. and G. Dix (2000), *Conciliation in Employment Rights Cases: User Feedback*, Research Paper 3. London: ACAS.

Hunter, L. and G. Thorn (1991), 'External Advisory Services in Labour Management: A Worm's Eye View', *Human Resource Management Journal*, **12**, pp. 22–41.

Huws, U., S. O'Regan and S. Honey (2000), *An Evaluation of Homeworking in ACAS*, Research Paper 2. London: ACAS.

Kerr, C. (1964), *Labour and Management in Industrial Society*. New York: Doubleday.

Kessler, I. and J. Purcell (1995), *Joint Problem Solving. Does it Work? An Evaluation of ACAS Advisory Mediation*, Occasional Paper No. 55. London: ACAS.

Kessler, S. and F. Bayliss (1995), *Contemporary British Industrial Relations*, 2nd Edition. Basingstoke: Mcmillan.

Knell, J. (1999), *Partnership at Work*. London: Department of Trade and Industry.

Legge, K. (1995), *Human Resource Management: Rhetoric and Realities*. London: Macmillan.

Lewis, J., A. Thomas and K. Ward (1997), *ACAS Conciliation at Industrial Tribunals: An Evaluation of an Experimental Scheme*. London: ACAS.

Lewis, J. and R. Legard (1998), *ACAS Individual Conciliation: A Qualitative Evaluation of the Service Provided in Industrial Tribunal Cases*, Research Paper 1. London: ACAS.

Lowry, J. P. (1990), *Employment Disputes and the Third Party*. London: Macmillan.

Marginson, P. (1998), 'The survey tradition in British industrial relations research: an assessment of the contribution of large scale workplace and enterprise surveys', *British Journal of Industrial Relations*, **36**, pp. 361–388.

Marsh, C. (1982), *The Survey Method*. London: Allen & Unwin.

McCarthy, W. E. J. and W. D. Ellis (1973), *Management by Agreement*. London: Hutchinson.

McCarthy, W. E. J. (1994), 'Of Hats and Cattle: or the limits of macro-survey research in industrial relations', *Industrial Relations Journal*, **25**, pp. 315–322.

McCrudden, C., D. J. Smith and C. Brown (1991), *Racial Justice at Work*. London: Policy Studies Institute.

Millward, N. (1994), *The New Industrial Relations?* London: Policy Studies Institute.

Millward, N., A. Bryson and J. Forth (2000), *All Change at Work?*. London: Routledge.

Millward, N. and W. R. Hawes (1995), 'Hats, cattle and industrial relations research'. *Industrial Relations Journal*, **26**, 69–73.

Millward N, Stevens M, Smart D and Hawes W R (1992), *Workplace Industrial Relations in Transition: The ED/ESRC/PSI/ACAS Surveys*, Aldershot, Dartmouth.

Millward, N. and M. Stevens (1986), *British Workplace Industrial Relations 1980–1984: the DE/ESRC/ PSI/ACAS Surveys*. Aldershot: Gower.

Ministry of Labour (1934), *Report on Collective Agreements between Employers and Workpeople in Great Britain and Northern Ireland*, vol 1. London: HMSO.

Ministry of Labour and National Service (1944), *Industrial Relations Handbook*. London: HMSO. Revised editions 1953, 1961.

Ministry of Labour (1965), *Written Evidence to the Royal Commission on Trade Unions and Employer Associations*. London: HMSO.

Mitchell , J. (1972), *The National Board for Prices and Incomes*. London: Secker & Warburg.

Mortimer, J. E. (1998), *A Life on the Left*. Sussex: the Book Guild.

Ross, A. M. and P. T. Hartman (1960), *Changing Patterns of Industrial Conflict*. New York: Wiley.

Sharp, I. G. (1950), *Industrial Conciliation and Arbitration in Great Britain*. London: Allen & Unwin.

Stone, N. (1993), *The Advisory, Conciliation and Arbitration Service: An example of the continuing success of tripartism against the odds, or anachronism in the era of anticollectivism*, unpublished MSc dissertation, Birkbeck College, University of London.

Tailby, S., E. Pearson and J. Sinclair (1977), *Employee relations in the South-West*. London: ACAS.

Taylor, J. and R. Woods (1994), *Pay strategies and Pay Determination in Scotland*. Glasgow: ACAS.

Towers, B. (1997), *The Representation Gap: Change and Reform in the British and American Workplace*. Oxford: Oxford University Press.

Weekes, B. et al (1975), *Industrial Relations and the Limits of the Law*. Oxford: Oxford University Press.

Wedderburn, K. W. W. (1971), *The Worker and the Law*, 2nd edn. Harmondsworth: Penguin.

Wedderburn, K. W. and P. L. Davies (1969), *Employment Grievances and Disputes Procedures in Britain*. Berkeley: University of California Press.

Whitfield, K. and G. Strauss (eds) (1998a), *Researching the World of Work: Strategies and Methods in Studying Industrial Relations*. Ithaca: Cornell University Press.

Whitfield, K. and G. Strauss (eds) (1998b), 'Retrospect and prospect', in *Researching the World of Work: Strategies and Methods in Studying Industrial Relations*. Ithaca: Cornell University Press.

2

Building bridges and settling differences: collective conciliation and arbitration under ACAS[1]

John Goodman

INTRODUCTION

It is over 25 years since ACAS was set up in 1974 as a tripartite body, independent of Government. It was charged inter alia with responsibility for the long established, state financed, supplementary and optional services aimed at assisting the resolution of industrial disputes which had not been settled by the parties in their jointly-agreed procedures.

This chapter's principal purpose is to describe and to consider ACAS's effectiveness in this role, and the contribution of ACAS's collective dispute resolution services to industrial relations over the past 25 years. The review is essentially retrospective, though inevitably it has implications for present and future operations. As the focus is on ACAS, other third-party conciliation or arbitration activities such as, for example, the Central Arbitration Committee (CAC), the various (now few) public or private-sector arbitral bodies and institutions like the former Wages Councils are not included. For an excellent review which includes this wider area of dispute resolution see Wood (1992). However it is necessary to touch on the fundamental economic, political, legal and other changes which have so altered British industrial relations from the situation of the early 1970s which led to the establishment of ACAS.

In resource terms collective conciliation and arbitration are minor ACAS activities, probably accounting for less than 10% of expenditure and dwarfed by individual conciliation activity. However, collective conciliation was instrumental in the creation and design of ACAS as a quasi-autonomous and independent body, and

[1] This is a review paper, based on literature and documents, supplemented by brief interviews with the then present and two former Chairmen of ACAS (John Hougham, Sir Douglas Smith and Sir Pat Lowry) and the present and immediate past Chief Conciliation Officers (Derek Evans and Dennis Boyd). I am grateful also to Simon Gouldstone (now Senior Case Manager, Central Arbitration Committee) for answers to several queries. All errors and views are my own.

arguably retains disproportionate influence in its public profile and rationale. Any review of ACAS's stewardship of these services requires discussion of both their *acceptability* and their *effectiveness*. Acceptability is crucial, for if the provider or the service is not acceptable to the parties in dispute, it cannot be effective. In order to establish acceptability, ACAS was designed to be *independent* (of governments) and not subject to ministerial direction in its operation, and *impartial* (as between the parties). The role and composition of its governing Council continue to symbolise these twin strategic objectives.

Applying the concept of effectiveness in the field of voluntary dispute resolution, primarily collective conciliation, has many potential hazards. For example, whilst having no objection to the specific third-party agency, the parties may react against the involvement of third parties per se, perhaps seeing it as an admission of failure, or regarding a particular issue as too complicated for an outsider to grasp all the intricacies and complications (Dickens, 1979). The involvement of third parties is often regarded as likely to lead to compromises, and issues of principle or preroga-tive are not readily amenable to compromise. Nor is some perceived or actual loss of control over the final outcome welcome. This may perhaps be especially feared in high-profile disputes, with the pressures generated via media attention. There are also other questions. For example, in disputes where industrial action has started, could ACAS have intervened earlier, or helped produce a settlement more quickly? How difficult was the problem, how big the gap between the parties, how good or poor their relationship, was the request made by one rather that both parties, how would it have been resolved in the absence of conciliation, and how good/durable/workable was the solution? The empirical research studies, most now rather dated, have largely bypassed these thorny issues (not least because of access problems) and instead have opted to survey the views of users. One fairly standard potential criticism, i.e. that on occasion collective conciliation may produce principally short-term stop-gap settlements, can readily be countered by the fact that the settlements are owned by the parties, and it is they and not the conciliators who make the decisions about short-term/long-term trade-offs. It is also possible to cite the increased use of ACAS-chaired Joint Working Parties (JWP) to follow up with longer-term strategic assistance after resolution of the immediate dispute.[2] On the other hand, these arguments may be less applicable to criticisms of some potential side-effects of arbitration.

The main sections of the chapter deal first with collective conciliation and second with arbitration organised by ACAS. These are preceded by brief background and contextual sections.

---

[2] JWPs, usually but not always operate under the 'Advisory Mediation' banner in ACAS, indicating some flexible blurring of activities at the interface of collective conciliation and advisory mediation.

BACKGROUND

The arrangements made by the state for the resolution of industrial disputes vary widely across the globe and between industrialised, democratic countries. The economic rationale for state intervention and expenditure in this area was succinctly set out by Laurie Hunter shortly after the establishment of ACAS (Hunter, 1977). Principal concerns typically include the minimisation of the economic and social damage arising from industrial disputes, and the promotion of employment/labour practices which optimise international economic competitiveness and growth. The nature and degree of state intervention varies, for example between legal and informal regulation, the scope and relative prominence of statutory prescription, and the conditions and institutions surrounding the lawful exercise of sanctions.

Within this mix the British system (in peacetime) was predominantly voluntary and informal within a wider 'collective laissez faire' regime (see McCarthy, 1992). Legal intervention and the involvement of lawyers was minimal, and the overriding values were that terms and conditions of employment and related matters were best left to voluntary collective bargaining, and collective bargaining was best left to the parties. The position of third-party agencies was generally that of optional extras, available if acceptable, to provide assistance in helping to unblock deadlocks or impasses which the parties, having exhausted their internal procedures, had been unable to resolve. This regime was interrupted in war-time with provisions for compulsory arbitration. It was supplemented by infrequently-used powers such as Courts of Inquiry, by the Industrial Court/CAC dealing mainly with specific statutory provisions, and—in extremis—Emergency Powers. This constituted the more or less settled position of third-party, state-funded, assistance. Its key characteristic was that it was voluntary and its use exceptional.

State-funded conciliation and arbitration have been provided as free services continuously in Britain for over a century, with ACAS thus accounting for almost a quarter of that period. Although there were earlier arrangements and experiments, modern provision is normally taken from the Conciliation Act 1896, which authorised the (then) Board of Trade to appoint conciliators to assist the parties, and where the parties agreed to do so, arbitrators. The conciliation function passed to the Ministry of Labour on its creation in 1917 and continued to be undertaken directly by this Government department until its transfer to ACAS in 1974. Arbitration, however, has had a rather more complicated institutional history, with the continuous use of ad hoc arbitration (our principal concern here) being supplemented in various ways at various times. Central amongst these was the Industrial Court set up in 1919, which arbitrated on a range of both voluntary and unilaterally referred statutory issues (e.g. the Fair Wages Resolution) through the period until its renaming in 1971 as the Industrial Arbitration Board, and subsequently (in 1975) as the Central Arbitration Committee (CAC). The CAC, which may also hear ad hoc voluntary arbitrations, was exceptionally busy in its early years with cases arising under

Schedule 11 of the Employment Protection Act 1975, but experienced a substantial reduction in its jurisdictions after 1979. Indeed it survived latterly on a rather slim diet of cases concerning disclosure of information for the purposes of collective bargaining. The new millennium, however, promises a much more prominent and significant workload as the key body in the new provisions on statutory trade union recognition in the Employment Relations Act 1999.

ACAS

ACAS was established by the Labour Government, initially as the Conciliation and Arbitration Service (CAS) in September 1974, without waiting for legislation, and as a statutory body from January 1976 by the Employment Protection Act 1975.[3] Its distinctive character was that though publicly funded it was to be *independent* of government, not subject to ministerial direction,[4] and run by a tripartite Council including equal numbers of representatives of the TUC and the CBI, balanced by independent members, initially mainly academics. The creation of ACAS removed from ministerial control the state's conciliation and arbitration functions, which successive governments had exercised for over 80 years. It followed significant dissatisfaction amongst employer organisations and especially trade unions at the withholding of conciliation by the Department of Employment (DoE) from certain disputes during the 1972–1974 incomes policy, and some uncertainty or ambiguity over the relationship between incomes policy and independent arbitration (see Hunter, 1983). These dissatisfactions had led to the creation jointly by the TUC and CBI of a (largely still-born) alternative service.

During the 1960s and 1970s there was much controversy and debate about the relationship between arbitration and incomes policies (see Hunter, 1983 for a full discussion). Should arbitrators be bound by the policy, and if not, just how much account should be taken of it? The ACAS Council resolved this very early on, and quickly demonstrated its independence from Government by affirming the primacy it would give to dispute resolution, rather than to interpreting, implementing or enforcing incomes-policy prescriptions. Copies of the relevant White Papers were sent to arbitrators 'for information', and they were recommended 'where appropriate' to include in their 'awards' a statement that they were not empowered to give an authoritative ruling as to whether the award conformed with the pay policy, and that if the parties had any doubts on that aspect they should seek the

---

[3] The statutory provisions relating to ACAS are now contained in Sections 210 and 211 of the Trade Union and Labour Relations (Consolidation) Act 1992.

[4] The 1975 Act provided that '... the Service shall not be subject to directions of any kind from any Minister of the Crown as to the manner in which it is to exercise any of its functions under any enactment' (Para 11(i), Schedule 1).

advice of the appropriate authorities (ACAS, 1976, p. 14). It is probable that this policy position contributed to the subsequent massive growth in both conciliation and arbitration cases immediately after the creation of ACAS.

The development of ACAS took place around the same time as the Department of Employment (DE) was 'hiving-off' other substantial activities into agencies, and at a time when civil servants were seeking to persuade ministers of the advantages of their being distanced from and thereby 'not responsible for doing something about' every industrial dispute which hit the headlines. ACAS was staffed in the main by civil servants from the DE Group, including staff with experience of conciliation and arbitration at the DE and the operation of the (disbanded) Commission on Industrial Relations (CIR). This continuity of staffing ensured that the established techniques and practice of collective dispute resolution and many of the values of the voluntary system were transferred to ACAS not only in the statute but also with the same people.

The terms of reference of ACAS, set out initially in a letter from the Secretary of State (ACAS, First Annual Report, 1975, Appendix B), and subsequently amplified in the Employment Protection Act 1975, were:

> to provide conciliation and mediation as a means of avoiding and resolving disputes, to make facilities available for arbitration, to provide advisory services to industry on industrial relations and related matters and to undertake investigations as a means of promoting the improvement and extension of collective bargaining.

Apart from the invited and not unwelcome loss of its role in the statutory union recognition procedure in 1980, subsequent changes (e.g. to ACAS's basic statutory duty in 1993) have had little or no impact on its collective conciliation or arbitration roles.

The absence of powers to compel the parties to suspend industrial action or to compel an unwilling party to co-operate with third parties in attempts to resolve collective disputes, was a well-established and (internationally-speaking) peculiar feature, indeed a dominant characteristic, of British state provision in this area long before ACAS was set up. It has continued to be fundamental to the ACAS philosophy and its mode of operation. ACAS is both a product of, and essentially an embodiment of, voluntarism. It has not only adopted but invariably advocated the efficacy of this approach to dispute resolution. It is seen as functional, more likely to produce workable and accepted solutions than compulsion.

CHANGED AND CHANGING CONTEXT

Much has changed in the economic, social, political and legal context of employment in Britain during the period since 1974. These changes, usefully highlighted in the opening chapter of successive ACAS Annual Reports, include: the enhanced scope and range of international competition in many product markets (EU 'single market' and 'globalisation'); major changes in technology, especially IT; the move away from Keynesian macroeconomic policies; a long period of high unemployment by 1945–1975 standards; the sectoral shift of employment from production to service industries; the decline of manual/blue collar, increase of non-manual/white-collar work; the growth in the proportion of female employees, part-time work, self-employment; and the privatisation of ex-nationalised industries, executive agencies etc. in the public sector.

In areas particularly close to ACAS's collective dispute-resolution work there have been possibly even more dramatic changes, for example: the continuous reduction in trade union membership (from 13m to 7m) and density; the reduced coverage of trade union recognition and of collective bargaining; the decline of industry employers' associations and multi-employer collective bargaining; the introduction of fundamental restrictive changes in collective labour law, particularly affecting strikes and other forms of industrial action; the substantial expansion in the scope and coverage of individual statutory employment rights, and their enforcement residually through Employment Tribunals; a major diminution in the incidence of industrial stoppages; and significant changes in organisational management—rise of human resource management (HRM) and neo-unitarism, downsizing, flexible labour forces, de-layering, team-building and so on.

The period may be characterised in many ways, but particularly significant for the work of ACAS are perhaps:

- the much enhanced role of statutory regulation in employment relations matters, employment standards etc, which—subject sometimes to length of service and other qualifications—seek to establish minimum rights and standards by statute, enforceable by individuals at Employment Tribunals; and,
- arguably, the heightened influence of what are sometimes categorised as neo unitarist perspectives, the often-asserted reduced emphasis on collectivist values and methods in the employment sphere, and the developing concept of partnership.

These developments have certainly changed the *context* of ACAS's collective dispute resolution work, and the emphasis and balance of its work. As suggested above, concerns about government influence on the availability of collective conciliation services and the thorny issue of what influence (if any) incomes policies should have on access to conciliation and on the decisions of arbitrators were key factors in the creation of ACAS in 1974. Collective disputes received massive media coverage, and the general public's perception of the *raison d'être* of ACAS (and possibly its only role) was to assist in the settling of these disputes. Few were aware of its advisory, preventive and individual conciliation activities. This impression was underpinned by the urgency usually attached to such disputes, if stoppages and perceived damage or inconvenience associated with them were to be averted or minimised. The ability of ACAS to help the parties resolve high-profile industrial disputes more rapidly than they would unassisted (and without, or with less, industrial action) was the obvious (if not only) criterion justifying the allocation of public funds. Whilst fire-fighting might be less strategic than preventive work, successfully assisting in settling often very complex collective industrial disputes attracted publicity, had urgency, carried significant prestige and not a little mystique. Thus ACAS's creation, its reputation and indeed at one or two points its survival rested disproportionately on its perceived and potential value in this field. Certainly Ministers (and governments) who loudly asserted their lack of involvement/influence/interest in some particularly prominent industrial disputes could see the merit of retaining an independent, autonomous body beyond their direction in this area when questions needed to be answered about what was being done to resolve such disputes. Being, or at least appearing to be 'hands off', was convenient and important to some views about the division of responsibility between ministers and managers.

COLLECTIVE CONCILIATION

Definitions and distinctions

State-sponsored collective conciliation has a long history as a very flexible means of intervention in industrial relations as a voluntary supplement to the parties estab-lished negotiating procedures. The latter have always been regarded as primary and it is a fundamental element of policy (and indeed incorporated into statute) that their authority should be upheld. Thus conciliation is normally considered appropriate only when these procedures have been exhausted or when the parties agree that other overriding considerations require it. This often presented difficulties and dilemmas when unofficial and/or unconstitutional strikes were widespread, and was a much-debated policy issue (see Kessler, 1980).[5] In recent years it has been less prominent. ACAS normally continued to deal with official union hierarchies, talking with unofficial strike leaders only when they formed part of official union teams or with clearance from officials.

Conciliation differs from arbitration in that the parties retain responsibility for any outcome, and from mediation in which the mediator is charged with making formal recommendations about the basis of a solution. Historically the distinction between conciliation and mediation has been sharp, with ACAS staff acting as con-ciliators and independent outsiders being appointed to conduct dispute mediation.[6]

---

[5] Sir John Wood observed that the Ministry of Labour's official policy that it would not intervene in unofficial strikes was a formal obstacle, but went on to suggest that 'too much importance should not be attached to this expression of rectitude, since no doubt unofficial soundings would often be made beyond the range of publicity ...' (Wood, 1992, p. 245.)

[6] Internationally such a fine distinction is less common, with the term mediation being widely used in the United States to describe processes for which the term conciliation would be used in Britain.

This fine line is important in that it maintains the official position that ACAS conciliators do not act as adjudicators. Whilst the conciliation/arbitration distinction is clear, that between conciliation and what ACAS now calls 'advisory mediation', and which includes JWPs, is less so. The latter are normally concerned with less urgent longer-term issues, and thus may be seen as more preventive or strategic than 'dispute mediation'. However, in some cases JWPs can in effect be an extension of conciliation, especially if undertaken against the background of a potential dispute or as part of a conciliated settlement. Finally, although the distinction between collective and individual conciliation activities looks clear in principle it can become complicated in practice—particularly in the area of multiple dismissals (and compensation) following industrial action, as at Wapping in 1986 and the 1995–1998 Liverpool docks dispute.

According to ACAS, collective conciliation:

> provides a means whereby employers and trade unions can be helped to reach a mutually acceptable settlement of their disputes by a neutral and independent third party. Its essential characteristics are that it is voluntary and that agreements reached in conciliation are the responsibility of the disputing parties. (The ACAS Role in Conciliation, Mediation and Arbitration)

ACAS conciliation: practice and process

Collective conciliation is normally characterised as a resumption or a continuation of the bargaining process—in effect *assisted bargaining*.[7] The conciliator's role is to facilitate a voluntary agreement. The principal processes are by acting as an intermediary in the exchange of information and ideas, by keeping the parties communicating, clarifying issues, establishing common ground, identifying barriers to progress, eroding unrealistic expectations, pointing to the costs and disadvantages if the dispute is not settled, developing possible solutions and creating confidence that an acceptable solution will be found. The conciliator has no powers other than those of reason and persuasion. The problem remains the property of the parties, as indeed does any emerging solution, irrespective of who may have first put it into the discussion. In its first Annual Report ACAS described the role of the conciliator as providing:

> a calm and informal atmosphere, a patient understanding of difficulties and a knowledge and experience of industrial relations. He probes and identifies the areas of agreement and disagreement, and acts as an intermediary between the parties in dispute conveying proposals without the formal commitment that direct negotiations sometimes require.

---

[7] Whilst this appears accurate in the great majority of cases, on occasion other characterisations may be applicable. For example conciliation may be sought as a *gateway* to other ACAS services, e.g. arbitration or mediation. (ACAS invariably offers conciliation first when approached with an arbitration request.) Parties to a dispute may also seek to use ACAS as an *external authority* (e.g. on employment law) whose endorsement may be sought via the conciliation process in order to persuade an employer or union members of the validity of a particular set of facts (see Jones *et al.*, 1983).

Conciliators, of course, are expected to put forward ideas or suggestions about possible ways forward and to use their judgement in a variety of ways, including not least the timing of interventions, the combination of formats of separate and joint meetings, and the use made of hints and suggestions made in confidence by the parties and so on.

Over the years of ACAS operation a more proactive emphasis has gradually replaced the earlier emphasis on the conciliator as a 'catalyst', a word which is now much less in vogue. Rather, the 1998 ACAS Annual Report suggested, 'The role of the conciliator is to be *a creative force* [emphasis added] in dispute resolution'. It is difficult to judge whether this reflects a greater degree of transparency in what has always been a somewhat blurred area, or a real change of emphasis.

ACAS has developed a range of operational manuals and training materials used internally, describing choices and alternatives both at different stages of the process (such as the classic conundrum of 'no talks until there's a return to work' versus 'the action will not be called off without an improved offer') and compilations of possible avenues of approach in disputes about different issues. The whole process is conducted on a confidential basis—a feature regarded by conciliators as critical to its success. This, however, has also in the past prevented observation by researchers, though some with direct experience of ACAS have shed some light on the process (see Fells, 1986, Lowry, 1990, pp. 24–26). For a full early account of ACAS collective conciliation methods, issues, roles and so on see the 1978 Annual Report, pp. 51–64.

In the main, ACAS becomes involved in disputes as a result of conciliation being written into voluntary procedures, those procedures having been exhausted or an impasse reached, or following a joint or unilateral request from parties with no procedures.[8] Thus, in most cases, the initial timing is determined by the parties. However, without any request from the parties, ACAS may become aware of a dispute via its networks or the media and may contact the parties to be briefed. In the ACAS in-house jargon this behind-the-scenes activity is called 'running alongside' a dispute. It may lead to a later intervention offering conciliation assistance. Maintaining these channels of communication is plainly a very important activity, perhaps especially so in cases where relationships have broken down, and in high-profile disputes. Figures for 'running alongside' were first published in 1982 and are given in Table 1.

Demand and usage levels

Collective conciliation is used in only a small minority of collective-bargaining situations. Most differences or disputes are resolved directly by the parties without outside assistance. Second, it must be emphasised that most of the work done by

---

[8] There is a separate statutory duty on ACAS to conciliate in disclosure of information cases to the CAC or failure to consult on redundancy applications to an employment tribunal.

TABLE 1
ACAS requests for collective conciliation

	Number of Stoppages	'Running Alongside'	Requests	Completed	Settlement or progress towards one	Conciliation Unsuccessful Number	% (rounded)	Head Office No[a]	%
1975	2332	n/a	2564	2017	1640	377	19	81	4
1976	2034	n/a	3460	2851	2188	663	23	84	2
1977	2737	n/a	3299	2891	2126	765	26	76	3
1978	2498	n/a	3338	2706	1997	709	26	69	3
1979	2125	n/a	2667	2284	1786	498	22	62	3
1980	1348	n/a	2091	1910	1467	443	23	54	3
1981	1344	n/a	1958	1716	1364	352	21	59	3
1982	1538	173[b]	1865	1634	1292	342	21	90	6
1983	1364	479	1789	1621	1370	251	15	120	7
1984	1221	453	1569	1448	1246	202	14	108	7
1985	903	379	1475	1337	1104	233	17	87	6
1986	1974	540	1457	1323	1117	206	16	95	7
1987	1016	500	1302	1147	955	192	17	95	8
1988	781	524	1163	1059	876	183	17	96	9
1989	701	423	1164	1070	910	160	15	100	9
1990	630	260	1260	1140	964	176	15	103	9
1991	369	238	1386	1226	1056	170	14	100	8
1992	253	168	1207	1140	971	169	15	94	8
1993	211	209	1211	1118	980	138	12	80	7
1994	205	304	1313	1162	1052	110	9	51	4
1995	235	366	1321	1229	1082	147	12	42	3
1996	244	355	1306	1197	1099	98	8	35	3
1997	216	301	1281	1166	1038	128	12	29	2
1998	166	263	1301	1214	1110	104	9	26	2
1999[c]	192	219	1465	1212	1111	101	8	24	2

Source: ACAS Annual Reports

Notes:
Excludes claims for trade union recognition under the statutory procedure
Excludes claims reported to ACAS under Schedule 11 of the Employment Protection Act 1975
[a] In some cases both region and Head office may be involved, either sequentially or simultaneously.
[b] Six months.
[c] Provisional

ACAS conciliators is carried out (usually quietly and unobtrusively) in the regions, for the most part to settle minor issues rather than major disputes. Head Office handles national level disputes, and those of special importance or national significance, a proportion which has never exceeded ten per cent of the caseload and is often substantially less. Third, for whatever reason, in the great majority of cases industrial action is avoided.

Traditionally, the number of stoppages has also been taken as a crude indicator of the scope for collective conciliation, despite the obvious limitations of this view. Many factors may influence changes in the number of instances when third-party collective conciliation may be requested or be feasible. For example, the level of demand may be influenced by increases/decreases in the number of bargaining units and the frequency of negotiations. Thus the reductions in the coverage of collective bargaining might be expected to offset the decentralisation of bargaining structures to local/establishment level. It might also be suggested that the relative inexperience of negotiators at these lower levels (e.g. in the public sector) may—at least initially— be more likely to lead to situations in which third-party assistance is sought. Wider macro variables such as labour market conditions, profit levels, rates of change in living standards and the presence or absence of incomes policies were also thought to have an impact (Hunter, 1977).

In the early years of its existence the demand for ACAS collective conciliation rose dramatically, to peak levels of over 3,000 in the three years 1976, 1977 and 1978, several times the volume of requests in the preceding years. It would be simplistic, however, to regard this as purely a huge positive response to the creation of ACAS, though it was a factor. The TUC urged affiliated unions to make full use of it, and the then largest union—the TGWU—adopted a policy of instructing officials to use ACAS before taking industrial action. The presence on its governing Council of leading figures from the trade unions and the CBI, and the early and decisive steps taken by the Council to place dispute resolution as its primary target, irrespective of the incomes policy prescriptions of the time,[9] were crucial to its acceptability amongst disputants.

The circumstances of the first few years were clearly exceptional, and demand fell markedly during the recession years of the early 1980s, and then more gradually to just under half the early peak in the mid-1980s. Writing in 1990, Lowry suggested a number of reasons for the decline in the conciliation workload, including:

- from 1979 Conservative governments were in power which '... commended the virtues of employers standing on their own feet';
- changes in the economic and political climate causing employers to 'think twice' before becoming involved with an agency created by a Labour Government;
- given ACAS's role in the 1975–1980 statutory trade union recognition process, '... there were undoubtedly some employers who denied themselves the use of the service because of its suspected bias';
- the change in the balance of bargaining power (due inter alia to declining union membership and recession) led employers who in other circumstances might have used ACAS conciliation deciding not to; and
- a fall in the number of strikes.

---

[9] Jim Mortimer, the first Chairman of ACAS, notes that under the Labour Government ACAS '... decided that (it) should not act as the interpreter, monitor and, least of all, as enforcement agent for the incomes policy' and under the Conservative Government it '... decided not to be involved in drawing up codes of practice on picketing and the closed shop' (Mortimer, 1981 p. 24) because in both situations it could be regarded as instrumental in carrying out government policy.

It has also been suggested (Jones *et al.*, 1983) that ACAS's (temporary) statutory conciliation caseload (Schedule 11 and statutory recognition) may have indirectly stimulated voluntary references, but their removal also then contributed to the subsequent decline. Lowry concluded that, provided it takes place in 'an improving climate of industrial relations', a decline in the collective conciliation workload of ACAS from its early peak '... is a healthy symptom' (Lowry, 1990, pp. 35–36).

Despite the continued major reductions in the number of industrial stoppages, trade union membership and coverage of collective bargaining, the number of requests for collective conciliation between 1987 and 1998 has been essentially stable (see Figure 1 and Table 1). Over these recent years it fluctuated only between a low of 1,160 in 1988 and a high of 1,380 in 1991, with a five year average of 1,300—virtually identical with demand in the latest year, 1998. This stability, at a level over twice that experienced in the years prior to ACAS's arrival,[10] is both curious and interesting (see below), particularly when contrasted with the recent substantial fall in arbitration—though certain special factors are relevant to that. It must be remembered that simple numbers of requests tell us nothing about the nature or relative importance of the dispute, nor its complexity or the degree of difficulty involved in reaching a conciliated settlement.

The subject matter

The tables in the text bring together statistics from the ACAS Annual Reports on a number of dimensions of ACAS collective conciliation activity. Table 2 presents completed case data on the number and proportion classified by 'cause of dispute'. As always such data need to be treated with caution, not least because not all disputes have a single, simple 'cause' which fits readily the classification used. The main features are:

- the unsurprising prominence of the compendious 'Pay and terms and conditions of employment' category, accounting for half or more of cases in all but six years—all in the 1990s;
- the relative importance of trade union recognition cases,[11] which were above the 10% level in every year until 1993, and rose again in 1998 and 1999—possibly in response to the anticipated legislation;
- the consistent flow (proportionately) of discipline and dismissal cases at or around the 10% level; and

---

[10] In the period 1960-64 the Department took conciliation action in between 300 and 400 cases, reaching 408 in 1964. The annual average for the five years 1965-9 was 439, but the number accelerated thereafter viz. 1968–472; 1969–516; 1970–647; 1971–716; 1973–866. For earlier periods see Goodman and Krislov (1974).

[11] In most collective conciliation situations, the parties already have a relationship and mainly expect it to be a continuing one. This is not the case where trade union recognition is being sought, and hence the approach, role and skills required of the collective conciliator may need to differ from other cases.

FIGURE 1
Stoppages and ACAS intervention, 1975–1999[a]

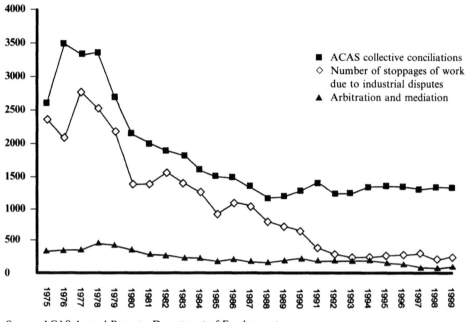

■ ACAS collective conciliations
◇ Number of stoppages of work due to industrial disputes
▲ Arbitration and mediation

Source: ACAS Annual Reports; Department of Employment
Note: [a] 1999 provisional

- the fluctuating share of redundancy cases, reflecting in part the incidence of the business cycle with record levels in 1991 and 1992.

Some issues are likely to be more readily referred to third parties than others, and some more likely to go no further than voluntary conciliation. The major contrast with the equivalent table of arbitration cases is the absence of recognition and redundancy categories (and probably cases) in the latter.

It is difficult to establish objective or systematic measures of the 'importance' of the disputes in which ACAS conciliates or arbitrates, particularly where industrial action is avoided and the conventional but crude and undiscriminating 'days lost' measure is not available. No figures are published on the number of employees involved in the cases. Employer resistance prevented ACAS attempting conciliation for example in the major Civil Service dispute in 1981, and at Wapping and P&O ferries until the final stages; whilst its attempts in the 1984–85 miners strike, although significant, ultimately proved unsuccessful. 'Importance' has several dimensions, and certainly some major regional conciliations can be just as 'important' as some lesser national ones. However, one possible proxy, despite its many limitations, is the number of disputes in which Head Office acts as conciliator. The criteria governing

TABLE 2
Completed cases by cause of dispute

Total		Pay and Terms & Conditions of Employment		Recognition		Redundancy		Dismissal and discipline		Demarcation		Other TU matters		Others	
		No	%	No	%	No	%	No	%	No	%	No	%	No	%
1975	2017	1148	57	416	21	102	5	208	10	24	1	49	3	70	4
1976	2851	1561	55	697	24	148	5	220	8	32	1	88	3	105	4
1977	2891	1601	55	635	22	134	5	239	8	32	1	143	5	107	4
1978	2706	1652	61	451	17	91	3	218	8	26	1	130	5	138	5
1979	2284	1336	59	392	17	90	4	219	10	20	1	125	6	102	5
1980	1910	1003	53	329	17	181	10	210	11	12	1	101	5	74	4
1981	1716	969	54	247	14	153	9	204	12	17	1	82	5	44	3
1982	1634	977	60	232	14	109	7	189	12	12	1	62	4	53	3
1983	1621	966	60	216	13	103	6	178	11	13	1	57	4	88	5
1984	1448	854	59	221	15	71	5	183	13	8	1	41	3	70	5
1985	1337	769	58	211	16	80	6	162	12	8	1	49	4	58	4
1986	1323	777	59	179	14	61	5	172	13	1	–	51	4	82	6
										Changes in working practices					
1987	1147	652	57	140	12	52	5	147	13	43	4	60	5	53	5
1988	1059	594	56	165	16	35	3	148	14	42	4	37	4	38	4
1989	1070	585	55	136	13	56	5	141	13	48	5	50	5	54	5
1990	1140	570	50	159	14	109	10	147	13	67	6	50	4	38	3
1991	1226	496	41	174	14	233	19	144	12	46	4	91	7	42	3
1992	1140	468	41	148	13	238	21	129	11	50	4	64	6	43	4
1993	1118	527	47	94	8	220	20	124	11	59	5	61	5	33	3
1994	1162	590	51	93	8	185	16	120	10	60	5	65	6	49	4
1995	1229	593	48	107	9	203	17	144	12	42	3	86	7	54	4
1996	1197	537	45	112	9	184	15	143	12	68	6	103	9	50	4
1997	1166	593	51	102	9	146	12	146	12	57	5	77	7	45	4
1998	1214	581	48	131	11	144	12	157	13	77	6	80	6	44	4
1999[a]	1212	610	50	151	12	153	13	122	10	60	5	59	5	57	5

Source: ACAS Annual Reports

Notes: Recognition excludes cases under section 11 of Employment Protection Act 1975 (repealed 1980)
% rounded   [a] Provisional

Head Office involvement have varied, being described at various times as 'cases involving industry-wide disputes or companies with several plants throughout the country' (ACAS Annual Report, 1976, p. 11), and 'those involving disputes of national significance and public concern' (ACAS Annual Report, 1984, p. 21) and 'disputes having a national dimension' (ACAS Annual Report, 1998, p. 39). The numbers are in Table 1 and show around 70 cases (1975–1982) rising to an average of 100 (1983–1992) followed by a rapid decline to less than 30 cases in the most recent years. The proportion handled at Head Office has fallen from a peak of around 9% in 1989 to around 2% currently.

The source of requests

The other statistical tables relating to collective conciliation in the Appendix also touch on the issues of acceptability and effectiveness. Table 3 traces shifts in the source of requests. It shows continuation of the long established very low proportion coming from employers alone. It also indicates a decline in the proportion of requests from trade unions alone (from over half in the early days), but an increase in joint requests, from around a quarter to consistently over 40%. As the number of requests has stabilised at around 1,300 this rise in joint applications has been suggested in several ACAS Annual Reports as an indicator of the continuing acceptability of ACAS. Whilst this development is obviously welcome on general grounds, it is open to the question of whether it can bear such an interpretation. Table 3 also shows what may be a significant influence on the maintenance of demand for collective conciliation, namely the sharp upward movement in the number and proportion of cases in which ACAS took the initiative—up from an

TABLE 3
Completed Cases Analysed by Source of Request %[a]

	Union	Employer	Joint	ACAS	Total
1975	56	17	24	3	2017
1976	56	17	24	3	2851
1977	54	20	23	3	2891
1978	56	19	22	3	2706
1979	52	17	29	2	2284
1980	53	14	31	3	1910
1981	48	13	36	3	1716
1982	42	14	40	4	1634
1983	40	12	45	4	1621
1984	37	12	48	4	1448
1985	40	11	47	2	1337
1986	36	12	50	3	1323
1987	32	11	53	4	1147
1988	32	10	54	4	1059
1989	33	10	54	3	1070
1990	32	9	54	5	1140
1991	37	9	48	6	1226
1992	36	6	51	7	1140
1993	31	11	50	9	1118
1994	31	9	47	13	1162
1995	35	11	43	11	1229
1996	35	11	40	14	1197
1997	32	11	41	16	1038
1998	32	10	41	17	1214
1999[b]	34	12	38	16	1212

Source: ACAS Annual Reports

Notes: [a] % rounded   [b] provisional

average of only 4% between 1975 and 1993 to an average of 14% over the most recent five years. Further analysis at regional level shows a remarkable increase in the number of collective conciliation cases in Scotland which more than doubled between 1992/93 and 1995/96. It is difficult to account for this increase in terms which do not include local initiative to improve contacts and communication with the collective conciliation constituency.

Although ACAS conciliation is not restricted to employees represented by trade unions it might be expected largely to reflect the narrowed areas where unions are recognised. Certainly some of the most heavily unionised sectors are well represented, with engineering and transport and communication prominent. However, over the years, the 'food drink and tobacco' sector has probably been the most consistently and most highly over-represented sector, with some of its constituent areas such as baking perhaps showing occasional signs of addiction. The media and banks have also been frequent users at times. No continuous data are available on the public sector/private sector division but health and education have become much more prominent in the 1990s.

'Success' rates

The question of effectiveness relates in part to ensuring that the parties are aware of and, where appropriate, utilise ACAS services. A second, and arguably critical dimension, is not only that the services are used in appropriate cases but that they are also largely effective in the time-worn phrase in 'achieving a settlement or progress towards one'. ACAS records the outcome of cases as being 'successful' either if a settlement is achieved (which includes a reference to arbitration and withdrawal of claims) or if there is progress (which includes movement back to direct talks or reference to mediation or a working group). Plainly this process involves a degree of subjectivity and self-reporting, and the stark terms 'success' and 'failure' may on occasion perhaps exaggerate the clarity of the outcomes. For example, some small disputes may fade away, not being sufficiently significant to be pressed to a conclusion, or perhaps having served a purpose as part of some wider developments. Sometimes ACAS conciliators move in and out of disputes at different times. There is also scope for debate about the categorisation on the outcomes in some cases— for example how voluntary recognition cases which do not lead to some form of recognition should be classified.

Whatever the weight of these considerations may be, they appear marginal relative to the predominance of reported outcomes. Table 1 indicates success rates improving from an already impressive level of over 70% in the early years to a moving average of close to 90% over the last five years. This is an outstanding achievement, and reflects great credit on the skilled ACAS staff involved. It is indeed difficult to envisage it rising further. Along with other aspects of collective conciliation it may benefit from independent study, and perhaps identifying separately the two component elements of reported 'success' would be useful.[12]

Surveys of users

Earlier research studies of collective conciliation have focused principally on the experience and views of the parties to collective conciliation. All reported in generally favourable terms. The earliest survey (1972) reported reservations about third-party involvement per se (greater than in surveys of other countries) but high levels of satisfaction with the behaviour and competence of the conciliators, with 75% of both parties saying they would not hesitate to use conciliation again in a similar dispute (Goodman and Krislov, 1974). Reporting on a sample survey of 1977/78 cases Jones *et al.*, 1983 noted that '... our survey evidence suggests that when ACAS does intervene both sides have a high regard for the service which is provided and would use it again if a similar issue arose'.

The most recent survey, albeit now 15 years old, was even more positive. Analysis of responses from the principal negotiators in a sample of 1984/85 conciliation cases (161 employer representatives and 174 union officers) showed scores of over 90% confirming, for example, that the conciliator acted impartially, had sufficiently understood the issues and had sufficient experience/knowledge about industrial relations. 90% also regarded the conciliator's contribution to the settlement as good, very good or excellent. These extremely high levels of positive response were underpinned by some reservations (particularly amongst managers) about becoming involved in the process, and strong emphasis from both management and union representatives on the importance of the process being voluntary and used only as a supplement to their own disputes procedures. 95% of union officers and 91% of managers in the survey said they would be prepared to use ACAS conciliation again for a similar future dispute. Interestingly this research (Burrill and Hiltrop 1988) also offers some insight into the reasons for the failure of conciliation in certain cases. Explanations included 'unrealistic trade union expectations'; 'intransigence'; employers 'take it or leave it' approach; 'lack of will'; the nature of the issues (e.g. indivisible/principle); original gap between the parties too wide; conflict not reached sufficient intensity to induce movement and one or other of the parties having entered conciliation as a manoeuvre (e.g. for public relations' reasons or as a bargaining tactic) rather than as a positive attempt to seek a settlement. Only four of the respondents in 'no settlement' cases regarded the role of the ACAS conciliator as a reason for non-settlement.

These studies offer impressive results, in terms of 'satisfied customers'. However they are confined to users, and can provide no information about non-users, and

---

[12] Research by Studd (1994, p. 89) looking at a sample of 1993 cases (a year in which ACAS claimed 87.7% success) found that conciliated settlements were achieved in 60% of cases.

thus about attitudes to ACAS collective conciliation more broadly across the employment relations scene.

Attitudes of government and the public sector

ACAS was created by a Labour government, and appeared vulnerable to possible abolition or radical overhaul or commercialisation at various points during the 18 years of Conservative Government from 1979 to 1997. During these years the Government was committed to deregulation of the labour market, made no secret of its distaste for collective bargaining, and 'set an example' by preferring confrontation to conciliation in many disputes in which it had direct influence over the employing organisation. An early example was the refusal of ACAS conciliation assistance in the Civil Service strikes in 1981, and several other instances might be cited during the 1980s. Such exclusions, whilst no doubt a disappointment to ACAS, not least for their wider 'exemplar' implications, may be considered to be legitimate where the Government was the direct employer. However it is beyond doubt that the Government's 'principled resistance' (Lowry, 1990, p. 30) was an important influence, particularly in other areas of the public sector including the then nationalised industries. For example ACAS recorded its concern at its delayed involvement in the 1981 13-week strike at the British Steel Corporation (8.8m. working days lost). Such exclusion or delayed involvement was not universal and 'principled resistance' appears to have applied selectively and pragmatically. ACAS was heavily involved, through a (rare) Committee of Inquiry in the major water dispute in 1983, and also appointed an independent panel (chaired by Sir John Wood) in an attempt to mediate in the 1985/86 teachers' dispute.

   The interface between ACAS and different parts of the public sector and different disputes within it is fascinating but often tantalisingly inaccessible. Often the references to this area in the ACAS annual reports are perhaps understandably but frustratingly bland—with the partial exception of ACAS's role in the 1984–1985 miners' strike where some detail is given. Sometimes public sector employer reluctance to involve ACAS is put down to the fact that ACAS staff 'are only civil servants', sometimes to the subject of the dispute, or to co-operation in conciliation being interpreted as a readiness to compromise where there is none. In some instances a rigid opposition to involving third parties in a particular dispute is announced; in others it is operated in a more discrete fashion, sometimes being presented for example by Ministers as matter solely for the management of the operation'. The reality or otherwise of such sentiments, and the public relations smokescreens and subtleties in this area of ACAS work are difficult for outsiders to unravel. This 'aloof' stance was compromised by press leaks in the water dispute in 1984. Resistance by governments as employer to the use of third parties in particular disputes, and influencing other employers to do likewise, however is not direct 'political interference' in the operation of ACAS. Seeking to influence when ACAS intervenes and when it holds off, however, could be.

There is plenty of evidence of ACAS conciliation activity in many parts of the public sector, not least in the railways and London Underground, and in various areas of local authorities. Lowry comments that '... despite the apparent misgivings of central government, ACAS has been officially involved in conciliations involving the NHS *at district level*; and even in the Civil Service protracted *local* disputes have eventually involved ACAS ...' (Lowry, 1990, p. 30). Unfortunately there are no continuous statistics about the number and proportion of ACAS collective conciliation cases in the public sector, though there are occasional figures. In 1986 and 1987, for example, national and local government (alone) accounted for around 10% of the ACAS conciliation case load (Beaumont, 1992). Cases in the public sector appear to have risen during the 1990s, with figures of 12% (1991) 16% (1992), 18% (1993) and around a quarter (1998). In recent years, ACAS Head Office conciliators have been involved in the prominent national disputes in higher education (1997) and in Royal Mail (1996). These illustrate that despite Conservative governments' reforms which often had the effect of removing, fragmenting or otherwise marginalising large national public-sector bargaining units a number of these remain. The public sector is an area of relatively high union density, where national level disputes and the threat of industrial action remain feasible. The new Labour Government elected in May 1997 has yet to face a major Civil Service or NHS dispute of national significance. If it does, its approach to ACAS conciliation involvement will be watched with interest. Its attitude to arbitration in such a case would be especially interesting.

Impact of changes in the law and strike patterns

Conservative legislation restricting and imposing new legal requirements if those inducing industrial action are to remain within the narrower limits of the traditional immunities have altered the scene. For many other reasons too, industrial action has probably become more difficult to organise and sustain, and open-ended strikes are very rare indeed. The availability of the law as a means of challenging industrial action means it is an option to be considered by any employer facing serious disruption. Its use involves an approach and a process, aimed more at stopping the action via assiduous attention to, for example, ballot rules, than to resolving the dispute itself. It seems probable that successful use of injunctions may increase employer resistance to third-party conciliation, though in some disputes, e.g. on London Underground, this has not always followed. The inter-relationship (and relative frequency of use) of the new legal avenues and traditional dispute resolution processes has not yet been resolved. However, the advantages of the latter (flexibility, cost, continuity of relationship etc) suggest that in most situations it is continuing to prevail.

The introduction of industrial action ballots may appear to complicate the conciliation process although they have now become an accepted and routine part of the process. They can have the effect of raising the profile of disputes, and thus offer 'early warning' of a dispute to ACAS. However the complex requirements for notifying employers, and the requirement that action must be taken within the 28-day ballot validity period seem likely to present hurdles and deadlines which may be unhelpful to conciliation. In this context it is interesting to note the provision in the Employment Relations Act 1999 for the possible extension of the ballot validity period from four weeks to eight weeks, where both parties agree to this. In an early assessment of the effects of ballots on conciliation ACAS (ACAS Annual Report 1985, p. 16) indicated that in some cases they prolonged conciliation slightly, with the parties declining to amend their position until the ballot result was known. However, ballots sometimes aided conciliation subsequently since the party against whom the result had gone was likely to be prepared to reconsider its position. Major difficulties arose only where strike action had been taken following support in a ballot and union officials chose to regard this as a mandate from which they could not diverge.

The very marked reduction in the incidence of (recorded) industrial action to record low levels—whether due to legal or other changes—is itself relevant to the context of conciliation activity. Whilst this might be seen in one sense to demonstrate the parties enhanced ability to resolve disputes without recourse to sanctions, it may also reflect reductions in trade union coverage and, from a distributive perspective, reductions in power. It is possible also that the increased difficulty of getting members to strike may be a factor in maintaining the caseload, particularly in adversarial situations with trade union officials seeing conciliation as a possible means of making progress. Where strike action does take place it now seems more likely to take the form of a series of one-day stoppages than an open-ended all-out strike. The former may make the conciliation process more protracted in that it may take longer to cause sufficient damage to concentrate minds. Particularly in disputes with media appeal, a weekly pattern of one-day strikes may undermine efforts at conciliation. If there is insufficient progress to call off the next scheduled strike, not only will that set things back but the parties may become involved in an acrimonious media exchange. This may remove the benefit of any past progress in conciliation and threaten to make it more difficult in the time available to secure enough progress to call off the next scheduled stoppage.

Overview of conciliation

For the past decade, in conditions which would tend to predict a downward trend, the numbers of requests for ACAS collective conciliation and completed cases have remained virtually unchanged. This suggests that although the incidence of major attention-catching disputes of national significance has diminished, ACAS has maintained its reputation and acceptability. There seems to be no sign of any lack of trust in its impartiality or independence, nor any evidence of doubts about the competence of its staff. Indeed, if the demand is in some way correlated to the incidence of (recorded) stoppages then arguably its acceptability has improved markedly. There is evidence that ACAS has been more proactive in various respects e.g. the number of running alongsides, the rising proportion of interventions recorded as at ACAS initiative, and improved contact-building and networking in some regions. There are also other possible reasons, including the legal and other difficulties trade unions have faced in pursuing industrial action and the spread/impact of ACAS conciliation references in procedure agreements.

VOLUNTARY ARBITRATION

Definitions and Distinctions

Voluntary arbitration as arranged by ACAS is a process through which employers and trade unions jointly agree to pass the responsibility for determining the terms of settlement of a dispute or difference to an independent person (single arbitrator) or a group of persons (a board of arbitration)[13] appointed by ACAS, and in so doing they agree in advance to accept the award as binding. Unlike private arbitrations, and those commercial arbitrations regulated by the Arbitration Act, ACAS arranged arbitrations are binding in honour only, not in law. Nonetheless, ACAS reports that the awards are invariably implemented.

The Employment Protection Act 1975 made it clear that a reference to ACAS—arranged arbitration may be at the request of one party but needs the consent of both; the dispute may be referred either to the CAC or to arbitrators appointed by ACAS; and that ACAS shall not normally refer a matter for settlement to arbitration unless the appropriate agreed procedures have been used and have failed to result in a settlement. Thus an unwilling party cannot be compelled to go to arbitration offered by ACAS. ACAS Council has at various times affirmed its belief that '. . . arbitration (and mediation) provide valuable means of resolving disputes, when conciliation has failed to forestall or curtail industrial action.' (ACAS Annual Report 1980, p. 25). ACAS also responds to requests from employers and trade unions for the names of people suitably qualified to act as arbitrators under 'private' arrangements made by them rather than by ACAS. As the frequency of use of these is unknown, exact figures on the use of voluntary arbitration are impossible to establish. Such cases were generally considered unlikely to equal the number of ACAS-arranged arbitrations.

Voluntary arbitration may be contrasted with both compulsory arbitration (as applied during war-time and for a period after 1945) and unilateral statutory

---

[13] Occasionally assessors are also appointed to assist with technical issues.

arbitration, which allows one party to refer a statutory matter for binding decision by an arbitral body despite the objections of the other. As well as hearing voluntary arbitration cases the CAC (and its predecessors) has considerable experience in the latter area e.g. in deciding cases under the Fair Wages Resolution, Schedule 11 of the EPA, the Equal Pay Act, statutory trade union recognition and disclosure of information. Unilateral access to arbitration is also found as the final stage of some voluntary collective agreement dispute procedures, such as the so-called 'new-style' agreements of the 1980s which were given so much publicity. Voluntarily agreed unilateral access arbitration provisions were formerly common in various parts of the public sector e.g. the Civil Service. They are now much less so following Conservative governments' very strong criticism of unilateral access arrangements in the 1980s (see below) though they have survived in some areas, such as the police. The change from unilateral access to jointly-agreed reference to arbitration of course allows one party to block any reference, and the change has certainly tended to reduce the use of arbitration (despite its continuing presence in procedures) in many public service areas. ACAS has provided the secretarial support for a number of standing arbitral bodies in the public sector.[14]

Voluntary arbitration organised by ACAS is also distinguished from two other relatively little used forms of third -party intervention, namely mediation and inquiry/ investigation. *Mediation* is broadly intermediate between conciliation and arbitration, in that the mediator (or board of mediation) may proceed initially by way of conciliation but is expected to make formal recommendations. These may form—or form the basis of—a possible settlement, but (unlike arbitration) the parties are not committed in advance to accept. However, like arbitration, dispute mediation is conducted by independent people, appointed on an ad hoc basis and not by ACAS staff. ACAS generally considers mediation to be appropriate in complicated, multi-issue disputes (e.g. major changes in pay systems or structures or work arrangements) and where the parties are reluctant to be bound in advance by an award. During the 1980s there was some experimentation with a hybrid format known as 'med/arb' where the person appointed was expected to bring the parties to mediated agreement on the various issues if possible, but (as a means of helping to move the parties)was to act as arbitrator on any where this proved impossible (see ACAS Annual Report, 1987).

ACAS also has powers to provide facilities for ad hoc Courts or Committees of Inquiry or Panels of Investigation.[15] The former have a long and distinguished

---

[14] Some public sector areas which included arbitration in their disputes procedures also made provision for it to be conducted not by ad hoc arbitrators but by standing arbitral bodies which could build up knowledge and expertise relevant to a particular sector and its agreements e.g. the Railway Staffs National Tribunal (RSNT) and the Civil Service Arbitration Tribunal. The pros and cons of such bodies are debated in the literature.

[15] The Government also retained the power available to it had under earlier legislation to appoint Courts of Inquiry.

history, being used sparingly in the past but being found useful in terms of publishing factual reports which often established the basis of settlements in important and large disputes. Building on a method used by the CIR, ACAS was given powers to inquire into any industrial relations topic or industrial relations in a particular organisation or workplace. Use of these formats appears dormant, with apparently none since 1990.

ACAS arbitrations: practice and characteristics

References to ACAS arbitration arise principally following conciliation at ACAS which has been either partially successful (e.g. narrowed differences) or unsuccessful, or as requests for arbitration stemming from the parties' agreed procedures. In the latter cases ACAS routinely offers to conciliate prior to arranging arbitration, and is usually involved in ensuring that there are agreed, precise and unambiguous terms of reference. ACAS then appoints an arbitrator, usually a single arbitrator (more rarely a board of three) from its panel of arbitrators, and advises the parties about the submission and exchange of their written cases and arrangements for the hearing. The hearings are conducted informally, with an investigative/inquisitorial style used by the arbitrator, as opposed to the adversarial method adopted in the courts. Unlike in conciliation (and some styles of mediation) the parties are present throughout. The principal aim of the hearing is to ensure that the arbitrator fully understands all the issues and implications, and that both parties have had adequate opportunity to make their cases. Legal representation is rare. Awards are not given at the hearing but are written and sent to the parties via ACAS Head Office, usually about a week or so after the hearing. There are inevitably many matters of detail, and the handling of these is considerably helped by the presence of a specialist unit at ACAS Head Office, ensuring consistency of handling, giving advice and so on.

History suggests that the acceptability of arbitration turns, inter alia, on the suitability, quality and acceptability of the arbitrator. Like its predecessor, ACAS maintains a list (panel) of persons suitable to act as arbitrators and also of people experienced as representatives of employers or workers able to act as side members of boards of arbitration. Most arbitrators are academics, mainly with knowledge of industrial relations, labour economics or law, although there are also some lawyers and former civil servants. The principal requirement, in addition to relevant knowledge, experience and appropriate skills, is that of impartiality. As Sir Roy Wilson, former President of the Industrial Court and the Industrial Arbitration Board put it:

> The most important of all qualities necessary for a good arbitrator is the personal capacity to inspire in the parties who come before him/her full confidence that she/he will hear and decide the reference with understanding and care and complete impartiality. (Cited in the internally circulated ACAS Guide for Arbitrators.)

In the past, recruitment to the panel was largely informal, but recently in antici-pation of implementation of the arbitration alternative to employment tribunal hearings of unfair dismissal cases, a more open recruitment and selection process has been followed. Unlike in some other systems, e.g. the USA, the majority of single arbitrators and chairs of boards are appointed to cases by ACAS without consul-tation with the parties. This enables hearings to be arranged reasonably quickly, and arbitrators to be selected taking account of factors such as the need for special expertise, geographical factors and availability. In the case of boards of arbitration, the parties normally select their side member from a few names supplied by ACAS of those experienced in this role—and thus aware of the subtleties and conventions of the process. Both practices thus tend to forego a source of potential legitimation for the arbitral process. They also provide for subtle 'quality control', and increase the interdependence between ACAS and its arbitrators.

There are a number of characteristics of voluntary arbitration as arranged by ACAS which are important and to varying degrees have been controversial at one time or another. Generally speaking ACAS has tended to maintain previous practice in most areas, rather than being innovative. For example voluntary arbitration is treated as a private matter, confidential to the parties, and ACAS does not publish the awards. This is often felt to help the parties agree to arbitration in the first place, but it has a number of implications, including maintaining a fairly low profile for the process, which may produce a degree of ignorance about it. Privacy, however, contributes to a second key characteristic, that of avoiding the development of precedent or 'case law'. Each arbitration is separate, considering the facts in each specific situation, giving a degree of flexibility many regard as crucial. This charac-teristic is further reinforced by the fact that arbitrators are part-timers, appointed on an ad hoc basis and, unlike standing boards, are rarely able to develop medium/longer-term relationships with the parties. This may be seen as weakness or a strength. ACAS policy is hostile to closely reasoned awards—on the grounds that these may be challenged by the disappointed party, and thus re-open and extend rather than settle the dispute. It is suggested that any general assessment or brief explanation of the factors that have been influential are best confined to 'consider-ations'. Arbitrators are also advised that recommendations be avoided, unless explicitly sought by the parties. The traditional separation of conciliation and arbitration is also maintained in that what has taken place in conciliation remains private to the conciliator, and is not communicated to the arbitrator. This maintains the integrity of both processes, and emphasises that the arbitrator brings a fresh mind to the issues in question. Finally, arbitrators are not normally required to operate against specified criteria.

Industrial arbitration is an industrial relations rather than a judicial process. Whilst on occasion (on average in about a third of cases) arbitrators have to decide a case one way or the other (e.g. in which of two grades a particular job should fall) in conventional arbitration the positioning of the award allows for compromise—as indeed do negotiation, conciliation and mediation. Arbitrators apply 'industrial wisdom' rather than the law in a narrow sense. They are expected to bring with them experience of how possibly similar problems have been resolved in other cases. Consequently they can take account of both situational and wider factors in making decisions, and seek where possible to resolve (as well as to 'settle') the dispute by producing equitable and workable solutions, which acknowledge day-to-day realities in the continuing relationship between the parties. Unlike in many court cases the relationship has not been ended, nor are the parties strangers. In interest disputes (i.e. where the future terms of the relationship are being established) the arbitrator is seeking to resolve the dispute, rather than simply deciding 'who is right and who is wrong' in a limited technical sense—if that is possible.[16]

Last offer/pendulum arbitration

During the 1980s this technique—used in various forms in the public sector in North America—gained disproportionate publicity here (see Bassett, 1987). In Britain it was a private-sector initiative, led mainly by the then EETPU, in so-called 'no strike' agreements introduced mainly (but not only) at greenfield sites of incoming overseas companies.

The technique has been examined and assessed in substantial depth elsewhere (see for example Wood, 1985; Singh, 1986; Kessler, 1987 and Lewis 1990). Its major advantages appear to lie in the pressure it exerts on the parties (in situations where unilateral reference to arbitration is an agreed part of the disputes procedure) to continue to modify their offers and claims to the point where the difference is readily resolved in negotiation, or in conciliation. In a sense therefore it is an 'arbitration avoiding' device, designed to overcome 'chilled' negotiations. On the other hand, when actually used in interest disputes there are a number of well-known potential difficulties, such as what were precisely the last offer and claim, is further movement allowed, and how is the technique to be applied in multi-issue disputes? Use of last-offer arbitration raises relatively few objections in rights disputes, but in interest disputes it plainly limits the discretion of the arbitrator (as intended) and gives a clear-cut result '... but may not necessarily stand the test of fairness or improve relations in the longer term' (ACAS Annual Report, 1984, p. 39).

Despite the publicity pendulum arbitration is found in relatively few disputes procedures, and (ambiguously perhaps) accounts for very few ACAS arbitrations. There were apparently two cases in 1997 but none in 1998. Unlike in North America last offer arbitration appears largely absent in the public sector.

---

[16] There are a number of accounts of the modes or patterns of thought which arbitrators may apply to the variety of cases and subject matter with which they are faced—see for example Lockwood (1955); Hunter (1983).

Trends in caseload

Voluntary arbitration is an infrequently-used technique in dispute resolution, partly due to the priority given to directly agreed or conciliated settlements under the voluntarist philosophy, and possibly to some extent due to some lack of knowledge or understanding of the process. Concannon (1978, p. 15) identified three broad post-war periods, viz. a quiet period 1952–1965 averaging 22 cases a year, a stable period 1965–1974 with a higher caseload of 44 cases a year, and a high activity period beginning in 1974. He goes on to note a marked upward trend in numbers during the first nine months of 1974, but also that after the creation of CAS in September there were as many references in the final three months as there had been in the first nine months. Thus, as with collective conciliation, the caseload of arbitra-

TABLE 4

Cases referred to arbitration, mediation and investigation/inquiry

	Total	Single arbitrator	Board of arbitration	CAC	Others[a]	Single mediator	Board of mediation	Courts & committees of inquiry/panels of investigation
1975	306	260	32	–	–	8	3	3
1976	323	265	31	5	4	15	2	1
1977	327	247	40	7	2	27	4	–
1978	421	346	39	5	1	28	1	1
1979	395	304	44	11	4	31	1	–
1980	322	237	34	10	10	26	5	–
1981	257	212	27	5	1	12	–	–
1982	251	194	26	10	4	15	1	1
1983	207	151	25	10	–	20	–	1
1984	202	158	20	7	2	14	–	1
1985	162	135	13	2	–	10	2	–
1986	184	164	8	1	–	9	1	1
1987	145	122	10	1	–	12	–	–
1988	138	123	4	2	–	8	1	–
1989	169	142	8	–	2	15	2	–
1990	200	171	8	–	6	10	–	1
1991	157	126	15	–	3	12	1	–
1992	162	145	7	–	–	7	–	–
1993	163	152	3	–	1	7	–	–
1994	156	146	2	–	–	8	–	–
1995	136	129	1	–	1	5	–	–
1996	117	107	4	–	2	4	–	–
1997	71	58	2	–	–	9	2	–
1998	51	40	2	–	1	8	–	–
1999[b]	72	64	4	–	2	2	–	–

Source: ACAS Annual Reports

Notes: [a] Includes at various times arrangements made by ACAS eg. Post Office Arbitration Tribunal, Police Arbitration Tribunal, under The Remuneration of Teachers Acts, Railway Staff National Tribunal (from 1989)   [b] Provisional

tions rose to a peak in the early years of ACAS (1978 and 1979). So too did mediation, with 32 cases in 1979. Thereafter the caseload declined sharply from over 350 cases to average below 200 in the early 1980s, generally fluctuating in the 130–180 range during the rest of that decade, but with a tendency to fall (see Table 4).

In the first half of the 1990s single arbitrations oscillated in a similar, if slightly lower range. With the exception of 1991 the number and proportion of boards (which tend to be used in some of the more important cases) fell. In the two years 1997 and 1998 the number of arbitrations organised by ACAS has fallen dramatically, to 60 and 42, figures which are close to those of the pre-ACAS period although at that time the Industrial Court/Industrial Arbitration Board was hearing on average about a dozen voluntary arbitration cases each year. By contrast, no voluntary cases have been referred to the CAC since 1988. Amongst the causes of the recent steep drop are two very specific factors—changes affecting the job evaluation grading scheme applied mainly in some Scottish universities and a reduction in the number of cases under the former electricity supply industry-wide disciplinary procedure. This has been retained by less than half the privatised companies, and has also been modified in some of these cases.[17] For many years these two specific arrangements made substantial and misleadingly disproportionate contributions to the number of recorded arbitration cases. This is shown in Table 5 for the period since 1991, demonstrating the scale of reduction in 1997 and 1998.

TABLE 5
Substantial sources of arbitration cases 1991–1999

Year	Former electricity supply industry disciplinary cases	Job grading appeals from universities	Combined	Aggregate total single arbitrations
1991	36	33	69	126
1992	41	38	79	145
1993	36	47	83	152
1994	25	53	78	146
1995	38	33	71	129
1996	16	41	57	107
1997	14	–	14	58
1998	19	–	19	40
1999[a]	11	–	11	64

Source: ACAS   [a] Provisional

[17] The former electricity supply industry arrangement was inherited by ACAS from the DoE, whilst the university grading appeals arrangement began in the mid-1980s. The electrical contracting Industry JIB, the only scheme exempt from the unfair dismissal provisions, contributed only 17 cases between 1981 and 1998.

TABLE 6

Cases referred to arbitration, mediation and investigation, analysed by Cause/Issue

	General pay claim/ Annual pay		Other pay matters and terms/& conditions of employ		Recognition		Demarcation		Other TU matters		Redundancy		Discipline and dismissal		Others		Total
	No	%	No	%	No	%	No	%	No	%	No	%	No	%	No	%	
1975	89	29	153	50	3	1	4	1	4	1	1	–	46	15	6	2	306
1976	11	3	255	79	–	–	2	1	1	–	4	1	33	10	17	5	323
1977	17	5	233	71	–	–	7	2	5	2	4	1	46	14	15	5	327
1978	15	4	345	82	–	–	9	2	4	1	1	–	39	9	8	2	421
1979	336 (85%)				–	–	4	1	4	1	–	–	40	10	11	3	395
1980	246 (76%)				2	1	1	–	1	–	4	1	51	16	17	5	322
1981	179 (70%)				3	1	4	2			5	2	62	24	4	2	257
1982	194 (77%)						3	1	1	–	3	1	49	20	1	–	251
1983	147 (71%)								2	1	3	2	51	25	4	2	207
1984	134 (66%)												63	31	5	3	202
1985	98 (60%)						1	1	2	1	4	3	43	26	14	9	162
1986	94 (51%)										2	1	61	33	27	15	184
1987	25	17	32	22			*Grading*						61	42	27	19	145
1988	35	25	24	18									54	39	25	18	138
1989	27	16	36	21			37	22					55	33	14	8	169
1990	20	10	33	17			77	39					52	26	14	7	200
1991	26	17	37	24			35	22					57	36	2	1	157
1992	22	14	32	20			47	29					56	35	5	3	162
1993	21	13	30	18			57	35					49	30	6	4	163
1994	27	17	22	14			67	43					34	22	6	4	156
1995	21	15	27	20			36	26					47	35	5	4	136
1996	17	14	24	20			43	37					30	26	3	3	117
1997	20	28	26	36			2	3					21	30	2	3	71
1998	11	22	22	43			1	2					13	25	4	8	51
1999[a]	29	40	20	28			1	1					19	27	3	4	72

Source: ACAS Annual Reports

Notes: The figures do not include cases where ACAS assisted with private arbitration arrangements.
% rounded   [a] Provisional

The subjects of arbitration

Table 6 details the broad categories of subject or issue dealt with by arbitration, mediation and investigation since 1975. The single largest issue is pay, including terms and conditions of employment. For the first decade this generally accounted for around 75% of all cases, though subsequently it has been lower. Typically, over the past decade, about 25 general or annual pay claims have been settled by arbitration. The other two significant categories of issue have been discipline and dismissal, which typically accounts for between a quarter and a third of all cases, with job grading cases being of a similar order until 1997.

Arbitration: the debate

Arbitration has many benefits and strengths when judged against the obvious alternative means of remedy, i.e. recourse to industrial sanctions or to the courts. It avoids the costs implicit in the former, and the formality, legalism and narrowness of focus of the latter. It is a leading example of 'alternative dispute resolution' (ADR) which appears to be becoming increasingly popular in areas of conflict where court legal processes are thought either sub-optimal or expensive or both.

Like other impasse-breaking techniques in industrial relations, arbitration can be seen from a variety of perspectives. Its distinctive benefit is that unlike conciliation or mediation it provides a definite settlement of an unresolved dispute. Its principal disadvantage, and this is particularly significant in an industrial relations system that gives such priority to jointly agreed outcomes, is that it removes responsibility for the terms of the settlement from the parties (albeit within what can be a very narrowly confined area, as defined and agreed by the parties in the terms of reference). It is largely for this reason that voluntary arbitration has always been little used in Britain. Arbitration has been much more prominent in Australia, New Zealand and North America.

This 'loss of control' ensures that issues regarded as substantial matters of principle by management, e.g. trade union recognition or a redundancy decision are unlikely to be referred to voluntary arbitration. Not all issues are considered as equally arbitrable. It is often contended that 'disputes of right' (i.e. concerning the interpretation or application of an existing agreement) are especially suitable for arbitration in that the issue is clear and confined and usually has to be decided 'one way or the other'. 'Interest disputes' (i.e. claims to change the terms of an existing agreement, such as by an increase in pay) may involve major issues of cost and the parties may be less inclined to pass up control, except within very narrowly constrained terms of reference. Issues like annual pay claims raise especially complicated issues in the public-service sector, given the Government's role as either employer or paymaster.

The reasons why the parties agree to refer a dispute to arbitration can be very varied. The dispute is plainly not capable of resolution by negotiation or conciliation, and thus may be intractable—otherwise being resolved perhaps only by costly industrial action, or by being allowed to lapse but probably continuing to cause a sense of grievance/irritation. Sometimes the parties have so driven themselves into corners by what they have said in the negotiations that they cannot alter their stance without 'loss of face'. In accepting arbitration they can continue to indicate they 'maintained their position', and blame the arbitrator for any change. Arbitrators often have to accept such criticism, but understand the role they have fulfilled in 'getting the parties off the hook'. There may also be internal 'political' reasons for a reference to arbitration, for example a trade union officer wishing to show constituents that a grievance or claim has been pushed as far as possible, short of industrial action.

Arbitration has been the subject of a number of criticisms, of which the following are perhaps the most prominent. Some of these may have a particular resonance in the public sector, which is considered below. First, as discussed earlier, it is sometimes argued that the loss of control involved in referring an unresolved dispute to arbitration is in effect an abdication of responsibility by both parties, but perhaps especially so by management. Secondly, particularly (but not only) where arbitration is built into disputes procedures it may—if frequently relied on—become addictive and thus erode the parties' ability to resolve their disputes through direct negotiations. Both criticisms are made particularly strongly against procedures which require access to arbitration as the final stage and/or allow one party to refer an issue unilaterally simply by failing to agree at an earlier stage. In these circumstances it is argued that direct negotiations become 'chilled', i.e neither party is prepared to move from an opening position in negotiations because it is doubted that this will be matched by reciprocal movement from the other side, and if not the party making the move/concession will have shifted the gap between them in favour of the other side. It was these considerations that led to the fairly recent development in the public sector in the United States of so-called final offer or pendulum arbitration. Thirdly, a further major, recurrent and somewhat contemptuous criticism is the allegation that arbitrators tend 'to split the difference' between the last offer made by an employer and the last claim of the trade union. This accusation is ambiguous. If it means finding the exact halfway point between the parties it is superficial and is easily discredited. If it means any other point between the two, however close it might be to one or the other, it is scarcely surprising.

ACAS has certainly explored the nature and outcomes of arbitration on a number of occasions (see Annual Report, 1981, pp. 27–28 and pp. 86–87, and Annual Report, 1986, p. 45) and has sought to dispel this cynical view. (See also Lowry, 1990, pp. 67–69; Brown, 1992 and Wood 1985; 1992). It is generally established that in about one third of cases the arbitrator has little choice but to opt for one position or the other (e.g. in grading and many disciplinary cases). In many of the remainder it is by no means easy to locate the award with any proportionate precision, particularly where there are multiple issues. The evidence suggests that where this is possible awards tend to be a compromise, but one which is often located close to the position of one of the parties (Lowry, 1990).

The public sector

Several issues surrounding third-party intervention in major disputes in the public sector were considered earlier in the section on conciliation, and the peculiarities and problems of industrial relations and especially pay determination in the public sector are well known and much analysed (e.g. Beaumont, 1992; Bailey, 1996). There is a long and continuing history of third-party involvement in various ares of the public sector, e.g. the current prominence of Pay Review Bodies, and this has clear attractions on a variety of grounds e.g. apparent equity considerations in monopsony conditions, the notional bargaining power of 'essential workers' and so on. However, the importance of pay in total public expenditure and the government's responsibilities and policies as 'fiscal guardian' can present substantial and often sharp difficulties. These are especially acute in the case of arbitration, as prior commitment to and subsequent acceptance and implementation of the award are essential to the process.

The Conservative governments elected in 1979 and 1983 were particularly critical of arbitration. As Beaumont (1992, pp. 134–135) puts it, Conservative governments '... were far from being well-disposed towards arbitration in general, and to its use in the public sector in particular'. Its use was rejected in the civil service and NHS strikes in 1981 and 1982 respectively and in the ambulance dispute of 1989. 'In the 1982 NHS dispute, for instance, the then Health Minister Kenneth Clark was strongly opposed to the use of arbitration on the stated grounds that arbitrators are not ultimately accountable to the public at large and tend to try and fashion compromise solutions by splitting the difference between the positions of the two parties in disputes'. Beaumont also cites a government report in the early 1980s

> ... which examined 17 arbitration agreements in the public sector recommended that in 11 of them the employers withdraw from and renegotiate the existing arrangements. The essence of the change was a move away from the right of unilateral reference to arbitration ... on the grounds that the existing arrangements (i) encouraged irresponsibility among the parties (in that they had no responsibility for the final agreement and thus tended to hold their original bargaining positions), (ii) favoured the union side and (iii) were potentially inflationary in that they tended to undermine the effective operation of the system of cash limits' (p. 135).

In many areas unilateral access was removed; in others the government's wider policies towards the public sector e.g. privatisation, de-centralisation, executive agencies, and the major transfer from collective bargaining to Pay Review Bodies of the pay of teachers and nurses, led to the disappearance or marginalisation of many formerly important national level public-sector bargaining units. The contrast is marked indeed with the (exceptional) year of 1980, when 'the annual pay settlements for approximately 1.3m workers—mainly in the public sector—have been dealt with by arbitration or mediation' (ACAS Annual Report, 1980, p. 24). Moreover many of the former standing arbitral bodies serviced by ACAS have disappeared or become largely inactive. With the possible exception of London Underground, the incidence of large public sector annual/general pay claims being referred to ACAS voluntary arbitration now appears unusual. Although there are no systematic figures, issues are referred from the public sector (e.g. fire service and other areas of local government) but they appear to be mainly local rather than national matters.

User surveys

As in its other activities ACAS has both conducted and given facilities for others to conduct research into voluntary arbitration, including surveys of users. There have been at least two such surveys, both showing high levels of user satisfaction. First a small sample survey by ACAS of trade unions and employers in 30 cases referred to arbitration in 1975, and a much larger, more recent and more authoritative study by Alice Brown (1992). The former reported that awards had been accepted and implemented in all cases and that the parties said they were prepared to use arbitration again. In two-thirds of the cases the parties agreed that arbitration had resolved the dispute to their mutual satisfaction. (ACAS Annual Report, 1976, pp. 16–17). The second, a survey of all parties to ACAS voluntary arbitration in 1988, was much more comprehensive and had a high (over 90%) response rate.[18] It showed exceptionally high levels of satisfaction with virtually all aspects of the arbitration process. 70% regarded the award as fair (18% said it was not)—a remarkably high level given that there would be at least one disappointed party in most disputes. 86% said they would use arbitration again if a similar dispute arose again in future with only 8% saying 'no' to this question. Large majorities considered that the arbitrator acted impartially, deployed appropriate skills and understood the issues (Brown, 1992).

Overview of arbitration

The values and traditions of dispute resolution in Britain in peace-time have generally restricted the role played by arbitration. This applies both to arbitration in general and to long-established ad hoc arbitration which ACAS has organised for the last 25 years, following its transfer from the Department of Employment. It is regarded as a valuable possibility in some collective disputes, but has been used sparingly, and in many senses as a last resort. In the early years of ACAS a combination of particular circumstances, including incomes policy, led to a dramatic increase in its use. Not surprisingly the volume of use fell quickly from the early

---

[18] Alice Brown's survey analysed responses relating to 139 single arbitrations, five boards and 54 cases under the electricity supply disciplinary arrangements. On the parties reporting of these, 65% were joint requests, 21% trade union side, 7% employer side. In 37% of cases the arbitrator was restricted to either the employer's or the trade union's position (or in other ways) but in 62% was free to award what was thought appropriate. 16% said they selected the arbitrator (from a list), with ACAS choosing in four-fifths of cases—either with or without consultation (Brown, 1992).

peak, to levels now akin to those of the years before ACAS took over responsibility for the service. Several factors have influenced this return to earlier levels, including the reduced coverage of collective bargaining, record low levels of (recorded) stoppages, and a changed balance of power which may accentuate employer resistance to 'losing control' of the outcome of issues. In the public sector, changed procedural provisions on arbitration are likely to have contributed to a similar effect, certainly in relation to major national disputes.

CONCLUDING SUMMARY

The major changes affecting ACAS's collective dispute resolution services have been stimulated more by the external environment in which they operate, rather than (despite some innovation and development) through changes in ACAS's own objectives, organisation and methods of operation. The labour market, industrial relations and the world of work are very different, including, inter alia, major reductions in the number of strikes. Nationally it would be very difficult to argue that the 'volume of business' in the high-profile collective disputes arena has not fallen from the levels of the 1970s. The balance of ACAS's work has shifted, with the spread of individual statutory employment rights, minimum statutory standards and the much increased jurisdictions of employment tribunals.

The creation of ACAS was associated with major surges in the use of virtually all of the collective dispute resolution services offered by the new agency, and positioned ACAS firmly in the public mind with tireless and usually successful interventions in major industrial disputes. Even then, however, such national disputes formed only a small part of the ACAS collective dispute caseload, which was generally devoted to smaller, less 'newsworthy' differences. Over the years, although ACAS was occasionally unable to intercede, and in some cases was unsuccessful when it did so, it has maintained and further enhanced its acceptability to the parties in most disputes.

The notion of organisational effectiveness has many dimensions, not least when applied to a public service which epitomises the voluntarist tradition and spirit. In these circumstances there is an inherent danger of mis-interpreting or exaggerating the significance of numbers, and regarding rates of utilisation as the only indicator of value. Simple volume statistics reveal nothing of the circumstances, difficulty or importance of specific disputes, and a reduction in collective dispute cases may widely be interpreted more positively than an increase. However there can be no doubt that ACAS has proved its immense value across the 25-year period that has witnessed a transformation in its field. Certainly this assessment of its custody of the publicly-provided collective dispute resolution services is very strongly positive.

ACAS's collective conciliation service has maintained wide acceptability amongst the constituency, demonstrated by levels of activity and involvement well in excess of those of its predecessor—despite the much changed context. The service's national and local networks, together with the proactive but necessarily unsung activity of 'running alongside' differences and disputes, appears to ensure that the availability of the service is communicated appropriately. No doubt tight resource constraints apply on this as on all ACAS services, but ACAS has achieved remarkably high apparent success rates in terms of outcomes in collective conciliation. User surveys of collective conciliation have also shown exceptionally high levels of satisfaction, though they are now dated and more contemporary data seems desirable.

More recent research amongst the users of ACAS arbitration has also yielded remarkably high satisfaction levels, but the caseload has recently fallen back very substantially following a period of rather slower reduction. Again, several environmental influences mentioned above appear to have influenced this. The deepening juridification of the employment field may also be relevant, contrasting as it generally does with the voluntary approach that is synonymous with the work of ACAS. In this context the possibility of using some of the established strengths of ACAS collective dispute arbitration (such as informality, speed and non-legalism) in the burgeoning field of statutory employment rights is of great interest. The imminent extension and adaptation of the 'ACAS model' of collective arbitration as a voluntary alternative to employment tribunals in unfair dismissal cases may provide a fascinating contrast between different adjudicative traditions and styles.

REFERENCES

ACAS Annual Reports. London: ACAS.
Bailey, R. (1996), 'Public Sector Industrial Relations', in I. Beardwell *Contemporary Industrial Relations: A Critical Analysis*. Oxford: Oxford University Press.
Bassett, Philip (1987), *Strike-free: New Industrial Relations in Britain*. London: Macillan.
Beaumont, P. B. (1992), *Public Sector Industrial Relations*. London: Routledge.
Brown, Alice (1992), 'ACAS Arbitration: a case of consumer satisfaction?', *Industrial Relations Journal*, **23**(3).
Burrill, D. and J. Hiltrop (1985), 'How effective is ACAS as a conciliator?', *Personnel Management*, January.
Concannon, H. (1986), 'The Practice of Voluntary Arbitration in British Industrial Relations', thesis presented for the degree of Doctor of Philosophy, University of Salford.
Dickens, Linda (1979), 'Conciliation, Mediation and Arbitration in British Industrial Relations in G. Stephenson and C. Brotherton (eds), *Industrial Relations: A Social Psychological Approach*. John Wiley & Sons.
Fells, R. E. (1983), 'Movements, phases and deadlocks', Master of Industrial Relations Thesis, University of Western Australia.
Gladstone, Alan (1984), *Voluntary Arbitration of Interest disputes: A Practical Guide*. Geneva: International Labour Office.
Guillebaud, C. W. (1970), *The Role of the Arbitrator in Industrial Wage Disputes*. Nisbet.
Hunter, L. C. (1977), 'Economic Issues in Conciliation and Arbitration', *British Journal of Industrial Relations*, **15**(2).
Hunter, L. C. (1983), 'Arbitration', *Oxford Bulletin of Economics and Statistics*, **45**(1).
Hyman, R. (1972), *Strikes*. Fontana/Collins.
Goodman, J. F. B. and J. Krislov (1974), 'Conciliation in Industrial Disputes in Great Britain: A Survey of the Attitudes of the Parties', *British Journal of Industrial Relations*.

Incomes Data Services (1988), Pendulum Arbitration, IDS Study, 409, May.

Industrial Relations Services (1990), Conciliation and Arbitration—A Survey of Agreements and Practice, IRS Employment Trends, 19 Oct, No 474.

International Labour Office (1973), *Conciliation in Industrial Disputes*. Geneva: International Labour Office.

International Labour Office (1980), *Conciliation and Arbitration Procedures in Labour Disputes*. Geneva: International Labour Office.

Jones, M., L. Dickens, B. Weekes and M. Hart (1983), 'Resolving Disputes: the Role of ACAS Conciliation', *Industrial Relations Journal*, Summer

Kessler, S. (1980), 'The prevention and settlement of collective labour disputes in the UK', *Industrial Relations Journal*, 11(1).

Kessler, S. (1987), 'Pendulum Arbitration', *Personnel Management*, December.

Leopold, J. W. and P. B. Beaumont (1983), 'Arbitration Arrangements in the Public Sector in Britain', *The Arbitration Journal*, 38(2).

Lewis, Roy (1990), 'Strike-free Deals and Pendulum Arbitration', *British Journal of Industrial Relations*, 28(1).

Lewis, Roy and Jon Clark (1993), *Employment Rights, Industrial Tribunals and Arbitration: the case for alternative dispute resolution*. London: Institute of Employment Rights.

Lockwood, D. (1955), 'Arbitration and Industrial Conflict, *British Journal of Sociology*, VI, pp. 335–347.

Lockyer, John (1979), *Industrial Arbitration in Great Britain*. London: Institute of Personnel Management.

Lowry, P. (1990), *Employment Disputes and the Third Party*. London: Macmillan.

McCarthy, William (1992), 'The Rise and Fall of Collective Laissez Faire', in William McCarthy (ed.), *Legal Intervention in Industrial Relations: Gains and Losses*. Oxford: Blackwell.

Metcalf, David and Simon Milner (1993), *New Perspectives on Industrial Disputes*. Routledge.

Mortimer, J. (1981), 'ACAS in a changing climate: a force for good IR?', *Personnel Management*, February.

Mumford, Karen (1996), 'Arbitration and ACAS in Britain: A Historical Perspective', *British Journal of Industrial Relations*, 34(2).

Sharp, I. G. (1950), *Industrial Conciliation and Arbitration*. George Allen & Unwin.

Singh, R. (1986), 'Final Offer Arbitration in Theory and Practice', *Industrial Relations Journal*, 17(4).

Owen Smith, E., B. Frikk and T. Griffiths (????) *Third Party Involvement in Industrial Disputes: A Comparative Study of West Germany and Britain*. Avebury.

Purcell, J. (1981), *Good Industrial Relations: The Unending Search*. Macmillan.

Studd, T. J. (1994), 'Is there a difference between the provision of procedure agreements for the solution of disputes and the use, conduct and outcome of collective conciliation?' M.A. Thesis, University of Keele.

Thomson, A. W. J. and V. V. Murray (1976), *Grievance Procedures*. Saxon House.

Wedderburn, K. W. and P. L. Davies (1969), *Employment Grievances and Disputes Procedures in Britain*. University of California Press.

Wood, Sir John (1985), 'Last Offer Arbitration', *British Journal of Industrial Relations*, 23(3).

Wood, Sir John (1988), 'Pendulum Arbitration: a modest experiment', *Industrial Relations Journal*, 19(3).

Wood, Sir John (1992), 'Dispute Resolution—Conciliation, Mediation and Arbitration', in William McCarthy (ed.) *Legal Intervention in Industrial Relations: Gains and Losses*. Oxford: Blackwell.

3
Doing more with less: ACAS and individual conciliation

Linda Dickens

INTRODUCTION

The legal framework within which ACAS operates permits, but does not require, its involvement in collective disputes. In disputes concerning individual legal rights, however, ACAS is under a statutory duty to provide conciliation. This is conciliation in the shadow of the law; ACAS individual conciliation is a stage in a process which begins with a legal claim being made to an employment tribunal (ET).[1] If conciliation fails to achieve a settlement, and the claim is not withdrawn, then it goes on to be determined by a tribunal. In the past 25 years ACAS has dealt with over a million cases arising from employment rights disputes. While the collective area of ACAS work—collective conciliation and arbitration—has declined over the 25 years, conciliation of employment rights disputes has been a growth area. This ACAS function currently accounts for over two-thirds of the Service's operational resources.

This chapter deals with this important ACAS function. It is informed by my own and others' published and unpublished research and reports,[2] supplemented by interview

---

[1] Employment Tribunals were called Industrial Tribunals until August 1998.

[2] Large-scale research into the operation of unfair dismissal and the industrial tribunal system was carried out at Warwick in the late 1970s and early 1980s (Dickens, 1978/9; Dickens *et al.*, 1985). There was another, small-scale investigation of conciliation in unfair dismissal cases around that time (Lewis, 1982) and other academic research investigated individual conciliation in discrimination cases (Graham and Lewis, 1985; Gregory, 1982, 1986; McCrudden *et al.*, 1991). Further insights have emerged from investigations concerned more generally with the operation of employment tribunals (e.g. IPM, 1986; Kumar, 1986), and work undertaken by or for the Department of Employment (e.g. Tremlett and Banerji, 1994; Lewis *et al.*, 1997). ACAS Annual Reports are a useful information source and a former ACAS chairman has published his overview of its work (Lowry, 1990). ACAS has recently undertaken and commissioned its own evaluation of individual conciliation (see Dix, this volume). Only one aspect of this work was in the public domain at the time of writing (Lewis and Legard, 1998). I am grateful to ACAS for allowing me to draw on some of the unpublished findings.

material.[3] The chapter explores the nature of ACAS settlements in employment rights disputes and how they are achieved. It details the growth in caseload over the 25 years and considers the implications of this for the way in which individual conciliation is performed. Increasing caseloads in a context of reduced resources demonstrates that ACAS is successfully 'doing more with less' but I question whether the cost effectiveness and efficiency to which this testifies are the only, or most important, criteria by which this function should be evaluated.

I argue that there is unrealised potential for individual conciliation in employment rights disputes to contribute to ACAS's wider mission and to further social policy. Recent reforms involving the settlement of employment rights disputes, however, are being driven by a search for cost saving through increased efficiency, rather than by concern with qualitative outcomes or longer-term benefits. Nonetheless, they may give rise to questions about the appropriate criteria for evaluating this function.

NATURE AND CONTEXT OF THE FUNCTION

ACAS's statutory duty to provide individual conciliation is now set out in the Employment Tribunals Act 1996 s18(2). This provides that where employment tribunal proceedings arise under a range of different statutes, it is the duty of the conciliation officer (on request or on own initiative) to 'endeavour to promote a settlement of the proceedings without their being determined by an employment tribunal'. ACAS also has statutory responsibility for dealing with cases where no formal complaint has been made but where such a claim could be made. These are known as non-IT1 cases (the IT1 being the tribunal application form).

Settlements agreed with the aid of ACAS have always had a special status, in that settlements seeking to preclude someone proceeding to an ET are void unless a conciliation officer has 'taken action' (Employment Rights Act 1996 s.203 2(e)). This special status was extended in 1993 to 'compromise agreements' reached without ACAS. Certain conditions have to be fulfilled including the applicant receiving independent advice from a suitably qualified, and appropriately insured, person.

The range of jurisdictions given to employment tribunals has increased considerably since they were set up in 1964 to hear appeals from employers under the Industrial Training Act. The first jurisdiction involving disputes between employers and employees was under the Redundancy Payments Act 1965, and this was followed by the unfair dismissal jurisdiction introduced in 1972. This provided for

---

[3] In researching this chapter I had meetings with ACAS staff in London and the Midlands region to discuss current operations and developments. I would like to thank all those who gave assistance, including Carol Davenport, Gill Dix, Derek Evans, Robin Isaac, David Taylor and Andrew Wareing. None of these people bears any responsibility for the contents of this chapter.

individual conciliation, at first performed by staff in the Department of Employment, and then transferred to ACAS when it was set up.

The mid-1970s legislation (Employment Protection Act 1975) also introduced other rights where ACAS had a duty to conciliate.[4] Around the same time the Equal Pay Act 1970 and Sex Discrimination Act 1975 came into force—giving ACAS a role to play in discrimination jurisdictions, soon extended to race (Race Relations Act 1976).

The 25 years of ACAS operation have witnessed an explosion in employment rights. Employment tribunals became the mechanism of choice (or, more accurately perhaps, the most expedient option) for handling these new rights. In 1998/9 nearly 92,000 applications were made to employment tribunals, the second-highest total ever. ACAS has a duty to conciliate in almost all the ET jurisdictions and so the range and number of cases in which individual conciliation is to be offered has increased considerably over the 25 years. Figure 1 shows a list of the majority of employment rights disputes where ACAS has a duty to offer individual conciliation. Table 1 indicates the proportion of total cases accounted for by the main jurisdictions, indicating trends over a decade. The increasing number of jurisdictions means that unfair dismissal cases form a smaller proportion of the total ET case load than they once did, but they still constitute the highest proportion and a majority of cases each year.

TABLE 1

Employment tribunal applications by jurisdiction 1985/86 to 1995/96

Jurisdiction	'85/86	'86/87	'87/88	'88/89	'89/90	'90/91	'91/92	'92/93	'93/94	'94/95	'95/96
Unfair dismissal	73.7	67.5	66.6	66.8	58.2	60	60.9	57.3	57.9	59.5	52.5
Redundancy pay	10.7	8.6	8.9	8.4	9.4	10.8	12.8	11.9	12.1	10.3	8.7
Wages Act	–	0.1	6	9.1	15.9	14.7	14.6	16.7	15.5	15	19.6
Race discrimination	1.9	1.8	2.5	3.5	3.2	2.8	2.1	2.1	2	2	2.4
Sex discrimination	1.2	1.6	2.7	3.1	3	4.6	4	6.7	4.1	6	5
Equal pay	4.9	1.6	6.1	2	3.5	1.4	1.3	1.1	1.5	0.6	0.9
EPCA 1978[a] Others	7.7	18.6	7.6	7.1	6.9	5.8	4.3	4.3	6.9	6.6	10.9
TOTAL	100	100	100	100	100	100	100	100	100	100	100

Source: *Resolving employment rights disputes: options for reform* 1994 and April 1997, *Labour Market Trends*, London: The Stationery Office.

Note: [a] Includes matters concerning trade union activities, guarantee payments, the transfer of undertakings, and appeals against training levy assessments and health and safety improvements and prohibition notices.

---

[4] These included guarantee pay during lay off; maternity pay; right to return after pregnancy; redundancy consultation protective awards; right to an itemised pay statement; time off to seek work in redundancy; rights relating to trade union membership and activities.

FIGURE 1

Main employment rights in which ACAS has a duty to conciliate

- unfair dismissal (including the right to return after maternity absence)
- disability discrimination
- equal pay
- sex discrimination
- racial discrimination
- guarantee payments
- suspension on medical grounds
- time off for ante-natal care
- offer of alternative work before being suspended on maternity grounds under health and safety regulations
- remuneration when suspended on maternity grounds under health and safety regulations
- time off for public duties and for trade union membership and activities
- time off in the event of redundancy to look for work or arrange for training
- written statement of reasons for dismissal
- itemised pay statements
- certain matters concerning redundancy consultation
- action short of dismissal on grounds of trade union membership and activities or non-membership
- certain matters concerning the transfer of undertakings
- unauthorised deductions from payment
- redundancy selection
- exclusion or expulsion from trade union membership
- unjustifiable discipline by a trade union
- unauthorised or excessive deductions from trade union subscriptions
- refusal of employment/service of an employment agency on the grounds of being, or not being, a union member
- breach of employment contract
- Sunday working (shop and betting workers in England and Wales only)
- suffering a detriment—health and safety cases and trustees of occupational pension schemes
- redundancy pay
- working time
- 'whistle blowers'
- National Minimum Wage

Much of the enlarged jurisdiction concerns rights given to individuals (employees, potential employees) to be exercised against their employers. But they also include rights to be exercised by trade unions against employers (e.g. redundancy consultation, where the sanction is an award to individual employees); and, since the Employment Act 1980, disputes between individuals and trade unions (e.g. alleged unreasonable exclusion from membership). The breach of contract jurisdiction (long-promised and finally given to tribunals by the Trade Union Reform and Employment Rights Act 1993) may involve claims by employers against employees.

The Donovan Commission (1968, para 573) had proposed that the jurisdictions of the labour tribunals (its suggested name for the employment tribunals) should include 'all disputes arising between employers and employees from their contractual employment or from any statutory claims they may have against each other as employer and employee'. But the Commission argued that matters arising between trade unions and their members should be excluded, and disputes between employers and groups of workers or trade unions 'must be settled by procedures of, or agreed through, collective bargaining' (para 576).

This distinction between collective and individual disputes is in practice difficult to draw; the fact that it is an individual worker who brings a claim does not mean there are not collective issues at stake. The proposal to leave collective issues to be resolved through collective bargaining procedures assumes the existence and health of collective bargaining—something which has changed dramatically since Donovan reported in the late1960s.

The large increase in employment rights mainly occurred during a period of deregulation under Conservative governments, an apparent contradiction. In 1980 statute required ACAS to offer conciliation in 16 tribunal jurisdictions; by 1991 it was up to 23, and rising. But a number of these new jurisdictions were driven by the need to comply with European legislation rather than a domestic agenda.[5] Some rights were part of a de-regulationary move. The Wages Act 1986, for example, was a deregulatory measure removing earlier restrictions and reducing the scope of Wages Councils, while protection for existing shopworkers who object to Sunday working was given when Sunday trading was deregulated under the Sunday Trading Act 1994. Other rights were linked to the legislative attack on compulsory union membership, the promotion of non-unionism, and the internal reform of trade unions (Dickens and Hall 1995).

The domestic agenda was concerned to reduce the burdens which employee rights were seen to place on employers. This, coupled with a pragmatic desire to ease the pressure on the tribunal system, led to changes which made it more difficult for people to bring claims to tribunals. The service qualification for various rights,

---

[5] For example, equal pay for work of equal value; rights on transfer of undertakings and the individual rights in the Trade Union Reform and Employment Rights Act (TURERA) of 1993.

including unfair dismissal, was increased from six months to a year in 1979, and then to two years in 1985. Additional filters and deterrents were inserted into the tribunal system. Pre-hearing assessments were introduced in 1980 to weed out weak cases by the threat of an award of costs if the unmeritorious party persisted. These were replaced by pre-hearing reviews at which a party may be ordered to pay a deposit in order to continue.

Substantive changes made it more difficult for applicants to succeed. The burden of proving the reasonableness of a dismissal was removed from the employer; and tribunals were required to give special consideration to small firms. The real value of awards was allowed to diminish by not uprating the maximum and the 'weekly pay' calculation unit to keep pace with inflation and earnings. In 1972 the compensatory award maximum was £4,160. In 1994 that was equivalent to £27,606 when uprated by the retail prices index. But the statutory maximum at the time was £11,000.[6]

Some ideas for attempting to deter cases being brought were not adopted, such as instituting an application fee and exempting new employees in firms of ten or fewer workers from unfair dismissal protection (proposed in the Deregulation Task Force 1996 report). Compliance with European equality law necessitated some wider access to rights (e.g. the removal of hours qualifications in 1993). Nonetheless, the changes outlined did hold down what would have been even greater increases in ET and ACAS caseloads.

CASE LOADS AND TRENDS

Change in ACAS individual conciliation caseload over time reflects the factors just mentioned: expanded jurisdictions and court judgements; changes in access to rights and the attractiveness of remedies. Unemployment also had an impact. Greater job loss increased applications, particularly unfair dismissal, at various times (e.g. 1980–85 recession and again in the early 1990s). The changing structure of employment is also a consideration. There has been a shift to employment in areas most likely to generate tribunal applications (particularly unfair dismissal). Characteristically the employers appearing most frequently as respondents in tribunal cases are small, non-unionised employers in the service sector (Tremlett and Banerji, 1994; Cully et al., 1998).

ACAS Annual Reports show a dramatic rise in cases over the 25-year period, with 105,812 actual and potential claims completed in 1998 (see Figure 2). ACAS counts each jurisdiction as a separate case, so cases where more than one jurisdiction is involved are counted more than once. This is misleading in some ways but the ACAS

---

[6] The ceiling on sex discrimination awards was removed in 1993 to comply with European law. The same principle was applied to race discrimination awards in 1994.

figures do indicate the increasing complexity of the cases with the growth of multi-jurisdiction claims. The majority of breach of contract claims are linked to unfair dismissal or redundancy pay and claims relating to unauthorised deductions (ACAS 1997, Annual Report p. 62). Multi-jurisdiction claims place additional responsibilities on conciliation officers, who have to ensure that all issues are discussed, clarified and understood by the parties and all outstanding matters covered in any settlement (ACAS 1995, Annual Report p. 51).

Figure 3 presents ACAS figures adjusted to show cases rather than jurisdictions, and indicates 78,243 cases were handled in 1998. Non-IT1 cases constitute 1.5% of this total. Ten years earlier, non-IT1 cases formed an amazing 36% of the total case-load, nearly all being initiated by employers in cases of job termination. A changed ACAS policy on handling non-IT1 cases (including a refusal to simply rubber-stamp agreements) was put into effect in 1990 (ACAS 1991, Annual Report p. 45). This, and the subsequent provision for compromise agreements to be reached without ACAS, led to a substantial decline in such cases.

The annual caseload may be distorted in any one year by a particular issue generating numerous individual claims against the same employer, or group of employers. This happened in 1988 for example, with 1,336 equal value complaints by speech therapists against 122 District Health Authorities, and in 1991 with 2,000 pregnancy dismissals cases against the Ministry of Defence. On hold currently are thousands of part-time pension cases awaiting a ruling from the European Court of Justice.

FIGURE 2
Total conciliation cases (jurisdictions)

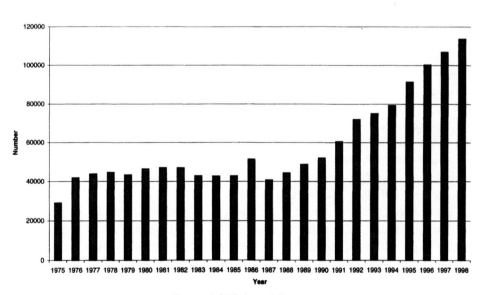

Source: ACAS Annual Reports.

FIGURE 3
ACAS caseload: individual conciliation (adjusted)

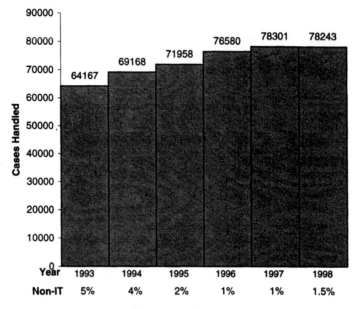

Source: ACAS, personal communication.

Although concerned with individual rights, some claims may have a collective intent, with multiple cases being lodged against a single employer in pursuit of a collective issue. The 1988 caseload included 1,212 complaints under the Wages Act 1986 where it seemed that a trade union was seeking to use the Act's provisions in this way (ACAS Annual Report, 1988). With the decline in the extent and depth of collective bargaining, some unions have sought to use the individual employment rights as a lever to get employers to the bargaining table and to exert pressure on them once there. There is no provision for class action (where one case can stand for many similarly situated) and unions cannot bring cases on behalf of members, so they have encouraged their members to make simultaneous individual claims against their employer. This has been done in some equal pay cases for example, where unions have used the lever of individual tribunal claims (or their threat) to persuade employers to negotiate new pay structures (e.g. in parts of the electricity supply industry and in the National Health Service).

We can also identify employer use of the provisions to individualise a collective issue, most notably in the News International dispute in the mid-1980s (ACAS Annual Report 1985, p. 89). Over 5,000 striking employees were dismissed, around 4,700 made unfair dismissal applications. Negotiations between the company and unions produced proposals to settle the dispute which were rejected by the dismissed employees. The company then offered to make the terms for compensation set out in its final package available on an individual basis to ex-employees if they would withdraw all claims against the company and take no further part in the dispute. Some 1,700 individual agreements were reached under the auspices of ACAS individual conciliation.

The upward trend in caseload is set to increase as recent jurisdictions such as working time disputes begin to produce cases, and yet more jurisdictions get added.[7] Further, the recent Employment Relations Act 1999 reduces the service qualification for such rights as unfair dismissal from two years to one, and increases the maximum limit on unfair dismissal compensation to £50,000.

ACHIEVING SETTLEMENTS

ACAS achieved settlement in 42% of cases in 1998; 31% were withdrawn and 27% went on to be determined by an employment tribunal (ACAS, 1998, Annual Report p. 77). The 'positive clearance rate' is high. Rates of withdrawal, settlement and cases proceeding to tribunal vary slightly over time but roughly speaking only about a third of cases go through to a tribunal hearing; around a third of cases are settled at conciliation and a third are withdrawn. There is variation by jurisdiction, as shown in Table 2. The rate of settlement in race discrimination cases (23% in 1995/6) is lower than in sex discrimination (40%) or unfair dismissal cases (38%).

ACAS literature explains to the parties that the conciliator can discuss the case with them; describe tribunal procedure; explain the way tribunals have dealt with similar cases in the past; discuss the options open to them; exchange information which is not confidential so that each side has a clearer understanding of the other's

TABLE 2
Outcome of cases 1995–1996 %

	Unfair dismissal	Equal pay	Sex discrimination	Race discrimination	Wages Act	Breach of contract	Redundancy pay
ACAS conciliated settlement	38	18	40	23	27	38	No duty
Withdrawal	30	66	41	38	43	33	54
To tribunal	32	16	19	39	30	29	46
Number of cases	38,557	694	3,677	1,737	14,391	3,495	6,390

Source: Labour Market Trends, April 1997, London: The Stationery Office.

[7] The DTI, for example, calculated that an additional 3,000–6,000 cases per annum could arise from implementation of the Working Time Directive.

position and tell each side any proposals the other has for settlement. The conciliator cannot express a view on the merits of a case or on the likely outcome of a tribunal hearing; or assist either party with their case (ACAS, 1998a).

The line between discussing the case, explaining the law and how tribunals handled similar cases on the one hand, but not expressing a view on the merits of the case or its likely outcome on the other, is not a particularly easy one to tread. Conciliators often try to get the parties to critically examine their own cases; to consider weaknesses as well as strengths. Describing what the law, as interpreted by tribunals, requires, and indicating what the party may have to demonstrate or prove in order to succeed can assist in this, as might conveying why the other party feel they are on strong grounds. This may relate to the substance of the case or their perceived superior ability to get the case across to the tribunal because of better access to evidence, witnesses, representation and so on.

Conciliators do sometimes act in a 'proactive' way (Lewis and Legard, 1998; Dix, this volume) giving their view on the strengths and weaknesses of a case, highlighting the advantages of settling, rather than adopt an 'administrative' or 'reactive' role, merely passing offers/counter offers and conveying the desire to settle. Some conciliators do give a view as to likely success of the case at tribunal—making it clear that they are not judges in the cases and that the tribunal may well take a different view. Even where a more indirect approach is adopted, the parties may perceive the conciliation officer as giving a view on the merits of the case. Parties can always discount the information given by the conciliator or take a different view on the merits of their cases, but this is less likely where a party has no other source of informed advice or information.

An analysis of reasons why unfair dismissal applicants in the Warwick survey settled their cases showed the largest proportion (22%) did so because they got what they asked for or thought was due to them, and a similar proportion (21%) considered they would get no more from the tribunal. In weighing up the pros and cons of proceeding it is not only financial considerations which are influential. 16% mentioned they did not want to go to the tribunal because of the fuss, publicity, stress or strain they thought this would involve. For others (14%) the trade-off was between the certainty of getting something and the risk of getting nothing if they lost a tribunal. Others (11%) said they settled because they were advised to (Dickens *et al.*, 1985).

For employers, the main factor (42%) leading to settlement was that it was a way of saving money/the cheaper option. This included some who feared they would lose at the hearing and also some who felt they would win who offered 'nuisance' or 'economic' settlements. It might be noted here that 19% of those employers who refused to offer a settlement because they thought they would win at tribunal did in fact lose their cases. This suggests that some so-called nuisance settlements may avoid rather higher tribunal awards in some cases, as well as the saving on managerial time and the costs of representation.

The 1992 survey of parties in unfair dismissal, redundancy, discrimination and Wages Act cases (Tremlett and Banerji, 1994) found over one-third of employers who made offers at the conciliation stage did so because they thought the applicant was entitled to it; 25% did so to avoid the expense of the tribunal, or the 'hassle' of it (13%); 6% because they thought they would lose and 17% wished to avoid a dispute and settle amicably.

It is clear that the parties' perceptions of what might happen at the tribunal and the relative advantages and disadvantages of proceeding are crucial in determining the likelihood of their settling or, in the case of applicants, withdrawing their claims. ACAS conciliation officers play a key role in shaping these perceptions and providing information upon which these assessments can be made. They provide parties with the ability to settle—a mechanism for settlement—but also help shape the desire to settle by marshalling and channelling pressures towards settlement that are present in the system.

The research indicates the depressing impact of the information a conciliation officer may impart when outlining the law and indicating what happened in similar cases. Graham and Lewis (1985) report some applicants in sex discrimination cases withdrew their complaints after conciliation officers had told them that sex discrimination was 'very hard to prove'.[8] They note that 'for a number of applicants such remarks would undoubtedly tip the balance against proceeding with the case'.

Helping tip the balance against proceeding with an unfair dismissal claim might be the facts that the substantive tests of fairness do not go far in challenging managerial prerogative. Most applicants lose their cases at tribunal (38% succeeded in 1995/6); re-employment is hardly ever awarded; and compensation awards are not high (median award £2499). In conciliation officers' explanations of the tribunal system it will become clear that the tribunal, although less formal than ordinary courts, requires parties to present their cases through examination and cross-examination, to call witnesses and to present evidence—a context within which skilled representation is an advantage, but no legal aid is available.[9]

Although depressing, information of this kind is what the parties—particularly unrepresented applicants—are looking to the conciliation officer to provide. The employment tribunal system provides a context within which conciliated settlements of whatever nature will often appear preferable to a tribunal hearing. Channelling

---

[8] There has been a shift in the burden of proof away from the applicant since this research, but in 1995/6 sex discrimination applicants succeeded in only 31% of cases heard by tribunals (*Labour Market Trends*, April 1997).
[9] The Equal Opportunities Commission (EOC) and Commission for Racial Equality (CRE) can provide assistance in discrimination cases but their resources are inadequate to help more than a small proportion of those who are sufficiently aware of the possibility to request such assistance. Although resources to aid employees enforce their rights against employers are scarce, the Employment Act (EA) 1988 established the office of the Commissioner for the Rights of Trade Union Members to give legal advice and assistance to trade unions members in enforcing statutory rights against their unions. The office has recently been abolished.

pressures for settlement is a legitimate tool for the conciliator to use, but the nature of the system means such pressures generally weigh more heavily on applicants, particularly those without representation.

Only a minority of unrepresented applicants, however, sees ACAS itself as a source of pressure. 16% of unrepresented applicants in unfair dismissal, Wages Act, and breach of contract cases agreed or agreed strongly that the conciliator tried to pressure them into resolving their case; 56% disagreed/disagreed strongly (ACAS, unpublished data).

NATURE OF CONCILIATED SETTLEMENTS

Generally speaking, settlements are on the basis of a monetary payment on average at about half the level of the average tribunal award (Tremlett and Banerji, 1994).

Reinstatement of dismissed workers (the intended primary remedy for unfair dismissal) is not quite as rare in conciliation as it is at tribunal but it is very much the exception. In 1998 re-employment was the outcome in 3% of unfair dismissal cases settled through ACAS. In 1995–6 tribunals awarded reinstatement (return to same job on same terms) or re-engagement (re-employment by the same employer) in 1.6% of upheld cases (0.6% of all heard cases). But conciliation does not restrict itself to the remedies a tribunal can award. In the Warwick research on unfair dismissal cases 10% of applicants obtained settlements on the basis of something other than reinstatement, re-engagement or compensation (the statutory remedies for unfair dismissal); 9% of them were given a written reference (Dickens et al., 1985). A reference may also be given alongside a sum of money—a way of 'clearing one's name' without needing to go to tribunal. A third of proposals for settlement from applicants in race discrimination cases studied by McCrudden, Smith and Brown (1991, p. 186) included a reference, and one-fifth an apology.

This illustrates one way in which settlements may be obtained. What applicants actually want to achieve by applying to a tribunal may not be an available remedy as such. Once the conciliation officer has unearthed what is really at stake/what is motivating the claim and what the applicant is really concerned about, this may facilitate settlement, especially where what is sought is much less costly to the employer than any possible tribunal remedy.

Conversely, settlement is less likely where what is wanted is outside the ability of conciliation to deliver. Conciliation cannot deliver a public hearing, 'a day in court'. It cannot provide 'justice' for an employer seeking exoneration from a charge of discrimination, nor for an applicant seeking public affirmation that discrimination occurred. Nor does it provide a demonstration effect intended to impact on other employees such as a legal ruling or clarification. Such outcomes appear to be sought particularly by parties in race discrimination cases and help explain why fewer such cases are settled (McCrudden, Smith and Brown, 1991, p. 191).

The law recognises that the inequality in the power relationship between employer and employee could be used to prevent workers exercising their rights. Hence, as noted, only certain agreements can stop a case going to a tribunal. The special status accorded to agreement reached when ACAS has taken action appeared to suggest that settlements with the involvement of ACAS were intended to be qualitatively different from those reached without ACAS. For some this implied the involvement of the concilation officer would 'provide some guarantee as to the fact that the settlement was reasonable and arrived at in a proper fashion' (McIlroy, 1980, p. 180). This view received little support from the courts, however, who have required ACAS to do very little in order to have 'taken action' sufficient to prevent a case being heard by a tribunal (*Moore* v *Duport Furniture Products Ltd* [1982] IRLR 31).

In practice (and as indicated by ACAS policy in non-IT1 cases after 1990) conciliation officers do more than the minimal amount indicated in the case law. But ACAS is not concerned with the fairness of any settlement judged by some external standard. The qualitative difference appears to reside not in the fact that ACAS settlements are reasonable or equitable ones but rather in the fact that the parties are reaching informed agreements. The parties should know their legal rights, understand what they are doing and the implications of settlement. The nature of the settlement is then up to them. The conciliation officer does not take a view as to the reasonableness or sufficiency of settlements. What conciliators can do—and often do when asked for guidance on amount—is indicate how tribunals calculate compensation. This gives the parties a yardstick against which offers and requests may be measured. But they are not required by statute to go through the heads of compensation in every case, and do not always do so (*Slack* v *Greenham Plant Hire* [1983 IRLR 271]). The statute mentions equity as a consideration for ACAS in performing its function only in relation to the terms of any reinstatement.

As noted, this remedy is rarely achieved through conciliation. There are grounds for arguing that there is scope for at least some parties to be reconciled to the idea of re-employment during conciliation even if tribunals are reluctant to award it (Dickens *et al.*, 1981, p. 171–173), but a careful exploration of these possibilities would require ACAS conciliators to adopt a positive approach to the specific remedies in their dealings with applicants and employers. Although acknowledging the requirement to attempt conciliation on the basis of re-employment, conciliation officers have been unwilling to pursue enquiries about this where it is thought the prospect of promoting any other form of settlement might be prejudiced (Lowry, 1990, p. 128).

The courts have rejected an interpretation of the statutory duty as requiring some positive initiative to secure re-employment. For the most part, where the worker has been dismissed, the emphasis is not on reconciliation and re-establishing the relationship but rather on the terms of ending it (Dickens *et al.*, 1985, p. 172). In 1991 ACAS strengthened its guidance to conciliation officers on re-employment 'to ensure the parties are aware of the practical advantages of re-employment before moving towards settlements on another basis' but a number of factors mitigate against this outcome being achieved (ACAS Annual Report, 1991, p. 47).

It is in the discrimination jurisdictions that ACAS's neutral stance in relation to settlements has come in for most criticism. ACAS concern for (and interpretation of) impartiality makes it impossible for conciliation officers to see themselves as guardians of fairness or promoters of equality, despite the intention of the discrimination statutes. Some of the criticism concerned how conciliation officers performed the statutory function (e.g. Gregory, 1982), but much of it questions the appropriateness of conciliation in such jurisdictions where a particular social policy is being pursued. Conciliation is seen as treating an alleged injustice as equivalent to a disagreement between parties (McCrudden, Smith and Brown, 1991, p. 193). There is a conflict between the search for compromise, which is at the centre of conciliation, and the pursuit of rights. Where there has been unlawful discrimination then, it is argued, conciliated compromise cannot be defended since it compounds unlawful behaviour (Graham and Lewis, 1985, p. 62). At the extreme this is an argument against having a conciliation stage, since 'parties might settle while leaving justice undone' (Fiss, 1984).

HOW THE FUNCTION IS PERFORMED: DOING MORE WITH LESS

The conciliation work is undertaken by conciliators based in the regions, with control and management functions performed by Conciliation Managers (CMs). There are around 300 staff currently employed in the conciliator grade, of whom 49% are female. In the early 1980s only 7% of the conciliators were female, and none of the CMs.

There is some variation across regions as to the degree of specialism among staff, although even in regions where a more generalist approach is favoured (where, for example, conciliators also get involved supporting advisory work), the increasing caseload means that in practice conciliators do spend most of their time on individual conciliation work. In was the practice that training in jurisdictions other than unfair dismissal (particularly discrimination jurisdictions) was given only to selected, more experienced staff after they had spent some time on unfair dismissal cases (Dickens et al., 1985, p. 150; McCrudden, Smith and Brown, 1991). Now, for case management reasons, all conciliation officers handle all jurisdictions.

The increasing range of jurisdictions and the increasing number of cases with which ACAS has to deal (over which it has no control), has not been matched by increased resources for ACAS. Indeed ACAS experienced staffing cuts, as did other areas of the public service in the early 1980s. In 1978 ACAS had a total staff of 819. Three years later this was down to 691, and it declined further during the 1980s so that by 1990 there were 574 staff employed. At this time about half the operational resources were being devoted to individual conciliation. Although there was a small increase in resources in the early 1990s the increased workload meant that the number of cases being handled by each individual conciliation officer increased. Resources had to be diverted into individual conciliation at the expense of advisory and other preventive activities (ACAS Annual Report, 1993, p. 49). ACAS maximised the resources devoted to operational activity; reducing Head Office (HO) staffing and making changes in regional management structures with a reduction in senior management posts (ACAS Annual Report, 1994, p. 71). Fears were expressed that opportunities for settlements might be missed since officers were unable to deal as fully with all cases as they would have wished (ACAS Annual Report, 1991, p. 44). It was noted (ACAS Annual Report, 1993, p. 27) that individual conciliation staff were working in their own time to keep up with the caseload.

Current annual caseloads are around 330 for each individual conciliation officer. This compares with around 300 in the late 1980s (Lowry, 1991, p. 120) and about 250 a decade earlier. New staff are being appointed (current total staffing for ACAS is 767 full-time equivalent staff) but numbers lag behind what is required to meet the ever-increasing demands. The Midlands region for example was resourced for a 13% increase in 1999, but experienced a 33% increase in cases. There is also an issue of where sufficient numbers of new staff are to be found. Since 1995, recruitment is from within the DTI group.

The impressive rise in productivity demonstrated by the caseload figures has implications for how the function is performed.

Joint meetings between the parties and the conciliation officer, which are the norm in collective conciliation, have always been an exception in individual conciliation where the individual conciliation officer conventionally meets with each party separately. Now any meetings involving the conciliation officer are exceptional. Increasingly individual conciliation is conducted by telephone. The unpublished ACAS survey of the parties shows under one third (30%) of unrepresented applicants met with a conciliation officer; 16% of unrepresented employers did so, as did 3% of applicants' representatives and 1% of employer representatives. Resource constraints make it impossible to undertake many visits.

There has been an increase in the use of representation at the conciliation stage but a significant proportion of applicants represent themselves at conciliation (36%) and 29% of employers have non-specialist, in-house representation (ACAS survey of conciliation officers, unpublished data). Conciliation officers tend to prioritise unrepresented parties for visits but clearly many in this category have dealings only by telephone. The ACAS research found telephone contact, while satisfactory for some (e.g. those with knowledge of the system), was seen by the parties to impede establishing good relations with the conciliator, making it difficult to discuss the case in detail and making it difficult to absorb complex information. Furthermore, without face-to-face contact to establish necessary confidence, there is a danger that the more 'proactive' style of conciliation discussed earlier, which was found to be more influential on case outcomes (Lewis and Legard, 1998) may be seen as bias on the part of the conciliator (*ibid*, p. 118).

It is likely that in practice the approach adopted by any individual officer will vary according to the nature of the parties and the circumstances of the case. This requires an ability to identify when particular approaches are appropriate, something which may be constrained when contact is only by telephone. The need for sensitivity and flexibility in adopting the most appropriate approach is indicated by those applicants in the early discrimination cases who apparently saw persistent, proactive intervention as undue pressure.

Where a party is represented, it is ACAS practice for the conciliation officer to deal with the representative. As shown in Table 3, the use of representatives has increased. Representatives are often repeat players in that they have dealt with tribunal claims before. Both applicants and employers are now more likely to have legal representation at the conciliation stage. ACAS conciliation officers reported dealing with lawyers as applicant representatives in 26% of cases and as employers' representatives in 47% of cases (ACAS, unpublished data). This compares to 21% of applicants and 31% of employers having this form of representation at conciliation in 1976/7 (Dickens *et al.*, 1985).

TABLE 3
Representation/involvement at conciliation

	1976/7[a] (representation at conciliation) %	1996[b] (CO dealt with) %
Applicants		
In person	57	36
TU official	15 ⎱ 17	13
ss/lay	2 ⎰	
Lawyer	21	26
Other Rep	5	
CAB/Law Centre		16
Claims Specialist		3
Friend/Relative		
Respondents		
Internal Company		
Law	41	29
Specialist	22	12
Solicitor	31	47
Employers' Association	4	4
Other	2	4

Source: [a] IRRU survey of parties in unfair dismissal cases, Dickens *et al.* (1985).
[b] ACAS Survey of conciliation officers handling unfair dismissal, Wages Act and breach of contract cases cleared during July/Aug 1996. Unpublished.

ACAS expressed concern about the growing incidence of legal representation in the 1980s, saying that the involvement of lawyers 'can hinder the informal, speedy, inexpensive and amicable settlement of employment rights disputes' and reduced the possibility of obtaining re-employment. It has been unenthusiastic about any extension of legal aid to tribunals, fearing an adverse effect on the individual conciliation process (ACAS Annual Report, 1995, p. 26). For their part, solicitors generally appear to find ACAS individual conciliation helpful (White, 1989, p. 281; Lewis and Legard, 1998; ACAS data, unpublished) although what they want from ACAS clearly differs from the needs of other parties, for example lay represented small employers and unrepresented applicants.

Dealing more frequently only with representatives and communicating by telephone has the effect of focusing conciliation narrowly on settling the individual case. This is, of course, what ACAS is required to attempt to do but there is also the wider ACAS remit, to which individual conciliation also can and should contribute, namely improving industrial relations and preventing disputes in the future. Having representatives, often legal representatives, as the 'client' at conciliation (rather than the employer or the worker) has implications for this wider contribution.

INDIVIDUAL CONCILIATION AND ACAS'S WIDER REMIT

ACAS aims 'to improve the performance and effectiveness of organisations by providing an independent and impartial service to prevent and resolve disputes and to build harmonious relations at work' (ACAS Annual Report, 1998, p. 112). Narrowly conceived, individual conciliation concerns only dispute resolution.[10] A broader conception of the role sees it as contributing also to dispute prevention and good industrial relations. Even where individual rights are being enforced against an ex-employer, ACAS's wider remit suggests the conciliator should be concerned with ensuring that the employer has policies, procedures, and, above all, practices in place which will minimise similar disputes arising in the future.

The nature of those employers who are found to have dismissed unfairly, for example, indicates that the likelihood of having tribunal claims made against them would be reduced if they paid more attention to procedural fairness. A recent investigation of the links between workplace disciplinary and grievance procedures and the tribunal system concluded that 'the message is still not getting through to many employers about the necessity for the basic requirements of fairness' such as proper hearings, investigation of the facts and an opportunity for employees to state their case (Earnshaw et al., 1998, p. 15; see also Tremlett and Banerji, 1994).

---

[10] Arguably it does not even necessarily involve resolving or settling the dispute, as opposed to disposing of the case. Although the case is compromised or withdrawn the dispute (grievance) may remain.

Individual conciliation potentially provides ACAS with an excellent point of contact with small non-union employers who lack professional personnel management advice. This gives ACAS the opportunity to bring to their attention, inter alia, the standards of fairness in its Code of Practice on discipline and to assist in developing practices likely to foster harmonious relations.[11] Where the employer may be assisted most appropriately by another body (for example one of the equality commissions) ACAS could facilitate this.

ACAS recognises that wider industrial relations problems may underlie an individual claim (e.g. ACAS Annual Report, 1994, p. 56). Annual reports give examples of where the advisory function has been called in as a result of individual conciliation and employers involved in employment tribunal cases have been encouraged to attend relevant ACAS workshops. However this would suggest that this broader role is constrained by lack of resources and an undue focus on positive clearance rates (PCR) as the key measure of the success of the individual conciliation function. The PCR is easily measured; other achievements of the function are less easily quantifiable, and may deliver benefits (e.g. positive change leading to fewer applications to tribunals) only in the longer term.

As already noted, the increased workload and pressure to maintain and improve clearance rates at least cost has reduced the opportunity for conciliators to visit the parties. Underlying issues are less likely to be detected, explored or resolved via the telephone. The increasing use of representatives at conciliation also constrains performance of a broader role. In their study of ACAS advisory work, Kessler and Purcell (1992, p. 7) noted that around one-third of the organisations using ACAS's in-depth advisory service in the two years to December 1990 had first been in contact through the provision of individual conciliation. The switch in operational resources away from advisory and preventive work into individual conciliation to keep pace with the demand for this service reduces ACAS's ability to provide any follow up input in cases where the individual conciliator does consider it would be useful. Dealing with representatives by telephone, who may not involve their clients at all, also reduces the opportunity to get ACAS known among employers as a source of such preventative advice.

EVALUATION OF INDIVIDUAL CONCILIATION

There are two aspects of this evaluation of individual conciliation. One concerns ACAS performance of the statutory function as defined and interpreted; the other concerns the function itself. While ACAS is rightly concerned primarily with the former, others have wanted to engage in debate also about the latter.

---

[11] The standards set out in the Code of Practice on disciplinary practice and procedures in employment, published in 1987, have informed procedural development. The then government's reluctance to approve a revised Code led ACAS to produce an advisory handbook *Discipline At Work* in 1987. This does not have the status of a Code of Practice which is to be taken into account by employment tribunals.

Performance of the statutory function

The recent (unpublished) ACAS surveys of parties in unfair dismissal, Wages Act and breach of contract cases, indicate general user satisfaction with the performance of individual conciliation.[12] Employers and representatives tend to have higher satisfaction scores than unrepresented applicants (i.e. those without representation at the time they make their claim). But even unrepresented applicants generally rate the conciliators' performance as 'very good/good'. This was assessed in terms of outlining the law (65% scoring 'good/very good' compared with 8% rating it 'poor/very poor'); explaining tribunal procedures (67% compared to 10%); promoting a settlement (56% compared to 14%); passing messages, proposals to and from the employer (63%; compared to 8%) and discussing the strengths and weaknesses of the case (52% compared to 17%). Almost 80% of applicants said they were likely (21%) or very likely (58%) to want ACAS involvement if they ever made a tribunal claim again (ACAS unpublished data).

Satisfaction in part depends on what the parties want from conciliation and different types of party tend to want different things. Where what is wanted goes beyond the statutory role they may be disappointed. This is likely to be the case for those looking for something more like conciliation in collective disputes where the conciliator may 'make constructive suggestions to facilitate negotiations' (ACAS Annual Report, 1997, p. 3) or those seeking something akin to adjudication of the dispute. For example frustration may be expressed if it was expected that ACAS would state what would constitute a reasonable offer of settlement (Lewis, Thomas and Ward, 1997, p. 15). Applicants who, mistakenly, think the conciliation officer will represent them in pursuing their cases are also likely to be disappointed in this respect. Despite ACAS's best efforts, misunderstandings about the role of the conciliator persist.

In addition to scoring well on user satisfaction, ACAS clearly operates as an effective, cost-efficient filter, preventing cases going to an employment tribunal. A crude calculation in 1992/3 indicated the cost (to the public purse) per case heard by an industrial tribunal was £966. The cost per case cleared by ACAS was £267. If all the cases withdrawn and settled in 1992 had gone to hearing they would have cost over £30 million whereas the total cost of ACAS conciliation that year was some £15 million (Employment Department, 1994, p. 16). ACAS now publishes unit costs in its annual report, along with its positive clearance rate, as key performance indicators. The cost of an individual conciliation case settled or withdrawn in 1997/8 was £266; and 68% of cases were withdrawn or settled without the need for a tribunal hearing (ACAS Annual Report, 1998, p. 101). The individual conciliation function scores highly in terms of administrative efficiency.

---

[12] Previous research indicates satisfaction may be lower in discrimination cases where a minority of applicants described ACAS conciliation as helpful (Graham and Lewis, 1985, p. 50; Kumar, 1986; Gregory, 1982, p. 80). More research is required.

Appropriateness of the function

In discussing outcomes in discrimination cases, it was earlier noted there is an argument against providing conciliation at all in rights disputes. Generally, however, abolition of the function has not been suggested. Rather, the arguments have been concerned either with ensuring a context within which the appropriateness of conciliation is less open to question, or with developing a rather different function for the conciliation officer (or others) to perform.

The first sees conciliation as appropriate in rights disputes where inequalities as between the parties have been addressed. This facilitates conciliation taking the form of assisted bargaining or negotiation between the parties, and arguably provides a more congenial context for 'proactive' conciliation. The description of conciliation as 'assisted bargaining' is commonly used of conciliation in collective disputes but appears less appropriate as a description of individual conciliation, particularly where one or both parties lacks skilled, independent advice or representation (Dickens *et al.*, 1985, p. 175).

One way of addressing inequalities is to ensure applicants (normally the disadvantaged party) receive sympathetic, expert assistance in pursuing their rights. ACAS can act as a broker; what is needed is someone to act as representative. The Justice Committee (Justice Report, 1987) for example, called for greater public funding of voluntary and other agencies such as Citizens Advice Bureaux (CABs), Law Centres and the equality agencies. There has been some increase in use of representation by applicants (notably CABs) but, as the Justice Committee recognised, providing more assistance to applicants at conciliation can only be a partial answer to current inequalities. Other aspects of the tribunal system and the substantive law would also need addressing.[13]

The rhetoric of conciliation emphasises the responsibility of the parties for any settlement reached, and in collective disputes ACAS's refusal to involve itself in the merits of any outcome is seen as crucial. It is at least debatable, however, that what is required in employment rights cases is a form of 'committed conciliation', that is conciliation designed to bring about agreed settlements promoting certain desired substantive ends. This need not conflict with conciliator impartiality (differently interpreted) but it would move the role of ACAS in employment cases away from individual conciliation as currently practised towards rights enforcement (Dickens *et al.*, 1985, 180). This is not a role ACAS wants. The fear is it would lead to perceptions that ACAS was biased towards the applicant and that this would undermine its acceptability to employers as an impartial provider of third-party services.

---

[13] Among other things, the Committee suggested the creation of investigative officers to collect information from the applicant and respondent; inspect and copy documentary evidence, so that a dossier could be presented to the tribunal; and facilitating inquisitorial rather than adversarial hearings. It noted that ACAS conciliators were well placed to undertake this job but that ACAS Council took the view that this could adversely affect their conciliation role. Currently no information gained in conciliation is conveyed to the tribunal.

Some commentators, however, have argued that it is a social-policy oriented, rights enforcement role concerned with the nature of settlements, rather than (or in addition to) neutral conciliation which is actually required within the tribunal system. This argument has been put most usually in respect of the discrimination jurisdictions, but it has also been advocated in relation to other jurisdictions where it has been argued that the conciliator in unfair dismissal cases should act to promote procedural justice (Collins, 1992 pp. 137–139).

Although committed conciliation or a rights-enforcement approach might improve the *quality* of settlements in the sense indicated, such settlements might take longer to achieve and there may be fewer of them. Where the administrative efficiency of the system rather than its qualitative outcomes drives reforms, such developments are unlikely. The recent reforms of the employment tribunal system indicate that concern for administrative efficiency is paramount.

RECENT REFORMS AND THE ROLE OF ACAS

The 1994 Green Paper, *Resolving Employment Rights Disputes—Options for Reform,* despite its title, did not herald a radical re-think of how employment rights disputes might be resolved. This can be seen as a missed opportunity (Cockburn, 1995, p. 285). Among other things, a more radical re-consideration might have included discussion of whether some of the jurisdictions of tribunals might more appropriately go elsewhere. For example, it has been suggested at various times that equal pay issues (and other 'polycentric' disputes) might be better handled by a body such as the Central Arbitration Committee (Hepple, 1983, p. 85); that there should be specialist equality tribunals (e.g. Equal Opportunities Commission, 1998, p. 12); that disputes relating to unions and their members might more appropriately be handled by the Certification Officer (Justice Report, 1987); and that a rights mediation body would be more effective in sex discrimination cases (Hunter and Leonard, 1996). There might have been discussion of whether there should be a greater role for enforcement by inspectorates and agencies, rather than relying primarily on individuals to bring cases to tribunals. Given the clear association between union organisation and the resolution of disputes within the workplace, rather than claims being made to employment tribunals, there might even have been a consideration of whether the promotion of workplace employee representation would be useful.[14]

---

[14] The Green Paper did invite views on how the wider use of the voluntary exemption procedure could be encouraged. An agreement with provision for independent arbitration or adjudication made between an employer and independent trade union, and which provides remedies on the whole as beneficial as those provided by statute, may be designated by the Secretary of State as exempt from the unfair dismissal legislation. Only one such procedure has been so designated and the minor change made by the Employment Rights (Dispute Resolution) Act [ER(DR)A] 1998 is unlikely to greatly increase this number (Lewis, R. 1998).

But the terms of reference for the Green Paper were 'to review the operation of the Industrial Tribunals with a view to identifying any changes which would help them cope with an increasing volume and complexity of cases with reduced delays, whilst containing demands on public expenditure' (Employment Department, 1994, p. 4). Its proposals were concerned with examining options for cost-saving through increased efficiency. Two proposals in particular had obvious implications for ACAS, one concerned conciliation at tribunal premises; the other an arbitral alternative to employment tribunals.[15]

It was suggested that having a conciliation officer within the same building as the employment tribunal might facilitate settlements before or during hearings. Cases could be adjourned where settlement seemed possible. An experiment on these lines was run in 1995. The independent evaluation (Lewis, Thomas and Ward, 1997) found it was favourably received by those few who had used it, but operated at high cost to the tribunal and ACAS resources. The experiment was not continued (ACAS Annual Report, 1996, p. 64).

The other proposal affecting ACAS was for voluntary arbitration as an alternative to a tribunal hearing. The ER(DR)A 1998 provides for ACAS to prepare a scheme for an arbitration process as an alternative for unfair dismissal claims. This has been done and it awaits approval. Arbitrators (who are not required to have legal qualifications) have been appointed and it is expected that the scheme will start in Autumn 2000. The main elements of the scheme are that both parties will have to agree to go to arbitration rather than the employment tribunal; and entry is via a compromise or conciliated agreement ending the right to go to a tribunal hearing. A single arbitrator will be selected by ACAS from its panel; standard terms of reference will apply; and hearings will be non-legalistic, inquisitorial rather than adversarial. The arbitrator will have regard to the ACAS Code of Practice and handbook on disciplinary practice and procedures (rather than legal precedent) in making a decision. As in the ETs, re-engagement, re-instatement and compensation are the available remedies if the dismissal decision is not upheld. Unlike in the ETs, the hearing will be private and the award confidential to the parties; there will be no appeal on a point of law; the arbitrator's award will be final and binding.[16]

The argument that an arbitral system would be better than adjudication in the employment tribunals has been around a long time (e.g. Dickens *et al.*, 1985, Chapter 9; Rideout, 1986). It was revived, and more actively promoted by Lewis and Clark (1993) whose proposed scheme was influential in subsequent policy debate

---

[15] The ER(DR)A 1998 also facilitated compromise agreements by widening the category of people who may give advice to an employee and contained a variety of provisions designed to streamline and shorten tribunal hearings. It also extended the ACAS individual conciliation role to disputes over redundancy pay.
[16] This description is based on the consultation document (ACAS, 1998b), not the final scheme which had not been published at the time of writing.

(Employment Department, 1994, p. 31). The reasons why an arbitral system, based on ACAS collective arbitration, was argued to be better than adjudication via the tribunal system related to differences in personnel, form, procedure, objectives, outcomes and the nature of the process (Dickens *et al.*, 1985). But the fact that arbitration could also be cheaper to provide and quicker than a tribunal hearing clearly carried most weight with the government at a time when the tribunal system appeared to be unable to cope effectively with increasing caseloads and was requiring increased funding.

Arguments about the merits or otherwise of adjudication by employment tribunals and determination by arbitration, and about the details of the proposed alternative continue (e.g. MacMillan, 1999; Rideout, 1999; Clark, 1999), but it is not appropriate to engage with them here. However, it is appropriate to raise a few questions concerning the implications of the arbitration alternative for the individual conciliation function which have been neglected in the current debate.

The conciliation officer is to be a key informant concerning the arbitration alternative, helping the parties make an informed choice whether to choose it in preference to the Employment Tribunal route. Information leaflets will be available but it is clear that unrepresented applicants in particular do not always assimilate information conveyed in this way. One issue is whether, if one side wishes to go to arbitration but the other does not, the conciliation officer should attempt to get agreement or merely accept, in effect, a veto. The former would clearly have implications for the time spent on a case. How the alternatives are described will clearly be important in influencing the choices the parties make. Arbitration could be described in terms of its claimed advantages over the tribunals (cheaper, quicker, less formal, non-legalistic and so easier for unrepresented parties; private; final). If so, it may appear not only as a more attractive option than a tribunal for some, but might also deter some people from settling or withdrawing their claims by removing some of the pressures toward settlement currently in the tribunal system. Whether this is seen as a 'good' or 'bad' outcome depends on the measures used. The implications of the scheme could be a decline in positive clearance rates and rise in unit cost of individual conciliation and thus a reduction in administrative efficiency as shown on current indicators. Other measures need to be brought into operation.

CONCLUSION: CHANGE AND CONTINUITY

This chapter indicates both change and continuity in individual conciliation over the past 25 years. The statutory function has remained unchanged, but the scale and range of employment rights cases has increased enormously. The increasing caseload has not been matched by increased resources, and ACAS has had to do more with less. It has done so successfully in that there continues to be general user satisfaction with the performance of individual conciliation and the clearance rates remain high. ACAS operates as an effective, cost-efficient filter, preventing cases going to tribunal.

But doing more with less has had adverse implications for the way in which individual conciliation is performed. It is conducted now mainly by telephone rather than face-to-face. This makes it harder to establish trust and confidence, and thus may make the more proactive style of conciliation problematic. It also restricts the ability of the conciliation officer to detect, explore and resolve industrial relations issues which may lay behind an individual claim. More conciliation is now conducted with representatives, often legal representatives, rather than with the parties them-selves and this too has the effect of focusing conciliation narrowly on settling (or disposing of) the individual case. Some of the implications of doing more with less, therefore, affect the opportunities for individual conciliation to contribute to ACAS's wider mission of dispute prevention and fostering harmonious relations at work.

There was another sense in which this chapter argued that doing more with less may not be enough. This concerned the potential contribution to furthering the social policy behind the employment rights legislation, for example in discrimination cases. This calls for a more committed (or rights-enforcement) form of conciliation, with concern for the quality and nature of settlements rather than just settlements per se. ACAS, however, does not want such a role.

Recent reforms have been driven primarily by concern for cost saving and admin-istrative efficiency. There appears to be little public policy pressure for a broader conceptualisation of the individual conciliation function. In practice however, the ACAS role within the proposed arbitration scheme, together with the new emphasis on the Service's wider role, may require some rethinking of the appropriate performance criteria for evaluating the individual conciliation function.

REFERENCES

ACAS (1975–1998), *Annual Reports*. London: ACAS.

ACAS (1997), *Preventing and Resolving Collective Disputes*. London: ACAS.

ACAS (1998a), *Conciliation in Tribunal Cases*. London: ACAS.

ACAS (1998b), *ACAS Arbitration Scheme for the Resolution of Unfair Dismissal Disputes*. London, ACAS.

Clark, J. (1999), 'Adversarial and Investigative Approaches to the Arbitral Resolution of Dismissal Disputes: A Comparison of South Africa and the UK', *Industrial Law Journal*, 28(4), pp. 319–335.

Cockburn, D. (1995), 'Changes to the Industrial Tribunal System', *Industrial Law Journal*, 24(3), pp. 285–291.

Collins, H. (1992), *Justice in Dismissal*. Oxford: Clarendon Press.

Cully, M. *et al.* (1998), *The 1998 Workplace Employee Relations Survey First Findings*. London: DTI.

Dickens, L. (1978/9), 'Unfair Dismissal Applications & the Industrial Tribunal System' *Industrial Relations Journal*, 9(4), pp. 4–18.

Dickens, L. and M. Hall (1995), 'The State, Labour Law and Industrial Relations', in P. Edwards (ed.) *Industrial Relations Theory and Practice in Britain*. Oxford: Blackwell.

Dickens, L., M. Hart, M. Jones and B. Weekes (1981), 'Re-employment of Unfairly dismissed workers: the lost remedy', *Industrial Law Journal*, 10(3), pp. 160–175.

Dickens, L., M. Jones, B. Weekes and M. Hart (1985), *Dismissed: A Study of Unfair Dismissal and the industrial Tribunal System*. Oxford: Blackwell.

Donovan Commission (1968), *Royal Commission on Trade Unions and Employers' Associations 1965–1968 (Donovan Report)*. Cmnd 3623. London: HMSO.

Earnshaw, J., J. Goodman, R. Harris and M. Marchington (1998), *Industrial Tribunals, Disciplinary Procedures and Employment Practice*, Employment Relations Research Series 2. London: DTI.

Employment Department (1994), *Resolving Employment Rights Disputes: Options for Reform*, Cmnd 2707. London: HMSO.

Equal Opportunities Commission (1998), *Equality in the 21st Century: A New Sex Equality Law for Britain*. Manchester, Equal Opportunities Commission.

Fiss, D. O. (1984), 'Against Settlement', **93** *Yale LJ, 10–72*.

Graham, C. and N. Lewis (1985), *The Role of ACAS Conciliation in Equal Pay and Sex Discrimination Cases*. Manchester: Equal Opportunities Commission.

Gregory, J. (1982), 'Equal Pay and Sex Discrimination: Why Women Give Up the Fight', *Feminist Review*, **10** Spring, pp. 75–89.

Gregory, J. (1986), 'Conciliating Individual Employment Disputes: A Shabby Compromise?', *Employee Relations*, **8**(1), pp. 27–31.

Hepple, B. (1983), 'Judging Equal Rights', *Current Legal Problems*, **36**, pp. 71–90.

Hunter, R. and A. Leonard (1997), 'Sex Discrimination and Alternative Dispute Resolution: British Proposals in the Light of International Experience', *Public Law*, Summer.

IPM (1986), *Industrial Tribunals Survey*. London: Institute of Personnel Management.

Justice Report (1987), *Industrial Tribunals*. A Report by Justice (Chairman: Bob Hepple). London: Justice.

Kessler, I. and J. Purcell (1992), *Evaluation of ACAS in-depth advisory service. First Year Report*. Oxford: Templeton College.

Kumar, V. (1986), *Industrial Tribunal Applicants under the Race Relations Act 1976*. London: Commission for Racial Equality.

Lewis, P. (1982), 'The role of ACAS Conciliators in Unfair Dismissal Cases', *Industrial Relations Journal*, **13**(3), pp. 50–56.

Lewis, R. (1998), 'The Employment Rights (Dispute Resolution) Act 1998', *Industrial Law Journal*, **27**(3), pp. 214–219.

Lewis, R. and J. Clark (1993), *Employment Rights, Industrial Tribunals and Arbitration: The Case for Alternative Dispute Resolution*. London: Institute of Employment Rights.

Lewis, J. and R. Legard, (1998), *ACAS Individual Conciliation: A Qualitative Evaluation of the Service Provided in Industrial Tribunal Cases*. Research Paper 1. London: ACAS.

Lewis, J., A. Thomas and K. Ward (1997), *ACAS Conciliation at Industrial Tribunals: An Evaluation of an Experimental Scheme*. London: ACAS, DTI.

Lowry, P. (1990), *Employment Disputes and the Third Party*. London: Macmillan.

MacMillan, J. K. (1999), 'Employment Tribunals: Philosophies and Practicalities', *Industrial Law Journal*, **28**(1), pp. 33–56.

McCrudden, C., D. Smith and C. Brown (1991), *Racial Justice at Work*. London: PSI.

McIlroy, J. (1980), 'Conciliation', *Industrial Law Journal*, **9**(3), pp. 179–183.

Rideout, R. W. (1986), 'Unfair Dismissal—Tribunal or Arbitration', *Industrial Law Journal*, **15**(2), pp. 84–96.

Rideout, R. (1999), 'Alternative Employment Remedies: The ACAS arbitration alternative', *Federation News*, **49**(2), pp. 54–69.

Stevens, M. (1988), 'Unfair Dismissal Cases in 1985–86 Characteristics of Parties', *Employment Gazette*, December, pp. 651–659.

Tremlett, N. and N. Banerji (1994), *The 1992 Survey of Industrial Tribunal Applications*, ED Research Series 22. London: Employment Department.

White, P. J. (1989), 'ACAS and the Lawyers—Some Survey Evidence', *Industrial Relations Journal*, **20**(4), pp. 280–285.

4

Operating with style:
The work of the ACAS conciliator in
individual employment rights cases

Gill Dix

INTRODUCTION

The factors which bring about an out-of-court settlement in a dispute are varied and complex. But one issue which is becoming recognised as of special significance is the use of different techniques, by the mediator, in handling the dispute situation. This aspect of dispute resolution has strong resonance within the Advisory, Conciliation and Arbitration Service (ACAS). If the Service is to continue to meet its statutory duty of promoting the settlement of cases brought to employment tribunal, against a tide of ever-increasing claims, more information is required about the process of conciliation, and why some methods and styles are more powerful than others. A recent evaluation of ACAS conciliation in employment rights cases (Lewis and Legard, 1998) identified the differing 'proactive' and 'reactive' techniques used by ACAS conciliators. These descriptions were derived from consultations with parties to cases yet, to date, there has been no systematic account of styles of operating as described by ACAS conciliators themselves.[1] This chapter redresses the balance.

The chapter explores the core dimensions of conciliation,[2] describing and discussing the different roles and styles as perceived and described by ACAS conciliators. Twenty-five years since the formal creation of ACAS, the picture of conciliation in individual employment rights is very different to that found at the birth of the organisation. Other chapters in this volume have charted in detail the change in

---

[1] Some preliminary work in this area was carried out as part of a wider evaluation of a pilot initiative, involving ACAS conciliators working at employment tribunal premises (Lewis, Thomas and Ward, 1997).
[2] Within ACAS the term 'conciliation' is used to describe the involvement of a neutral third party acting as communicator between parties and encouraging a move towards a resolution, but without offering suggestions. This contrasts with ACAS 'mediation', a process including offering suggestions to parties to help them move towards a settlement. In other spheres beyond ACAS however, the term 'mediation' is used more generally, and can include activities ACAS categorise as conciliation. Research findings on other 'mediation' initiatives reported in this paper relate to the latter wider categorisation.

emphasis within the Service from conciliation in collective disputes to conciliation in the rapidly expanding volume of employment tribunal cases (Dickens, Goodman, this volume). But the change has not just been numerical. The entire arena of individual employment rights, in which ACAS is a player, has changed dramatically. The period has seen an increase in the number of employment rights jurisdictions: ACAS has a statutory duty to conciliate in more than 50 employment rights jurisdictions (Dickens, this volume). Cases are more complex—in 1998, just under half involved more than one jurisdiction (ACAS 1998, Annual Report p. 72). With the growth in legislation, and the exercise of these rights, has come a vast swathe of case law, and perhaps not surprisingly, more and more parties engage representation. In spite of the Donovan Commission's (1968) vision of labour tribunals providing an 'easily accessibly', 'informal' and 'inexpensive' procedure, today, around 40% of cases dealt with by ACAS are handled by a formal representative.

Such change has placed new demands on ACAS conciliators: they must now be capable of managing the vast array of legislation and the varied circumstances and knowledge levels of parties and representatives dealing with claims. The result is that conciliation in employment rights cases is, at its best, a highly sophisticated service. Discussions with conciliators reveal that the roles they play are both varied and highly responsive, according to the demands of individual cases. Conciliation is not formulaic. The disposition of conciliators is likely to influence the nature of their interventions, and by looking at styles of working, it is possible to gain an insight into the relationship between attitudes and actions.

Here we present a systematic account of the different *roles* played by ACAS conciliators in employment tribunal applications. These are described in the first part of the chapter which sets out a model of conciliation interventions. The second part looks at the different *styles* of conciliation, exploring the *manner* by which different roles are fulfilled. Again, a model is used as a vehicle for exploring conciliators' working styles. It becomes apparent that the different roles of conciliation, and the varied styles of operating are interlinked and it is this relationship that forms the essence of conciliation. The third part examines the interaction of roles and styles, exploring the discrete components set out in the chapter and considers the relationship between these different dimensions. The diversity and complexity of employment tribunal cases call for a finely tuned approach on the part of ACAS conciliators if they are to be effective in fulfilling their role.

METHODOLOGY

The material in the chapter is based on a series of in-depth interviews conducted with ACAS conciliators. The interviewees were selected to reflect a mix of length of service and gender, and were drawn from across the ACAS regional offices. The study used qualitative techniques to explore the ways in which conciliators construct their roles, and to identify the nature and range of tactics they use in their work. The chapter provides an understanding of the perceived merits and benefits of different approaches. However, the reliance on qualitative data makes it impossible to discuss, in any statistical way, which techniques are associated with successful conciliation. To achieve the latter would require a different research approach based on quantitative data, and factors determining case outcomes.[3]

Included are verbatim quotations taken direct from transcriptions made from the taped interviews. On occasion, words are added in parenthesis by the author to bring greater clarity to the interview extract. Throughout the text considerable emphasis is placed on reporting the language of conciliation as used by conciliators. This helps give a feel for the way conciliators describe their work, and adds definition to what is becoming a growing vernacular in ACAS conciliation. The exception to this is found in the model at Figure 1 which draws on the terminology of other research on mediation.

THE ROLES INVOLVED IN CONCILIATION

A model of conciliation interventions

Figure 1 sets out a model describing the large array of roles that conciliators identified when describing their work. The different actions are grouped under three broad headings as follows.[4]

A reflexive role which is concerned with responding to the needs of parties and establishing a positive working relationship, and at the same time giving the conciliator a greater orientation in the case.

An information provider which involves clarifying the details of a case and conveying factual information to parties. In acting in an informative role conciliators are, amongst other things, attempting to redress any imbalance in the knowledge of opposing parties, aiming to ensure that both sides are equally aware, for instance, of the legislative dimensions of their case.

A more substantive involvement may be required of conciliators in order to move parties to resolve their dispute. This may involve: exploring with parties the strengths and weaknesses of a case; assessing where parties interests lie; what is achievable within the confines of the law; and, where possible, promoting a settlement.

---

[3] Quantitative research within ACAS is currently underway examining determinants of outcomes in employment rights cases. Other studies have used quantitative measures to examine factors associated with successful conciliation and mediation. See, for example, an earlier study of ACAS collective conciliation by Hiltrop (1985).

[4] The model draws on previous studies examining mediation in social conflict, including labour as well as family and community disputes. In particular it takes ideas developed by Kressel and Pruitt (1985; 1989) who identify three basic tactics—reflexive, substantive and contextual—used by mediators. See especially Carnevale *et al.* in Kressel and Pruitt (1989). For a useful overview of mediation typologies see Pruitt and Carnevale (1993).

FIGURE 1
A model of the roles of the ACAS conciliator

Type of intervention	Reflexive	Informative	Substantive
Aims of intervention	To build the trust of parties	Place parties in a more informed position Redress a balance between parties Establish interest in ACAS, case and non-case specific	To narrow the gap in parties positions and precipitate a settlement
Tasks	Building professional confidence and trust Building personal rapport Being sensitive and flexible in dealing with parties Acting as a buffer	Clarifying issues of case Explaining ACAS role Explaining ET process and purpose Explaining case law	Identifying and ordering issues in a case Bringing realism to parties expectations Facilitating communication Examining strengths and weaknesses Promoting the settlement

Each dimension is considered in detail in the following sections. First, some caution is required in interpreting the model. While it provides a useful vehicle for exploring conciliation, like any model, it is by no means perfect. For instance, the identification of a series of distinct roles may suggest that for conciliation to be productive each type of intervention is required in each case. This is not necessarily so since, as the chapter demonstrates, different people and cases call for a different array of interventions. Second, the division of roles into three discrete areas is somewhat misleading suggesting that conciliation is a single dimensional, linear, process in which conciliators move from a reflexive to an informative and then substantive intervention in cases. In some instances this may be true: early contact with parties may indeed focus on building a positive relationship while later contact will focus on actively finding a resolution to the dispute. However, in reality, conciliation is an iterative process. Conciliators may act simultaneously to fulfill a range of functions itemised in the model, switching back and forth between roles as a case progresses, and the needs of the parties alter.

The reflexive role in conciliation

This element of conciliation refers as much to the nature of conciliators contact with parties, as to the purpose. The need to establish a trusting relationship with parties was central to the thinking of the conciliators interviewed in the study, and it was by taking a reflexive or responsive role with parties that trust was most likely to be gained. Gaining trust was important since it was felt to have a powerful bearing upon whether or not the parties respect and believe information given by the conciliator. Winning the confidence of parties was also a gateway to allowing conciliators to successfully promote a settlement. As one conciliator put it:

> ... the first thing that I am aiming for is to get their trust and confidence. I feel that once I have got that trust and they realise that I am totally neutral—I have got no axe to grind with either party—I find that if it's going to settle you can manipulate, conciliate, which every way you want to look at it.

Conciliators identified a number of dimensions to this reflexive role, all relating to the process of winning the confidence of parties as well as becoming attuned to cases. Aspects of the role are discussed below, and summarised in the model at Figure 1.

Gaining the trust of parties

Conciliators must win the parties' trust, both on a personal level, and in their professional knowledge and judgement. The tactics for achieving the two are often interlinked. Conciliators placed considerable emphasis on 'building rapport' (a phrase repeatedly used in the interviews), and it was widely perceived that face-to-face contact with the parties, especially those without representation, provided the most effective means for succeeding in this. Much was felt to depend on the demeanour and presentation of the conciliator at the point of introduction, but also the way the conciliator responded throughout the case. Conveying professional knowledge and experience was important, and this partly involved explaining the impartial stance of ACAS, and then maintaining integrity in this stance throughout their dealings with the parties.

Gaining trust and rapport meant being alert to the *sensitivities* of the parties in all types of cases. There was a widely held view that conciliators needed to be particularly aware of the sensitivities associated with cases relating to sex or race discrimination. However, it was stressed that grievances related to loss of employment or loss of wages, for instance, can have equal weight in people's lives and that conciliators needed to be alert to the reactions of the parties in all circumstances:

> It is one of the things you have got to be—sensitive ... if you are talking about a week's wages in lieu of notice, it can generate more passion for some than sex and race cases can. So I think you have got to be sensitive in every case. That is what the job is about. Getting the feel of it, and responding to the needs of the parties and the situation at the time.

> I think you would perhaps be, try to be, more sensitive maybe with sex or race (cases). At the same time, losing your job is very distressing, so you can't necessarily say that you would be less sensitive there.

Being responsive involved being a good listener. Parties unfamiliar with the employment tribunal system may feel daunted by the prospect of a tribunal, or by the bureaucracy surrounding claims. In such circumstances, some conciliators saw it as their role to make the party feel they could turn to ACAS for clarification and information, but also as a 'hand to hold' in the initial stages. These roles were felt more relevant to unrepresented parties:

> I think it (the role) is to try and, I suppose, offer some comfort—in that someone knows about it and is doing something about it. They are not just lost in a vast machinery ... it is just to offer them that hand to hold initially.

> I think the role is such that you need people from all backgrounds and all walks of life really because of the very nature of the job and the people you are dealing with. The key attribute would be really an ability to take on board and listen.

Yet this dimension of the job could be time consuming. Conciliators spoke of the need to devote time for instance with unrepresented parties, to allow them to recount their case in detail and visit all their concerns. This contrasted with some of their more expedient dealings with solicitors where conversations were confined to discussion of a settlement. Allowing parties to speak was seen as beneficial in giving them a chance to release their feelings. Listening to the detail of people's experiences was also important to progressing conciliation. It was the main means by which to gain an in-depth understanding of a case, and of the interests and motivations of parties. But it was also of 'human interest' to conciliators. Nevertheless it could also be stressful, placing a 'burden' on the conciliator and some felt the need to curtail parties with a propensity to talk at length about their case. The demand for this 'hand holding role' needed to be balanced with the time constraints faced by conciliators in having to manage their full caseload—'you certainly have not got the time to be agony aunts'. Some also spoke of feeling 'impatient' with parties, or becoming 'hard faced' about problems, and this was sometimes felt to stem from doing the job for a long time.

Winning the confidence of parties involves not only listening, but acting as a buffer to anger or frustration; to be a 'calming influence' while retaining impartiality. Such demands called for much patience and attentiveness, even when the conciliator felt under stress. These roles were relevant to applicants and employers alike:

> So sometimes you find your initial telephone contact is about allowing an employer to get their feelings off their chest. Let them have their say, and gradually try to persuade them that you are there to service them in an equal capacity to the applicant.

> A lot of people are defensive, and a lot are very hostile. They say things that could be defamatory, and they can have misconceptions. You have a professional job to sort the cases out, and you have to approach with 'I can see you are very upset about it'. And you let them gather themselves and calm your voice. ... You have people who are always shouting and you let them shout it out, and then pick out points that are obviously wrong.

Developing a flexible approach

In describing their approaches to building trust and rapport, conciliators emphasised the need for *flexibility* in dealing with different people in different circumstances. This sometimes meant simply varying the range of issues they may cover in discussing a case. With some solicitors, for example those well-versed in employment law, it may not be appropriate or welcome to discuss case law, or the merits of a case. Yet on occasions, the use of legalistic terminology may provide an assurance to a party of the competence of the conciliator. Some situations, for instance with less knowledgeable parties, warranted less technical or legalistic language, since it may be confusing.

Yet building trust may involve less palpable differences in approach. Gaining the respect of parties was sometimes easier if the conciliator demonstrated a sense of empathy with the circumstances or concerns of a party. Regional accents could have some bearing on the way parties relate to a conciliator:

> You respond to the needs of the case, and you respond to the attitudes of people you are dealing with. It even goes so far as the sort of language that you use. A colleague once remarked that she felt it was more difficult for her to do the job than it was for me because she came from (another town) and she felt it difficult to have an affinity with local people ... your accent varies, depending on who you are talking to. It becomes stronger or weaker. You do whatever gets you onto their wave length. It's a fascinating job ... you make adjustments without ever realising ... it just comes naturally.

> The language that you use varies according to who you are talking to and you don't say that particular language to an applicant, that to a respondent. You can be talking to half a dozen respondents, and your approach is totally different to every one. It all depends on the individual.

Creating a rapport with a party, or 'getting on the same wave length' as parties was not only confined to language and terminology. It might be appropriate to draw on one's own personal background in creating an affinity; or where appropriate introduce humour as an 'ice breaker'. The secret lies in a flexible approach. Here the words of the conciliators best describe their sentiments:

> Your flexibility is in how you approach the people and your attitude and its about your style I think. That's the way I see it anyway. ... You don't come on as Jack the Lad to the Managing Director of ICI, whereas there are other people you can do that with, and build up a rapport much more quickly.

> The only change to my approach is the person I am dealing with. The way I present myself. I come to work—black trousers and dark shirt, and I am quite comfortable. If I go to see an employer, I am wearing a business suit, cuff links, shiny shoes, and all the bits. It's just presentation.

Reaping the benefits of a reflexive role

The process of getting to know parties allows conciliators to orientate themselves to the dispute, and the respective positions and goals of parties. But a good working alliance was also widely regarded as having other short and longer-term benefits. First, good relations were seen as crucial to promoting a settlement. Having created a sense of empathy with parties, conciliators were able to use their position to 'feed back' to parties 'in a way that makes sense to them, and they are liable to accept'. Gaining trust was also believed to have longer-term benefits, particularly in relation to employers having future contacts with ACAS. Positive contact on a case was more likely to result in positive contacts in the future. As one conciliator pointed out 'you wouldn't buy another car from a dealer if you'd got a poor car previously'. Finally, in seeking to gain the confidence of parties, the good reputation of ACAS was sometimes felt to be helpful. This reputation was for integrity, in playing an active role in attempting to bring parties to some form of agreement, and at the same time in maintaining impartiality:

> I think the big thing ACAS does is gain the trust of people. I think it's the impartial, friendly advice. When I started someone said to me, the people who will generally be let into people's homes are vicars, doctors and ACAS officials. ... I think a lot depends on the initial contact and then the rapport you build up with people. But I think the big bonus is ACAS has got a good reputation and it's trusted.

Protecting this reputation was regarded as important. This required consistent and sound judgement and ensuring that conciliation stayed within the bounds of impartiality whilst at the same time seeking to influence the outcome of a case. These dual roles of the conciliator are discussed throughout the chapter.

Information provider

Conciliation also involves conveying information on issues related both to the employment tribunal process and to the case in question. The aim is to ensure that each party has sufficient understanding of the various dimensions of their case, and the proceedings surrounding it, to allow an informed consideration of the options for resolving their dispute (the latter, according to the model, involves a more substantive intervention by ACAS). Providing information to parties was described by some as the 'first block in terms of the conciliation process', 'the foundation for building on':

> I see my role as two-fold. Firstly, to make sure that both parties... have the same information—in other words, to explain the system of the Tribunal, what the compensation awards are, and the kind of things a Tribunal will look at. That's very important, before you get to the second stage which is obviously to try and facilitate a settlement. But you can't get to that stage unless the parties have got all the information.

Information conveyed could and should be referred back to at all stages of conciliation, to refresh the memories of parties. In particular the role of the conciliator was described as one of ensuring an even balance in the knowledge of opposing parties such that neither was disadvantaged by lack of information. The role had particular significance in cases where there is an imbalance in representation where the onus was to focus most on an unrepresented party:[5]

> I think with the unrepresented parties, we have an even greater role ... because a lot of them have never had a tribunal case, they haven't a clue what it is about. They are at risk of incurring massive legal bills. What I tend to say is 'perhaps you would like to see me and I can discuss all the options with you, and if you feel then it's appropriate (to find a solicitor) then obviously, go ahead'.

There were exceptions when conciliators felt they had a role in conveying factual information to solicitors. Some legally-trained professionals may not specialise in employment law, or not encounter as many cases as an ACAS officer. In such circumstances, the conciliator may recognise the benefits of conveying relevant

---

[5] Evidence from a study carried out within ACAS in 1996 suggests that in around 50% of cases both parties are represented; in 15%, neither party was represented; and in around 35% of cases there was an imbalance in representation, with either the applicant or the employer being represented.

information to the representative, but to do so in a way that would not cause offence—'we have got to be seen not to be implying that they don't know what they are doing'.

Pacing the flow of information to parties was important. Once contact with a party was established, or visit arranged, there was some pressure to review all aspects of the case, the options facing the parties and thoroughly describe the role of ACAS. Face-to-face contact provided a good opportunity for covering a wide range of issues, though in practice visits were relatively rare, taking place in around 10% of cases and almost exclusively with unrepresented parties. At the first point of contact, parties are at different stages in their understanding of their cases and of the employment tribunal process. Conciliators spoke of the need to judge carefully how much information to pass to parties, at what pace and when. They need to consider how receptive parties are to a mass of information and new ideas, but balance these considerations with their own constraints on time as well as the competing demands of other cases. These demands mean that conciliators often have no choice but to cover a vast amount of information in their first discussion with a party but 'good conciliation' was felt to involve constantly reiterating the technical issues involved in a case.

The following provides a description of different aspects of the information role performed by conciliators.

Clarifying the issues of a case

With unrepresented applicants, the first contact may involve exploring in detail issues raised in the application form. A similar role may be played with unrepresented employers. However where an employer written a formal response (by completing a Notice of Appearance form), there was some wariness about entering into detailed discussion since the conciliator may, inadvertently, convey information about the applicant's position that would otherwise not be known.

Clarifying the facts of a case may involve ensuring that a claim is 'within scope' by seeking clarification of length of service, or length of time elapsed since an alleged unfair dismissal. Other aspects of the parties' misunderstandings were more complex, for example relating to their conception of a tribunal as a forum which can 'sort out' any perceived injustice at work. An example given was a claim brought by a party for alleged bullying at work, an allegation which the party believed could be dealt with under the discrimination jurisdiction.

Describing the role of ACAS

At the outset of a case ACAS sends an introductory letter and leaflet, explaining the role of ACAS to the parties. Conciliators generally check that this information has been received during their initial contact with the parties, and in the main, the parties report to have read and understood the material. However, conciliators said that as discussions progress there are often signs that the parties are confused about the exact role and status of ACAS.[6] They may be unaware of the independence of ACAS and may perceive ACAS to be in a 'policing role' or likely to 'impose' a settlement or be biassed towards one type of party. It was important to remind parties of the parameters of conciliation since misunderstanding could result in parties acting 'defensively' towards suggestions made by the conciliator. Working with employers to build their confidence in ACAS and to ensure they understand the impartiality of the organisation was felt to be especially valuable since it is the employer who holds the balance of power in deciding whether or not a settlement can be offered:

> You have got to be very careful with a respondent that they don't feel that you are on the side of the applicant. This is particularly true when you have got Wages Act cases and Breach of Contract ones where you almost seem as though you are approaching them for money on behalf of an applicant, and they can see that as your role.

> I think some people find it very difficult to understand. There are a lot of people who actually think you are representing them. ... Employers tend more to think that you are representing the applicant, and they talk about 'your client'. Now solicitors do this as well—'your client'. I say, 'No, he's not my client'. And they say things like 'Well will you take instructions from our client?', 'Well no, because I am not a representative'. So you do need to keep reminding people.

Explaining employment legislation and case law

A further dimension of the information-provider role was in making parties aware of provisions in employment law, and relevant case law both potential sources of information in helping parties understand the likely outcome of their case. While there was wide recognition of the value of conciliators having some knowledge of case law, in practice there was reported to be considerable variation in the extent to which case law was discussed with parties. Discussing case law with representatives was regarded as important, in part to ensure that conciliators were respected for their knowledge of the subject matter. Yet conciliators often make the decision not to introduce case law when talking to parties since they sometimes feel wary about how it may be interpreted, particularly among those unfamiliar with the notion of legal precedent. Some feared that referring to previous cases could be off-putting, and unhelpful to parties new to tribunal proceedings. Others felt that this process carried the danger that parties may interpret the information as the conciliator saying that 'this is what is *also* going to happen in your case'. With these concerns in mind all of the conciliators interviewed said they chose to use case law sparingly, or avoid it:

---

[6] Research with parties similarly finds that they often feel they do not fully understand the role of ACAS (Lewis and Legard, 1998). This may in part be due to the need for conciliators to place more emphasis on explaining the purpose of ACAS, but is also due to the parties' inexperience of the role of an impartial, third party in resolving disputes.

Earlier on (in doing IC work), you get very bogged down with case law, trying to prove that the person has got a weak case, by bombarding them with case law and whatever. Often (it) doesn't help the person because they just become sort of alienated.

A compromise for some conciliators was to avoid using what they described as 'glossy' case law, meaning well-known cases, in favour of referring to cases which had been heard at their local tribunal, and which they sometimes had been directly involved in:

I tend not to use glossy case law, the lead cases. I usually try and find a similar one (to that heard at) the tribunal they are actually going to go to, which I think has much more impact.

Exploring Employment Tribunal procedures

Conciliators try to deal with parties misunderstandings about tribunal proceedings in order to alleviate concerns and fears about appearing in court. Here the conciliator can help by explaining all aspects of proceedings: the composition of the panel; the way the day is organised; the role of witnesses; the use of witness statements; the role of preliminary hearings and pre-hearing reviews; and the use of 'further and better particulars'. One suggestion was that parties, unfamiliar with proceedings, visit a tribunal before hand—'go along and sit in the back'. Giving parties a clearer understanding of the employment tribunal process was important in helping parties recognise what they want most to achieve from their case, and whether or not they wish to go through to the hearing stage:

We have got to tell them about the tribunal because it's one of the issues that helps them to decide whether they want to go or not ... I explain to them it's quite a formal situation. It's not that you sit around a table and have a cosy chat about something ... I definitely think that is our role ... I think that helps them to put into perspective any offers of settlement there might be, whether they really want to go or not.

Maintaining a boundary between information and advice—remaining impartial

Drawing a boundary between an information-providing and an advisory role presents a constant challenge for conciliators, but one which they are highly sensitive to in wishing to remain impartial. Clearly the manner by which conciliators present information, including case law and tribunal proceedings as discussed above, can be subject to considerable variation, and can be used more or less as tools of persuasion. The same is true of many of the dimensions of conciliation described so far, and in the next section on 'substantive involvement' in cases.

Much too depends on the different styles of individual conciliators (again discussed in the next section), but nevertheless all of the conciliators interviewed spoke of the constant pressure on them from parties to give personal views on the merits of a case, and how best to proceed. This was particularly the case with unrepresented parties, some of whom look to the conciliator to respond to the 'nitty gritty of running their case', as well as advise on the likelihood of their case succeeding.

Drawing the line between information and advice was a challenge. It involved reading and interpreting the case and the parties motivations, and offering real help without overstepping the mark. Some conciliators felt that achieving the right balance came with experience. Others spoke of their inherent tendency to feel sympathy for the 'underdog' who in the context of employment tribunal cases was normally the unrepresented party, or the applicant. Conciliators have their own 'rules of thumb' on how to deal with these kinds of demands. Some distinctions were made:

- it may be the conciliator's role to inform an employer about the timescale for completing an IT3, but not to assist him or her in presenting the arguments for rejecting the allegations of a claimant;
- conciliators may describe the detail of the tribunal process, inform parties of the role of witnesses in a hearing, and tell them the value of a prepared witness statement, but do not, in contrast, see it as their role to assist in rehearsing for a tribunal, or selecting witnesses; and
- a conciliator may be prepared to respond to a request for simple, factual information—'What are "Further and Better Particulars"', but not respond to questions seeking direct advice, such as 'Which piece of evidence should I be taking to the tribunal?'

It's like all things in this job. You talk about where that line lies. It can be difficult sometimes, particularly where you have sympathies with one party or the other, and the other party is represented.

They say 'they are offering this, do you think that this is a good offer?' and I say again that it isn't for me to decide. 'What would be a good offer for me may not be for you. What would be a lot of money for me ...' And then it's usually approached from 'Well I have explained to you how the Tribunal view things, and you really need to look at how you feel the Tribunal would view what you are going to tell them in the light of this offer. But I can't recommend it to you'.

Substantive involvement

Beyond rapport building, and informing parties of procedural issues, conciliators identified a wide range of roles which they undertake in endeavouring to meet their central objective of promoting a resolution of parties' disputes. Following the model at Figure 1, the likelihood of ACAS being successful in helping parties to reach a resolution—be it a settlement or a withdrawal of the case—is far stronger if a good working alliance has been developed (reflexive intervention), and parties are on a more sound footing if they fully understand the options open to them, are aware of tribunal proceedings and understand the role of ACAS (influenced by conciliators playing an informative role). Yet the stage at which the conciliators are required to make a substantive input is where conciliators can have most direct impact upon the outcome of the case. This involves dealing directly with the facts and details of a case; getting parties to explore issues in a critical fashion; considering the strengths and weaknesses of the claim; and look realistically at what may be the most acceptable outcome.

How an ACAS conciliator approaches this element of the work will vary depending on the style of that conciliator. As Kressel and Pruitt found in other areas of mediation, some mediators may be non-directive leaving much of this substantive work to the parties; at the other extreme, mediators will grapple directly with the issues, seek new ideas and advocate them vigorously to parties (Kressel and Pruitt, in Kressel and Pruitt, 1989). A similar range of approaches is likely to be found across the 300 or so conciliators operating in ACAS and the different styles of conciliation in seeking to influence case outcomes are discussed later in the chapter. Whatever the approach however, this element of conciliation is undoubtedly the most tactical, requiring a high level of skill and diplomacy on the part of the conciliator.

An important goal of ACAS intervention at this stage, according to conciliators, is to reassert to the parties what the options have open to them—either to settle the case, for the applicant to withdraw, or to seek an outcome via a tribunal hearing—and most importantly to inform parties of the implications of each course of action. There was a marked variation in the ways conciliators described how they go about exploring each of these options. In particular, they differ in the timing, and degree of emphasis they place, on asserting the ACAS' role in resolving cases. While the range and quality of information given to parties does not appear to differ according to the prominence given to ACAS settlements in discussion, some conciliators are clearly more vigorous and explicit than others in pursuing this outcome. The following quotation demonstrates some of the considerations in deciding a course of action:

> It's very easy for someone to withdraw and really you could argue that no action need be taken. But I don't see it like that. I think that we are here to offer a service. If someone wants to withdraw, we can deal with that. If they want to pursue it, we will conciliate. So I think there is a service to offer. To let them know the range of what they can do, and I like to feel that they know what their rights are ... If they want to withdraw because they don't want to carry on, that's fine. But if they are not sure, or if they have been frightened off, then I let them know what the options are. It's tailoring it to what you are faced with really. Yes, it's when I feel that they are not fully informed, we have a role there to inform them, and if they still want to withdraw, then fine.

The following sections explore the kinds of tactics associated with conciliators' substantive interventions in cases.

Clarifying the issues of the case

An important role for the conciliator is to assist each party to examine more critically the issues of a case and the arguments presented in defending their position: a task defined by one conciliator as stemming from the 'need to put questions their way' in order to 'open up new lines of thought'. For the conciliator, this will involve highlighting and explaining the strengths and weaknesses of each party's position and sifting through all their concerns in order to focus on those issues most pertinent to a case; most importantly, it involves helping parties to understand the 'position of the other side'. Identifying key issues in this way was a tactic for 'build(ing) momentum' (Kolb, 1983), and moving parties towards a settlement. In exploring these avenues, the issues covered are likely to be diverse, depending on the jurisdiction of the case, and influenced by a time as far back as the circumstances leading to the claim. For instance, with an employer, the conciliator may explore what lies within the range of 'reasonable conduct', or what 'represents a fair procedure', but may also involve seeking to explain some of the reasons why the applicant feels particularly aggrieved. With an applicant, the focus may be on what records or evidence the applicant has to support his or her position, and talking through precisely which internal procedures, if any, the employer used, for example before a dismissal:

> I think that once they (the parties) have decided what their case is, if you like, what their version is, I think it's then our role to point out to them where the strengths lie and where the weaknesses lie.

> We try and encourage people. I call it Brownie Points. I tell them that they have a Brownie Point there, 'because the Tribunal will chalk that one up for you'.

This kind of role was considered to be more relevant with unrepresented parties:

> If there is a solicitor acting, I think the phone calls are very short and to the point. You don't tend to get too bogged down on the merits of the case—you would, may be, just have one or two comments to be made about the strengths and weaknesses. You would take it really as read that the rep' was actually able to see what the strengths and weaknesses of the case were.

The role of encouraging a more critical analysis of a case was felt to have extra potential benefits when dealing with employers who may benefit from a more in-depth discussion by taking action to avoid future claims:

> ACAS is a vehicle for understanding. ACAS is a way of asking 'Why has it happened?' 'How has it happened?' 'Would it happen again?'. I mean, if we achieved nothing else, I would like to think that when we get a case, that by our role, we have a chance of it not happening again.

Having a good rapport with the parties was seen as crucial to being successful in helping people assess their case critically. A good relationship helped ensure that the parties are comfortable and confident about hearing the conciliator give a critical appraisal of a case. The timing of such interventions was also important. A critical, or harsh, assessment made too early in a case may inappropriately reduce a party's confidence in their case; yet leaving a detailed discussion of the weaknesses of a case too late may by implication lead to a party having false expectations of what they may achieve:

> If you are going to point out the weaknesses in their case, you have got to choose your moment for doing it, and it may not be a good idea to go in feet first at the beginning. It may be better as time goes on—let them down gently that they have not got perhaps the strongest case.

Although the value of this kind of careful intervention was appreciated by conciliators, constraints on their time was sometimes felt to hinder as thorough an analysis as would be considered desirable. One conciliator reported that pressure on time mean that he tended to simply 'look at the points (issues in a case) that stick out and hit you, and concentrate only on those'. He added that it may be that other issues would emerge if more time was spent talking to the parties.

Talking through how a tribunal would view a case

One tactic for highlighting the strengths and weaknesses in a case, and bringing about a more critical understanding of the issues involved, is to explore the likely perspective of the tribunal. In some instances this might involve a strategic reference to case law (though see earlier discussion on the use of case law). It may also involve looking at the compensatory side of the claim and the nature and size of award the tribunal may grant. It may mean offering some guidance on the likely viewpoint of the tribunal panel in relation to aspects of the case: with an applicant, explaining how their current circumstances may affect a tribunal's interpretation of a case (for example, if they have a new job); and with an employer explaining what kind of procedures a tribunal may perceive as 'fair'. One conciliator described the purpose of this stage of conciliation as explaining to the parties the 'hurdles they need to get over' if their case is heard at a tribunal. The aim of posing challenging questions was not necessarily to confront or question the party, as much as to encourage the parties themselves to assess the likely perspective of the tribunal:

> With employers (I say) 'This is what they look for in procedures. This is how they would expect a reasonable employer to act'. And you say to them 'Well, you need to put yourself and what you are going to say, to the tribunal. Ask yourself what they are going to make of your particular statement, your particular case.' I think it's a case of a lot more input (from ACAS) there, because generally speaking they don't appreciate what tribunals are all about.

> You would normally explain to them the way the tribunal system works, and you would paint a picture for them of what could happen if it went their way in tribunal, financially. Explain to them the way the awards are calculated and explain to them one of the things the Tribunal is going to be looking at would be how much they were the architect of their own downfall, because that is going to affect the award.

Taking the parties through this process was seen as a powerful tool in ensuring that they critically assess their cases. One constant challenge was handling requests for direct advice about how to deal with a case, or responding to parties who want to know whether the conciliator felt their case was 'good' or 'strong'. One tactic for dealing with such a query while retaining impartiality, was to refer to how a tribunal may view the case. Equally where a case is genuinely unclear, or sensitive, it can be helpful to draw on the possible perspectives of a tribunal in order to clarify a party's thinking. For example in handling a discrimination case, where a claim of discrimination on grounds of race is based not on 'blatant evidence' but on the apparent attitudes of the employer, conciliators may rehearse with an applicant how they may have some difficulty 'proving their case' to a tribunal. This approach was seen as favourable to the conciliator himself or herself trying to make clear the apparent 'weaknesses' of the party's position:

> You would look through the incidents that have occurred and then try to say 'Well, the Tribunal will be looking to see if you have suffered any sort of detriment and the Tribunal will be seeing your evidence. If it is subtle then you (the conciliator) may be able to say 'The burden of proof is on you at the Tribunal, so you may not be able to prove it. You may convince me as an individual possibly, but you may not be able to win at a Tribunal because you have to ... show that discrimination has occurred and it is not easy to define unless there is a blatant act.'

The process is not without difficulties. Anticipating the issues a tribunal may pick up is more predictable in some cases than others such as, for example, fair selection for redundancy, or where allegations relate to whether or not certain actions were taken or a series of events took place. Conciliators stressed the need to exercise caution in the level of certainty they attached both to areas that an employment tribunal would consider, and what their likely perspective may be:

> Take a redundancy case. What I would normally say to people (is) the sort of issues that a tribunal looks at are. Was it a genuine redundancy situation? What were the selection criteria and are they reasonable? How were the criteria applied? How was the consultation done? ... Sometimes you are being more prescriptive ... Where it's clearer what should be done, you are able to say to them 'You haven't done that'. In other areas, perhaps where it's an area of fact that is in dispute as to whether something was done or not, in that situation it is difficult.

Bringing realism to the parties' expectations

Another role identified by conciliators was to help the parties achieve a more realistic assessment of what they may achieve by pursuing a claim. The very process of getting them to achieve a greater understanding of the merits and weaknesses of their case may have the immediate effect of reducing or raising expectations. But conciliators sometimes needed to be more direct in pointing out areas of misunderstanding.

Unrealistic expectations sometimes related to the sum of money they expect a tribunal to award. Applicants may be influenced by national press coverage of employment tribunal cases attracting large settlements. Employers, in the same way, may be aware of high-profile cases and fear the likely outcome of a claim brought against them. ACAS conciliators said they felt it important to stress early in discussions with parties that very high settlements are quite rare. Calculating an actual sum of compensation that a tribunal is likely to award was a useful tactic in helping parties have a more realistic feel for the likely outcome of a case, though it was stressed by some that this process should always be couched by a degree of uncertainty about how a tribunal may view the case:

> People think that if they go to tribunal, it's going to be like winning the lottery. Of course, it's just not like that. The way the tribunals calculate compensation is very prescriptive.

> Sometimes you can identify a case that will only win a small sum of money because they have got a new job, and they have already been paid their redundancy money. So you can immediately say, 'What are you expecting to get from a tribunal?' And they say 'I think they should be paying me £5000'. And you then say that you have just worked it out and they could only win £500 or whatever. Once you have established something like that, it gives out a realistic prospect as to what they can do.

Other unrealistic expectations related more to the range of issues that a tribunal will cover in making an assessment of a case. Conciliators spoke frequently of encountering applicants whose prime goal in submitting and seeing through a case was to 'clear their name', and in so doing, bring a sense of 'justice' to their case. By bringing a claim to a public hearing, and 'winning' their case, they believed their reputation would be exonerated, and their employer will be publicly admonished. For applicants holding this view, the privacy of an ACAS settlement provided little attraction.[7] Clarifying with the parties what issues a tribunal is likely to address often involved getting applicants to accept that these kinds of outcome were unlikely to be forthcoming with the weight of tribunal decisions resting on procedural issues. This element of conciliation, of 'seeking some outcome other than retribution' (Peachey, in Kressel and Pruitt, 1989) was reported as time-consuming, and complex. Parties holding such views tended to be firmly entrenched in their beliefs and conciliators needed to constantly restate the purpose of tribunal hearings. Applicants who were unwilling to grasp this dimension were unlikely to agree to settling their case:

> It's amazing the number of people who think that when they get to tribunal, they see it as a forum for them to express their grievances in general, as a public humiliation of the employer and this sort of thing, and of course it isn't about that.

> He wanted to clear his name. This was obviously taking over his life and it took a lot of explaining to him that this isn't what a tribunal is for. That whatever the outcome of the tribunal, he wasn't going to clear his name (of alleged fighting at work). He wasn't going to get anything more than a decision on how the respondent had treated him.

Other parties simply have unrealistic expectations of the action a tribunal may take. One example was that the tribunal may 'force an employer to re-employ' the party. Some may have genuine misunderstandings about what a tribunal might consider to be a fair procedure, or acceptable action on the part of the employer.

Interestingly, while many of the tasks of the conciliator were associated with building the confidence of parties, in some circumstances, it was considered appropriate to diminish the parties' confidence in their cases. An instance given was where an applicant felt particularly angry about the poor treatment they had received from their employer to an extent that they were unable or unwilling to see weaknesses in their case. In such circumstances, some conciliators saw it as within their role to question directly with the party, how 'water-tight' their case really was. Similarly, conciliators cited examples in which employers had felt confident that they had behaved appropriately towards an employee; saw the claim as a 'waste of time'; and were determined that representation or advice was not necessary in their case. Once again, disabusing such employers was felt to be a legitimate role for the conciliator:

> When I first started, I always remember (my manager) saying something to me that stuck in my mind. He said 'What you are trying to do in a way is tug the rug'. Not to say they haven't got a case, because we certainly wouldn't go down that avenue at all, but quite a lot of people are so cock-sure that they have got a cast-iron case.

> I have always thought that was part of our role—to destabilise the parties. Actually to make them think that maybe they could lose—both sides.

---

[7] Settlements agreed through ACAS are private with details available only to the parties involved. This contrasts with employment tribunal decisions, the details of which are in the public domain.

Promoting a settlement

So far, this section has explored the substantive roles identified by conciliators in bringing parties to a more realistic and informed understanding of their cases. In carrying out all, or some, of these tasks, conciliators aim to bring the parties to a greater awareness of the options open to them, including the possibility of pursuing a settlement involving ACAS.

This final section on substantive interventions considers some of the wide range of tactics that conciliators use in promoting and pursuing a settlement. At its simplest level, conciliation involves a third party conveying offers and counter offers between parties yet, in negotiating parties acceptance of the terms of a settlement conciliators draw on a range of strategies and tactics. These can be summarised as follows.

1. One tactical approach is to seek to alter the parties' perceptions so that they are closer together, and can agree some common ground on which to agree a settlement. This involves conveying the other side's viewpoint in an impartial fashion, and listening and talking through the most acceptable compromise for both sides:

> You are there basically to listen to what both sides have to say and to try and just really reach some sort of compromise on whatever position both sides have. To try and just really reach some sort of compromise ... giving people as much information as you can so that they can make the best decision for themselves.

> The key attribute would really be an ability to take on board and listen, understand each other's view point and being able to impartially convey someone's view point to the other side—in a way influence them to move away from their own entrenched position to consider someone else's viewpoint.

2. In seeking to influence parties it may be appropriate on occasions to play 'devil's advocate'. This was a concept referred to frequently by conciliators and involved posing new questions, or turning questions round to bring a new insight into the case, for one or both parties. 'Playing devil's advocate' thus involved taking an active role as a third party. The approach could provide a challenge to the parties' thinking and contribute to their considering a settlement. Yet this was not a tactic favoured by all conciliators, or of use in all circumstances. Some feared that it was an approach that antagonised parties, and could create negative feelings towards the conciliator:

> People talk about playing the devil's advocate ... But actually, you usually find that often it just makes the person feel very negative towards you, and the whole question of settlement.

3. Where the parties are particularly entrenched in their position or for example, are worried about the implications of the case for their reputation. It is sometimes appropriate for the conciliator to intervene by taking action on their behalf, but not directly under their auspices. This kind of action was known as 'face saving'. It involved for example the conciliator putting an option to an employee which may open the door to a settlement, but doing so without admission, and thus 'loss of face' for the employer:

There are just ways of raising things. I think an awful lot of it is face saving. You are trying to put things to them so that they can say 'Yes, I will do that' but almost without a loss of face which I think for them is very important. I might say 'Well look, I know you probably feel you have got a very strong case ... but would you like just as an option, for me to find out ...' I think it's how you put it, and you have got to spend quite a lot of time in phrasing things the right way so that you really achieve what you want to achieve.

4. Similarly, in certain circumstances, employers were reported to feel more comfortable speaking 'off the record' to the conciliator for example about some evidence which is not widely known regarding the case. In suggesting the terms of a settlement, a party, or representative, may also speak 'off the record' to a conciliator about the lowest, or highest figure they are prepared to meet, or accept. This kind of dialogue was welcomed by some conciliators as a positive stage in successful conciliation, and an achievement which they believed resulted from careful building of the confidence of the party in the conciliator. Other conciliators felt uncomfortable when the parties invited them to speak 'off the record' seeing this as compromising their impartiality.

5. At different points in the conciliation process, and for different reasons, conciliators may suggest that a party seek advice elsewhere about their case, and may propose that a party seek formal representation. This may occur where it is clear that the case has a number of flaws, but that a party appears unwilling to acknowledge areas of weaknesses. Similarly where a party is looking for advice, for example on how good the case is, or whether to accept an offer, the conciliator may suggest that the person approach another advice agency or solicitor who could provide 'more pointed', or direct advice, than ACAS can provide.

Let them down gently that they don't have perhaps the strongest case, or get them to get advice which tells them that they haven't got the strongest case so that you are not then the bearer of the bad news. They always shoot the messenger sort of thing.

STYLES OF CONCILIATION

Following this discussion on roles and tactics involved in conciliation this section provides a further layer to the canvas of conciliation, discussing the different styles used by ACAS officers. The data reported is derived first, by asking conciliators to describe their own style; and second, by inferring something of the conciliator's style from the language and terminology used when describing their work.

Conciliation styles model

Again as a reference point, a model is used to describe conciliation styles. Here, approaches are described as operating on three broad dimensions, each of which is presented as a continuum between two extremes. These are set out in the model at Figure 2.

FIGURE 2
A model of conciliation styles

A	B	C
Reactive Responds to calls Works to high-priority cases and Employment Tribunal dates	**Message bearer** Conveys offers	**Passive** Makes parties think Turns issues upside down
Proactive Promotes contact with parties Chases Probes Works to high and lower-priority cases	**Influences** Works within framework of bands Uses 'natural pressures' 'Speaking off the record' Opposes bearing message that may antagonise	**Forceful** Makes the odds explicit Bullying—'others do it'

A   Reactive–Proactive. The first is a continuum describing the extent to which conciliators are active and persistent in initiating and responding to contact with the parties.

B   Message Bearer–Seeking to Influence. The second relates more closely to the goal of conciliation, but also suggests a style of working. In acting as a third party in disputes, some conciliators see their role as primarily a message bearer conveying information from one side to another. Others see themselves as more actively engaged in the detail of the case, and in attempting to influence parties' decisions about whether or not to settle a case.

C   Passive–forceful. The third dimension refers less to the substance of conciliators' involvement in cases, and more to their approach to the parties, and the ways in which arguments are presented. In particular, it describes the extent to which conciliators are assertive in seeking to influence (B) the parties in the resolution of a dispute.

Conciliators have each developed their own terminology to describe how they approach their work. While the terminology used is drawn entirely from the words of conciliators, it is worth noting that some of the terms are in practice used interchangeably having quite different meanings for different conciliators. Most noticeable is the very different uses of the terms 'reactive' and 'proactive', which, whilst part of the everyday conciliation vernacular, are used to refer to all three dimensions summarised in the model. This is apparent in some of the quotations used in the following text.

Reactive–proactive styles

This dimension of style refers to the way in which conciliators manage their cases, and their caseloads. Are they proactive, or reactive in contacting the parties? 'Proactive conciliators' will tend to initiate first contact, while a reactive approach is associated with waiting for the parties to make the first call to ACAS. Proactive conciliators are more likely to follow up contacts swiftly, maintain frequent contact and respond efficiently to the parties' calls or queries. Conciliators adopting a more reactive approach may leave long or indefinite periods of time between contacts, or may, after an initial discussion with the parties, leave the onus on them to contact ACAS. Another element of a proactive style of conciliation is ensuring that high priority be given to swiftly passing offers and counter-offers between two sides in a case. This approach is akin to the characteristics of the 'persistent' approach identified by parties and reported in Lewis and Legard (1998):

> Good conciliation involves consistent contact, not necessarily early contact, but consistent. Once having established contact, maintaining that relationship and being persistent.

> It is not just a question of making contacts in the beginning and you get nowhere, that's it, forget about it, put it in the drawer, that's the end of it. My involvement is one of a sort of continuous means of contact with the parties to see if the situation has changed.

> I am very proactive in that I keep the pan on the boil ... the parties moving. Whereas a lot of them (conciliators) think once we have done our bit ... then some of the willingness should come from the parties. I still think its more productive to keep having a go.

A proactive approach was regarded as an essential ingredient in 'gaining control' of individual cases and also important in managing a full caseload. In contrast, there was some evidence to suggest that reactive conciliation tended to be associated with a less rigorous approach to handling cases, either implying a considered *laissez-faire* approach or, less positively, a sense of cases being beyond the control of the conciliator. In the case of the latter, a reactive stance was often accompanied by a sense of the conciliator feeling over-burdened by the job, or by the number of cases on the desk.

Nonetheless, reactive conciliation was also felt to have a place. As one conciliator pointed out, a reactive approach was on occasions regarded as a positive tactic since it allowed the parties time to reflect on their case and possibly change their position. Another view was that repeated contact from the ACAS officer could be misinterpreted by the party as equating to a 'strong case' with a good chance of winning:

> I am a great believer that sometimes isolation is a great conciliation tool. You give them the ammunition and leave them to think about it for a while. I think there is a danger in being too proactive sometimes, not all the time, in that you can give someone the impression that their case is far more important than probably it is. Say if you are an unrepresented applicant and I ring you every couple of days—'Oh, I must be on to a good thing here. ACAS keeps ringing me'.

While 'proactivity' may be the favoured option for many, conciliators are often, in practice, constrained by the style which they can adopt. Their options may be limited by *external factors* especially pressure on time, or having to deal with a rising caseload, or new areas of jurisdiction, all of which may lead to a more reactive approach to cases. Sometimes the *particular circumstances of the case* have a bearing on the type of approach adopted. Indeed the circumstances of a case may require a varied approach to conciliation at different points in its duration. Finally, it is likely that the *individual disposition of the conciliator* (including their judgement of how best to proceed with conciliation) will shape the way they approach case management, and influence the vigour and enthusiasm with which they go about contacting, and dealing with the parties:

> It (conciliation) can be a bit of both (pro-active and reactive). I would like to think in an ideal world conciliation is pro-active, but I think because of the time limits (between receipt of IT1 and issue of a hearing date) that are on us, we must react to particular situations in that we alter our opinion or conception of the job. But I think it is probably 50:50.

Message bearer–seeking to influence outcome

In describing the way the conciliation role can be approached, conciliators draw a comparison between being a 'message bearer' on the one hand, which involves simply conveying information about the case and offers made between parties, and on the other hand actively 'seeking to influence the outcome of a case'. These two approaches equate to the 'administrative' versus the 'analytical' role identified by Lewis and Legard in their discussions with conciliation parties (Lewis and Legard, 1998).

Conciliators seeking a more 'influential' role in cases were more likely to vigorously pursue the range of interventions and techniques described earlier in this chapter, and particularly those described under the categories of reflexive and substantive roles. Where the end goal is to influence the parties' decisions, a conciliator may feel it is essential to build a strong working relationship and develop the trust of the parties. She or he may also see it as essential to work with the parties in weighing up the strengths and weaknesses of a case; posing new questions, playing 'devil's advocate', presenting how a tribunal may view the case, and encouraging the parties to move to a greater awareness of the perspective of the other party. One conciliator explained that successfully influencing the parties involved working on the 'natural pressures' that exist in the case in order to bring about a compromise. Another described the process as 'exploiting the weaknesses of a case that make them (the parties) more amenable to settlement'. Conciliators have their own definitions of what conciliation should seek to achieve, as the following quotations demonstrate:

> Some people do want you to be a passer-on of messages. Now to me that is not what conciliation is about. Perhaps to some extent towards the end of the life of an application, that's what it can be, but I think for it to be meaningful conciliation, it is not just a question of passing on messages. You have got to inform as well.

> Perhaps persuasion is not quite the appropriate word ... in terms of the conciliation officer having an influence on whether the case settles or not. I like to operate in such a way that my involvement is an influential involvement rather than simply a process of carrying messages between parties.

The key attribute would really be an ability to take on board and listen ... being able to impartially convey someone's view point to the other side and, in a way, influence them to move away from their own entrenched position to consider someone else's viewpoint.

One of the things that was drilled in when I first came to ACAS is that ACAS is impartial, and it takes a while to twig to the fact that conciliation is not a passive process. Conciliation is very much an active process and being impartial doesn't mean the same as never expressing a view, or sitting on the fence.

According to the last of these quotations, the construct of conciliation involves the conciliator as an active third party in a case. She or he adopts a dynamic role in conveying information but also acts as a stimulus in challenging the views of parties. In one sense it is an approach which is regarded as a high-risk strategy, placing the conciliator in a more vulnerable position with a danger of falling out of favour with the parties, or making a poor judgement—'sometimes you have to stretch yourself and put yourself almost in a lions den'. Yet, from another perspective, it is an approach which is empowering, and for those who favour this method, potentially more fulfilling:

In my experience, I think the conciliation officer is calling the shots in so much as they are weighing up the strengths and weaknesses, and going back to either party pointing out the problems that could occur if they go to tribunal.

None of the conciliators interviewed favoured the 'message bearer' as a predominant role at all times in the conciliation process. Nevertheless, almost all saw a potential role for the conciliator in simply conveying messages at certain points in the life of a case. This was especially true towards the end of a case in which a series of offers and counter-offers were to be passed between parties. Simply conveying the words of one party to the other was sometimes a tactic for the conciliator:

If the offer is £5 and you just know the guy isn't going to settle for £5, you relay the offer, wait for the rejection, and then start again. The messenger boy. It's as simple as that. Convey it. Tell them to think it over. Make sure that you follow it up if they don't come back. It's as simple as that.

Conciliators, then, see quite diverse roles for themselves according to the parties involved. Whilst with unrepresented parties, they tended to identify a broader 'more influential role', where the party has a representative it may be highly appropriate to act as message bearer. Even when dealing with representatives however, the role as messenger may not be insignificant. An example given was where representatives for each party 'did not get on particularly well' and ACAS was the 'person in the middle', objectively conveying facts of the case between the two sides with no overt vested interest. Equally, acting as a message bearer was more feasible where conciliators felt less pressurised by time. Where they felt more pressure on their time, they felt a greater onus to hasten parties to a more analytical assessment of their case:

If you have a heavy caseload, then maybe something has to go out of the window ... If you are perhaps not as busy, then you might be prepared to go along to a certain extent with passing on messages, whereas if you are very busy you literally can't go along with that in the hopes of maybe developing it at a later stage into a positive outcome.

Yet in certain circumstances, conciliators took exception to acting as a message bearer. This was particularly the case where a party asked ACAS to convey information which in their judgement would antagonise the opposing party. In response, the conciliator may indicate the dangers of a particular offer, for example, in creating a stalemate and making it clear that the party is unlikely to find the offer acceptable. Where they adopt the strategy of conveying offers, for example which they know to be lower than a party's expectations, they may do so in carefully chosen language, or by using appropriate intonation, to imply their awareness that the offer is unacceptable:

> I will make it clear to the employer that I know that (an applicant's suggested settlement) is more than what could be awarded at tribunal, but the applicant has requested it. It works the other way round. When employers say 'Tell them they can have £50 to go away', and they want £5000, I will ring and say 'They are offering £50!!.' There are times I would like to be in a position to say 'No come on, this is nonsense, and I don't want to do this', but we don't do that. You might try and point out that this is probably unreasonable, but at the end of the day the duty is to put the proposal without comment' .

These kinds of strategies allow conciliators to protect their own credibility. Whilst acting message bearers, they are simultaneously bringing some 'influence' on parties decisions, albeit at a low level. Here the boundaries between the 'message bearer' and 'influential' stances of ACAS become less clear.

Forceful—Passive

In the process of attempting to resolve a dispute, the conciliator may apply pressure tactics in an effort to push disputants towards an agreement. A recent evaluation of a pilot mediation scheme for the county courts found that some mediators chose to focus rapidly and heavily on the disadvantages of litigation, and uncertainty of a trial outcome (Genn, 1998). These mediators tended to a 'head-knocking' approach to influencing case outcomes, an approach which often attracted criticism for creating a pressure to settle. There is a prevailing ideology that such a standpoint is alien to good conciliation (Kressel and Pruitt in Kressel and Pruitt, 1989 p. 412). This sentiment was echoed widely among the ACAS conciliators. Yet where there is a commitment to an 'influential' style of conciliation, as discussed above, the boundary of what may and may not be acceptable in terms of pressure is difficult to define.

The challenge for the conciliator is to find a position on a notional scale between being 'forceful' and 'passive' which is dynamic and persuasive, yet acceptable to the parties involved, and within the norms of the ACAS role. One conciliator described this process as working 'within a framework' in which the goals may be clear, but within which the fine lines between 'pressuring' and 'coercing' are difficult to tread:

> I think the important thing you need to know is that the framework in which you are required to operate is not a standard 'this is what you must do', 'this is what you must say'. But its like you have got to know the band into which you can operate. There's a very fine line between what is influencing the parties, and what's actually coercing them, putting pressure on them. You have got to be careful not to overstep it. It's a bit hairy sometimes.

We do influence whether a case is going to settle because our job is to weigh the strengths and weaknesses of the case. I mean we never ever go and say to an applicant 'You haven't a hope in hell—withdraw this case.' It's just not on. If they are hell bent on taking that case to a Tribunal, that is their right to do so.

One alternative may be a more passive 'cajoling' style of bringing about a greater level of awareness and understanding of the case by the party. This may involve carefully posing questions about a case, and presenting difficulties inherent in the parties' arguments which lead to a desired outcome for the conciliator. Bullying or being aggressive was felt to be inappropriate, not least because it was feared that such an approach would negatively affect the conciliator's acceptability to the parties, both in the current and future potential cases (see also Kolb, in Kressel and Pruitt, 1989). None of the conciliators interviewed confessed to this style of conciliation, though it was believed to be an approach that 'others', probably a minority, in ACAS had adopted. Nevertheless, conciliators clearly do see opportunities for applying pressure to parties. Remaining influential without being perceived to place pressure on parties was a 'difficult path to tread'. Experience gave conciliators confidence to tread this path more effectively. Through experience, conciliators felt more able to judge the responses of the parties:

In some ways (it is) a difficult path to tread because if you tread the influential path you have got to be careful that you don't go too far in the way of pressure or perceived pressure.

You have to be careful that you don't use that pressure in a way which causes the person to feel that you, as the conciliation officer, have used undue influence, and it is hard to describe where the lines are.

Second, in one conciliator's view, his vast experience of doing the job for ten years had enabled him to make judgements about the likely outcome of a case. Where he felt on 'solid ground' about a case, he may say to a party 'you are in a mess', or that 'there was no point in taking this case forward'. In his experience, parties tend to welcome this direct advisory stance. He emphasised that it was an approach which he may use 'sparingly', and where he feels that the parties have confidence and trust in his judgement. Nonetheless this was an approach which other conciliators would most certainly feel at odds with.

Another expression of this dimension was how *direct* conciliators felt able to be in dealing with the parties. Here conciliators were again divided in their views. Whilst for some giving a personal view direct to the parties was an overt infringement of impartiality, there was a view that actively persuading parties of the merits of settling was felt to be both acceptable, and a good service:

It may have taken the penny a long time to drop with me, but I think you have got to actively persuade people to settle. I don't see anything wrong with that. It says in the (legislation surrounding ACAS) that conciliation officers should 'endeavour to promote a settlement', and promoting a settlement to me means trying to persuade people to settle. It's as simple as that. (Later in the interview) I am not prepared to go so far as to bully people into doing things that they don't want to do, but I do honestly think that if I can identify what's important to a person and feed that back to them in a way that satisfies, that's good enough.

Being direct requires judicious interpretation on the part of the conciliator—they can only do this where they feel they have built sufficient understanding of the parties to have a strong sense of what the party wishes to gain from a case. Experience allowed conciliators to more effectively tailor their style to match the confidence of the party. Where a party is more confident about themselves, and the nature of their claim, it may be possible to be more up-front about the likelihood of success at a tribunal; whereas being direct with a less confident party may precipitate a speedy, and sometimes inappropriate withdrawal:

> It depends on the person, because I think if the applicant is quite confident, you feel quite confident in putting your side of the case to them. Now I think there is a danger where somebody is very unsure that if you say 'Well you have no hope at all' that they immediately say 'Well ACAS said I have no hope, so therefore I'll withdraw my claim'. I think where you have got somebody who will weigh what we have said against what they know, I think you can be more forceful.

THE INTERACTION OF ROLES AND STYLES IN ACAS CONCILIATION

The chapter has explored the roles and styles of ACAS conciliation. These descriptions are underpinned by what conciliators believe to be the goals of conciliation, and how they go about achieving these goals. By taking the two sets of information—on roles and styles—together, it is possible to build an in-depth understanding of the conciliation process. While conciliation in employment tribunal cases is a statutory function for ACAS, and conciliators are guided by organisational policy set out in internal guidance, it is apparent that there is a considerable amount of discretion left to individuals in the way they go about their work. Not all of the interventions discussed were mentioned by all the conciliators. Some identified a wide range of goals, but others clearly gave preference or priority to certain tasks or certain approaches. It is clear from conciliators' descriptions that no one simple model can be applied either to what conciliation involves, or what constitutes 'good conciliation'.

Conciliators in practice will make, and are required to make, different kinds of interventions in cases, and may possibly draw on a wide range of styles of conciliation, depending on a number of factors. These factors are:

- the circumstances of the case and the jurisdiction;
- the parties involved, especially whether or not the conciliator is dealing with the party direct, or a representative;
- their current workload, especially the time available to them; and
- the interests, personality and disposition of the conciliator involved.

Considerable emphasis was placed on the need to take on board the particular circumstances of the case and to use discretion in how best to proceed with a case. As discussed earlier, the information requirements and level of analytical interventions needed and requested by unrepresented parties are likely to be greater than those from legally qualified, and experienced, representatives. Equally, parties will have different confidence levels; may be less or more open to absorbing complex information at different points in the life of their case; and may be less or more sensitive or susceptible to forceful, or persuasive techniques by the conciliator. The complexity of a case, the level of interpretation required and the scope for influencing parties are likely to be greater in some jurisdictions than others. Many conciliators are aware of these differing demands and articulated them in the interview situation:

> Each case is individual so how I react to each case would be different. But my actual way of thinking or outlook is to reach a settlement if I possibly can. How I set out to achieve that would obviously be different in different cases.

> I think that one of the things with this job is that you can't say we always do it this way, or we always do it that way, because every case is different and we have always got to be slightly different in the way we approach things in some cases, than you are with others.

> There has always been this argument about are we just a messenger, passing messages between the two parties, or do we have a more pro-active role. I think the role varies depending on the case, and the parties to it, and whether they are represented or not.

So it is clear that the conciliation process is a complex arena. The interventions and style explored in this chapter closely interact and shape the conciliation process. It is likely that across ACAS, different 'types' of conciliators may be identified. For example:

Type A—may use a wide range of reflexive, informative and substantive interventions, operating in a clearly proactive style which seeks to actively influence the outcome of cases.

Type B—may focus most closely on reflexive roles, of rapport building and gaining the trust of parties in order to seek to influence the outcome of cases.

Type C—may be more concerned with the informative role of ACAS, aiming to ensure that parties are fully aware of the procedural issues surrounding their case and the options open to them—but may act purely as a message bearer, leaving the prime decisions and thought processes to the parties.

There are a range of other 'types' that could be envisaged using the models of interventions and styles described. Equally important, some conciliators will shift between different 'types' depending on the nature of the case, on their current workload, and the pressures and constraints on their time. This flexibility comes more easily to some conciliators than others. Those who are more adaptable are likely to be more able to judge the precise demands of the case. They may draw skilfully and selectively from a 'kitbag' of possible roles they can play, and styles which they can adopt in seeking to affect the outcome of a case. Others may feel more comfortable operating a formulaic approach to conciliation, or utilising a single style and mode of operating. It was apparent from these interviews that many types of conciliator are operating in ACAS. Nonetheless, attitudes in this study, and from consultations with parties to cases (Lewis and Legard, 1998) point clearly to the merits of a flexible and adaptable approach as the optimum way of operating, and maximising the chances of settlements in cases.

As the verbatim quotations throughout this chapter suggest, some conciliators are very much in tune with the different demands of their job. Indeed, it is the challenge that emerges from the different circumstances that they encounter, and the scope afforded them as individuals to respond, which makes the job so attractive and fulfilling for them. Other conciliators were less able to reflect broadly on the tasks and goals associated with their work. It is not easy to find a clear pattern of explanation for this. One possible reason was that the more reticent conciliators simply felt less comfortable in the interview situation. It may also have been associated with lower levels of experience in doing the job. Finally, it is likely that these conciliators may have been of a less analytical disposition than some of their colleagues, and that this affected both the way they responded in the interview, and more broadly, the way they approach their cases and their conciliation role.

CONCLUDING COMMENTS

There has clearly been a recent growth in the number of alternative dispute-resolution systems throughout the civil justice system, but many schemes are new, and there has been relatively little evaluative research on the benefits and techniques involved in the process. Within the British context, ACAS with its experience of handling employment rights cases over the past quarter-century, arguably, stands as the 'grand old man' of conciliation, making it well placed to share its experiences and knowledge. The messages in this chapter are likely to have significance to other spheres of conciliation and mediation.

The study has demonstrated that flexibility and responsiveness are the cornerstone of good conciliation. This involves the ability to adapt to the demands of different people and different cases. ACAS has clearly responded to the challenges which have emerged from the expansion in employment rights, jurisdictions developing a service which has the potential for a high level of sophistication and professionalism. Yet the future holds further challenges for ACAS.

First, the messages from conciliators is that good practice is widespread, and the means for *best* practice are understood. But there is also evidence of variation in the current quality in standards. ACAS must look to consolidating and spreading understanding of the methods of conciliation which are most effective, through training, mentoring and developmental initiatives. One idea is that the skills and knowledge required for the job should be formally recognised through accredited training. This may be a sound move, though any accreditation system tailored to ACAS conciliation must clearly place equal weight on the interpersonal and cognitive skills required for the job, as well as the technical knowledge base.

A second challenge will be to maintain a high standard of service in the face of a rising tide of cases. New recruits to ACAS conciliation must be taught the tactics of the job which have been developed during quieter times. Current and longer-serving conciliators must strive to retain the range of influencing techniques which they know to be most powerful in determining case outcomes. Yet ultimately the danger is that pressures caused by the increasing volume of cases will have a bearing on the time afforded individual cases, and the creativity needed in responding to a varied caseload. Top of the agenda must be the imperative for ACAS to maintain settlement rates—the *raison d'être* of the Service. But beyond settling cases, the extra benefits of ACAS involvement, of bringing clarity to parties' understanding of their cases and the entire employment tribunal process, are also important. However, these achievements may well be predicated upon the highly responsive, depth, and often protracted conciliation which ACAS has, over the years, devised. ACAS must continue to meet its statutory duty while allowing conciliators the opportunity to operate with the style that is most fitting to effective conciliation.

RESEARCH ACKNOWLEDGEMENTS

The chapter reports on one element of a broader evaluation of conciliation in employment rights cases carried out within ACAS. I am grateful to Bill Hawes and Chris Reid from ACAS for their support in the conduct of this qualitative study, and to Barbara Kersley for her invaluable assistance in conducting the interviews. Special thanks go to the conciliators at ACAS who participated in the study, giving their time to talk freely and frankly about their work.

REFERENCES

ACAS (1998), *Annual Report*. London: ACAS.
Carnevale, P., R. Lim and M. McLaughlin (1989), 'Contingent Mediator Behaviour and Its Effectiveness', in K. Kressel, D. Pruitt and Associates, *Mediation Research*. San Francisco: Jossey Bass.
Donovan Commission (1968), *Royal Commission on Trade Unions and Employers' Associations 1965–1968*, Cmnd 3623. London: HMSO.
Genn, H. (1998), *The Central London County Court Pilot Mediation Scheme: Evaluation Report*. London: Lord Chancellor's Department.
Hiltrop, J. (1985), 'Mediator Behaviour and the Settlement of Collective Bargaining Disputes in Britain', *Journal of Social Issues*, **41**, pp. 83–99.
Kolb, D. (1983), *The Mediators*. Cambridge, Mass: MIT Press.
Kolb, D. (1989), 'Labor Mediators, Managers and Ombudsmen: Roles Mediators Play in Different Contexts', in K. Kressel, D. Pruitt and Associates, *Mediation Research*. San Francisco: Jossey Bass.
Kressel, K. and D. Pruitt (eds) (1985), 'The Mediation of Social Conflict', *A special issue of the Journal of Social Issues*, **41**(2).
Kressel, K., D. Pruitt and Associates (1989), *Mediation Research*. San Francisco: Jossey Bass.
Kressel, K. and D. Pruitt (1989) 'Conclusion: A Research Perspective on the Mediadtion of Social Conflict', in K. Kressel, D. Pruitt and Associates, *Mediation Research*. San Francisco: Jossey Bass.

Lewis, J. and R. Legard (1998), *ACAS Individual Conciliation: a qualitative evaluation of the services in industrial tribunal cases*. London: ACAS.

Lewis, J., A. Thomas and K. Ward (1997), *ACAS Conciliation at Industrial Tribunals: An Evaluation of an Experimental Scheme*. London: ACAS/DTI.

Peachey, D. (1989), 'What People Want from Mediation', in K. Kressel, D. Pruitt and Associates, *Mediation Research*. San Francisco: Jossey Bass.

Pruitt, D. and J. Carnevale (1993), *Negotiation in Social Conflict*. London: Open University Press.

5
Learning through ACAS:
the case of union recognition

Stephen Wood

INTRODUCTION

Recognition by the employer of a trade union is a core element of decentralised industrial relations systems. The extent to which employers agree to bargain with trade unions effectively defines the characteristics of the system at any one point in time. This is thus especially significant in the UK and North America, while in most other European Union countries industrial-level bargaining and/or constitutional rights underpinning union representation mean that trade unions are not so dependent on the goodwill of employers. The consequence is that, within the former (Anglo-Saxon) countries, it becomes 'impossible in practice to separate problems of freedom of association from those of trade union recognition' (Donovan Commission, 1968, p. 55, para 219), whereas in countries like Sweden the concept of trade union recognition is unknown (Bercusson *et al.*, p. 1998: 25). In both systems, unionism depends on members joining the union—though the French case reminds us that membership can still be low. But in the decentralised system, if an employer recognises a trade union for bargaining purposes, it ought to be easier for the union to persuade people that there are benefits to union membership. The employer can also use a failure on the part of unions to recruit members as an excuse for dismissing any claim by a union for recognition. Thus, as Dickens and Bain (1982, p. 81) note, 'In attempting to use their own strength to overcome employer opposition to recognition, unions are caught in a vicious circle ... the absence of recognition is one of the major factors impeding the development of strength'. This problem was particularly highlighted by Bain's (1970) theory of unionism in which management attitudes and public policy are a determinant of membership growth.

Legal provisions to ensure that an employer recognises the union when specified conditions have been met are one way of attempting to overcome the 'vicious circle' facing unions—although the experience in the USA, where the requirement is that the majority of employees in a bargaining unit have to indicate through a ballot that they want that union to represent them, suggests that this may not always be successful (see e.g. Gould, 1993; Wood and Godard, 1999). The British system of industrial relations was for so long characterised as voluntaristic on the basis that employers and unions entered into bargaining arrangements of their own volition and their agreements were unregulated by law. Given that employers are generally reluctant to concede union recognition to trade unions, the acquisition of representation agreements may be a major source of conflict, and thus may be a core issue for any state conciliation or arbitration service even in such a voluntary system. Moreover, if employers' attitudes to union representation are important to the achievement of collective bargaining, and the promotion of this means of conducting industrial relations is government policy, these attitudes may become a major obstacle to the realisation of that policy. It was the expectation that the State's policy was to encourage collective bargaining through the medium of representation that led the Donovan Commission (1968, p. 64, para 252–256) to accept the proposal that it had received from Allan Flanders that there should be 'a permanent public authority empowered to hear recognition disputes and to make recommendations for their settlement'. In separating the recognition issue from other conflicts, the Commission was effectively acknowledging that union recognition is the fulcrum of British industrial relations. Flanders argued that the body would not simply arbitrate between the parties' claims, but rather would have to collect its own facts and employ its own judgements to arrive at a recommendation, which itself would have to be backed by reasons. His expectation was that the agency would have to evolve a set of principles in order to ensure consistency over time. He also implied that support for the union, rather than actual union membership would be an important criterion by which the authority would decide on cases (Donovan Commission 1968, p. 64, para 252–256).

The Commission on Industrial Relations (CIR)—first between 1969 and 1971 as a Commission and subsequently as a statutory body from 1971–74—effectively applied Flanders' principles since an employer, a union, or the Secretary of State could refer a recognition dispute to the CIR. Its influence was limited, not least by the fact that the post-1971 procedure could only be used by unions that registered under the Industrial Relations Act 1971, and few did. But its recognition work was incorporated into the terms of reference of the Advisory, Conciliation and Arbitration Service (ACAS) which superseded the CIR when the former was established under the Employment Protection Act (EPA) 1975. The then Labour Government's commitment to the development of collective representation was reinforced by the singling out of the extension and reform of collective bargaining within the EPA's statement of its general duty of promoting the improvement of industrial relations (EPA s. 12). Its commitment to voluntary methods of achieving this was equally reflected in its giving ACAS the role of conciliating in union recognition disputes, all such conciliation being voluntary. ACAS was, however, also given the role of operating a statutory union recognition procedure designed along the lines of Flanders' original proposal and drawing on the experience of the system operated by the CIR. The dual responsibility of operating the voluntary and statutory procedures was to be a major factor behind the abandonment of the statutory system only five years after its introduction. For the next 20 years there was no legal support for recognition in the UK, but the Labour Government when elected in 1997 announced its intention to honour its manifesto commitment to reintroducing such a system, along the lines that the TUC had been urging throughout the 1990s (see e.g. TUC, 1995). The statutory system was introduced in the Employment Relations Act 1999 which came into effect at the time this chapter was published.

This chapter will analyse the work of ACAS in the union recognition area. Its purpose is not, however, to simply provide an historical overview. It aims additionally to contribute to current debate. More specifically it is oriented towards the following issues: (a) whether the problems associated with the involvement of ACAS in statutory procedures in the 1970s are replicated or avoided in the procedures under the Employment Relations Act 1999; (b) what might ACAS's role be in the more legalistic context of the future and whether the voluntary route, in which ACAS still has a potentially important role, can take precedence over the statutory procedure, with this remaining a long stop, as the government (and seemingly the CBI and TUC) intend.

The chapter will be divided in two parts: the first part will deal with ACAS's union recognition activity, beginning with the statutory system before dealing with its conciliation activity; the second with the questions involving the Employment Relations Act 1999 and the future role of ACAS. The material used for the chapter relies on documentary evidence, and particularly ACAS's Annual Reports and its reports on the inquiries it conducted as part of the Employment Protection Act's statutory procedure, and interviews with key national and regional ACAS officials.

ACAS'S UNION RECOGNITION ACTIVITY

The 1970s statutory procedure

The Employment Protection Act of 1975 established both ACAS and the statutory provisions for union recognition disputes—the 'Section 11 procedure'—that it was charged with operating. It involved a looser legal framework than the 'tight' regulative regime (Simpson, 1991, p.10) that had operated between 1972 and 1974, under which the CIR was responsible for resolving union recognition disputes. Because unions could only use the CIR procedure if they registered under the Industrial Relations Act 1971, and the vast majority did not because of their opposition to it, the procedure was only used by one trade union, the National Union of Bank Employees, which was expelled from the TUC because it had registered under the Act. It brought five of the 18 cases to the CIR, the remainder involved staff associations.

Because ACAS was charged with particularly promoting collective bargaining and it was given responsibility for both a voluntary and compulsory method it was envisaged that union recognition would be an important part of its work. Under section 2(1) of the Employment Protection Act (EPA), ACAS could provide conciliation in recognition disputes (the voluntary route), and an independent union (but not an employer or the Secretary of State, as under the 1971 Act) could refer a recognition issue to ACAS (this plus the sanctions imposed on employers constituted it as the compulsory route). The framing of this legislation was intended to encourage voluntary methods and to give ACAS a good deal of discretion in the way in which it carried out its tasks. ACAS's underlying approach 'to the conduct of references' was in practice 'based firmly on its general belief in the value of voluntary consent in the resolution of industrial relations problems' (ACAS, 1977, p. 42). Even when a union referred a case to ACAS, the initial aim was for ACAS to settle the dispute by conciliation; if it could not it had to conduct an inquiry and, if the issue was still not settled, to publish a report outlining its findings and recommending whether a union should be recognised. ACAS was given discretion as to how it went about these inquiries and how it interpreted the level of support for unionism. The rules about how it should conduct a formal ballot, if this option were chosen, were, however, specified by the Act. When developing its *modus operandi,* ACAS (1981, pp. 80–81) was strongly influenced by some of the principles that the CIR had developed, and particularly the principle that the level of potential support for unionism, rather than actual membership, should be the criteria for deciding recognition. I shall now discuss its procedures, focusing on the following: the recognition criteria, the recognition processes, employer rights, the mandated scope of bargaining, the first agreement, enforcement mechanisms, union security, and the right to strike.

Recognition criteria

Any occupational group could seek recognition, and there were no fixed criteria for recognition laid down in the EPA. ACAS, having insisted that there could be no 'strict' or universal criteria for handling bargaining unit questions or deciding the level of support for unionism required for recognition, sought to establish 'whether effective collective bargaining arrangements between the employer and the applicant union could be established and maintained on the basis of the group of workers covered by the reference' (ACAS, 1981, p. 80).

The bargaining unit and the appropriate bargaining agent had to be determined jointly and account had to be taken 'both of the diversity of circumstances surrounding recognition issues and of the different views of employers and unions' (ACAS, 1978, p. 45). In settling bargaining unit disputes, ACAS was guided by the experience of the CIR (analysed in CIR (1974) Study No. 5) and the Code of Practice issued under the Industrial Relations Act 1971 (ACAS, 1981, p. 81). This outlined a range of factors which should be taken into account, including the nature of the work, the extent to which a group of employees has interests in common, the wishes of the employees concerned and the need to fit the bargaining unit into the pattern of union and management organisation. These were all factors stressed in the ACAS annual report in which it outlined its basic approach to Section 11 references (ACAS, 1978, pp. 21–22). Four main criteria were presented: practice in the industry with regard to union recognition for particular categories of employees, trade union policies and any agreements which the employer may apply; collective organisation and the wishes of the employees including their membership of the union and wishes for collective representation; the nature of the work being done and associated requirements such as skills; and employer's organisational structures and employment policies, including working arrangements such as hours, shifts and payment systems.

The emphasis given to potential support for representation and bargaining by the referring union when assessing employees' orientations was consistent with ACAS's statutory obligation to promote collective bargaining. It echoed the CIR's earlier view that union membership is likely to grow following recognition and acknowledged the importance of the vicious circle whereby the absence of recognition is an impediment to membership growth. In fact in less than 5% of the cases to reach the final stage of the procedure was the support for representation by the union making the reference less than the actual union membership, and in several of these ACAS still made a positive recommendation. In one of these cases ACAS explicitly attributed the differential between actual membership and support for bargaining to employer interference in the inquiry.

From the outset ACAS 'avoided any commitment to a single figure as determining whether or not to recommend recognition' (ACAS, 1978, p. 47). The mean level of support for the claim for recognition was 65% in those cases where recognition was granted, as compared to 38% in those cases where it was not, while the level of union membership at the time of the inquiry was 51% in those cases where recognition was recommended, as compared with a figure of 27% in cases where it was not.

The use of additional criteria meant that in 33 cases where union support was below 50% and in 13 cases where it was below 40% ACAS still recommended recognition, while in 19 cases where support was over 50% it did not propose recognition (ACAS, 1981, p. 83). Though decisions not to recommend recognition were normally based on insufficient employee support, the criterion of 'not-being-in-the interests-of-good-industrial-relations' was evoked in a number of cases. For example, the application for recognition from the United Kingdom Association of Professional Engineers, a non-TUC body, in an engineering firm, W. H. Allen, was rejected on the ground that recognition of a trade union in this company 'must be consistent with established [multi-employer] collective bargaining arrangements in the company and industry' (ACAS, 1981, p. 84).

ACAS (1981, p. 86) reported that attempts were made to agree upon operating criteria that involved the CBI and TUC, but 'the traditional views on recognition of the two bodies proved impossible to reconcile'. It therefore continued to operate on a case-by-case basis, an approach which in its judgement (*ibid.*) had 'succeeded'. None the less, in the majority of cases there was disagreement between the parties in the reference about the content and coverage of the negotiating group (ACAS, 1981, p. 82), and in a number of cases a consensus could not be reached on this. Similar problems arose over the level of required support for the union. In the latter part of the 1970s these problems were only resolved by the introduction of vote taking within the Council, a move that ACAS reported (ACAS, 1981, p. 87) as introducing 'strain into the decision making process'. The cases brought to ACAS decreased in the late 1970s (see Table 1) and statistical analysis confirms that a union claim was significantly more likely to be supported in the first 18 months of the system's life and significantly less likely in the last year of the statutory procedure, which reflects to some extent the fact that the unions would have brought the easier cases to ACAS earlier.[1]

TABLE 1
Outcome of ACAS recognition cases by period

Period	Number of cases	Recommendation			
		Yes		No	
		Number	%	Number	%
1976		8	89	1	11
Jan–May 1977	29	24	83	5	17
June–Dec 1977	54	39	72	15	28
Jan–May 1978	39	25	64	14	36
June–Dec 1978	26	10	39	16	62
Jan–May 1979	14	11	79	3	21
June–Dec 1979	20	16	80	4	20
Jan–May 1980	22	14	64	8	36
May–Aug 1980	14	8	57	6	43

Source: ACAS, EPA (1975) s. 12 Reports.

Recognition processes

The actual recognition process consisted of three stages: consultation, conciliation and inquiry (Dickens, 1978, p. 162). Of the 1,610 references that did not get to the final inquiry phase, the union was fully or partially successful in securing recognition

---

[1] The results of this are available from the author.

in 1,115 (ACAS, 1981, p. 117), which is indicative of the importance of the conciliation role. An analysis by Dickens (1978) of the core recognition cases between 1975 and 1978 shows that employer opposition to the union in principle or on the basis of perceptions of the virtues of non-union arrangements was the main reason why cases went to the inquiry stage.

Once the issue was deemed incapable of settlement through conciliation, the inquiry that ACAS was required to conduct could, in the terms of the EPA, involve any 'inquiries' that it thought 'fit', but should include 'the opinions of workers to whom the issue relates', though again it could ascertain these by what ever 'means' it thought 'fit'. In practice the views of employees were normally sought through a postal questionnaire survey to employees, though in some cases—23 out of 91 of the cases analysed by Dickens (1978) in her study of Section 11 cases—the number of employees was small enough to permit individual interviews. The main purpose of the inquiry was to establish whether the reference group was the appropriate group of workers for negotiating purposes (the bargaining unit), the support for the union amongst the workers concerned and any other industrial relations considerations that needed to be taken into account. Questionnaires were designed for each case, but in line with ACAS's emphasis on potential support for the union, questions on the support for the union, were it to achieve recognition for the purposes of collective bargaining, were a central element in all. What became known as the standard questionnaire (reproduced in ACAS, 1980, pp. 132–133), which was increasingly used as the template, asked employees if they wanted their terms and conditions determined by collective bargaining, which trade union (or other body) would they like to represent them and whether they would join the union (or other body) were it to be recognised for bargaining purposes, though the intention to join the union tended not to be recorded in the reports.

Cases which went to the final stage took on average over a year to process: 12.1 months in cases where recognition was recommended, compared to 15.0 months in cases where it was not. Over 20% of these cases took more than 18 months (ACAS 1981, p. 80). The average was higher for claims involving white-collar employees (14.9 months) than for those from manual employees (10.6 months). This was deemed at the time as excessively lengthy by trade unions. Dickens (1978, p. 174) notes that such critics particularly felt that too much time was spent on conciliation, and thus that ACAS did not do the third, inquiry stage early enough. The worry for trade unions was that the longer the elapsed time before employees' attitudes were surveyed, the more likely it was that support for the union would diminish and that employees would be susceptible to employers' counters to the union threat. The fact that half of the cases which lasted over 18 months did not result in ACAS recommending recognition, when the figure was 38% for all completed enquiries; suggests that the union's prospects were affected by the time taken for cases to be processed (ACAS 1981, p. 80). The length of time it took for each case also had the effect of creating an excessive backlog of cases, so when the procedure was revoked in 1980, 248 cases (15.4% of all references) were at the inquiry stage. For only 28 of these were draft reports written.

Managerial un-cooperativeness and, in a number of cases, inter-union disputes, contributed to the delay (ACAS, 1981, p. 79) — as many as 90 cases were in suspense because of inter-union problems at the end of 1978 (Mortimer, 1998, p. 322) and 79 at the end of 1979 (*ibid.*, p. 314). Dickens (1978, p. 175) concluded from her analysis of reports as of 1978, that it was not, however, 'always possible to find this kind of explanation' for the delay and no decisive judgement about the significance of these two factors was possible since not all reports indicated the time spent on each stage of the procedure. She also commented at the time that 'the problem with attempting to speed up the procedure is that the conciliation stage is clearly valuable and by its very nature conciliation cannot be rushed'. Yet she and Bain (Dickens and Bain, 1982, p. 86) subsequently noted that the emphasis on conciliation certainly 'provided opportunities for employers to seek to frustrate union attempts to gain recognition'.

Employer opposition was disproportionately from small firms (ACAS, 1979, p. 29) though large firms (e.g. Michelin Tyres) also were resistant. This un-cooperativeness was often focused on the questionnaire, as employers would argue in favour of additional questions and against some standard questions on the grounds that they were biased. They particularly objected to questions aimed at gauging potential support on the grounds that these were hypothetical, and argued for a question addressing whether the employee preferred existing arrangements to prevail. ACAS (1981, p. 78) reported that it allowed for some of the objections to the questions on potential support in order to complete an inquiry, but that it always treated the inclusion of a question about the employees' support for collective bargaining by the applicant union as 'non-negotiable'. It resisted asking about preferences for the status quo 'on the grounds that the issue before it was ... recognition of the applicant union' (ACAS, 1981, p. 78).

Several court challenges resulted. The last of these, by the National Employers Mutual General Assurance Limited involving a reference from the Association of Scientific, Technical and Managerial Staffs, argued primarily that the questionnaire was biased and had thus failed to ascertain the true opinions of the workers. The court ruled that the questionnaire design was for the discretion of ACAS and that the court could only interfere if ACAS had used this discretion unreasonably. In this case, the conclusion was that it had not. Following this case, ACAS increasingly used the standard questionnaire which was probably beyond challenge.

Employer rights and obligations

Employers were not obligated to grant access to union representatives prior to recognition, nor were they required to give employees' names and addresses to either the union or to ACAS. There were also no legal constraints on attempts by employers to influence employees' views on union recognition. Thus employers could seek to influence the way employees replied to the questions raised in the ACAS enquiries.

Since the EPA did not give ACAS the power to demand information and access to employees, in several instances the employers simply refused to help the inquiry or give employees' names and addresses. Though ACAS still made recommendations in such cases on the basis of the information that they could acquire, this led to legal challenges in the courts (Simpson, 1979). The watershed case involved a photographic processing company in North London, Grunwick.[2] In that case, the House of Lords decided that ACAS, having been impeded by the employer from making a satisfactory survey of employees' views, had not fulfilled its statutory duty to carry out such an inquiry. The ruling made it clear that, where the employer did not co-operate, ACAS had to carry out its inquiries by other means; and, if it could not do this, it was in no position to make a recommendation. The judges could not read the Act to include the idea that ACAS's duty might end where the employer had effectively made its execution impossible. Without any corresponding duty on the part of the employer, ACAS could not fulfil its obligations. Following this case, ACAS (1981, p. 77) felt debarred from making a recommendation in six cases that had reached the inquiry stage because it had not secured an adequate response; while in five more it decided that it could not satisfactorily ascertain the opinions of the employees because of the lack of co-operation from the employer and so was unable to carry out its statutory duty.

Employers' non-cooperation subsequently increased so that, at repeal, ACAS (1981, p. 77) was experiencing difficulties in over 50 of the 248 outstanding cases. It is reported that delaying tactics by the employer often 'had the same effect as outright non co-operation'. Yet in 210 of the 228 cases which led to final reports, ACAS achieved response rates to its questionnaires of at least 65% (ACAS, 1981, p. 83) and the average response rate was over 80%, despite employer resistance and interference in its distribution.

The scope of bargaining

The EPA, as had the Industrial Relations Act 1971, imposed a duty to recognise on employers, since a union could file a complaint if it deemed an employer was not complying with an ACAS recommendation of union recognition. Recognition was defined as 'recognition of the union by an employer, or two or more associated employers, to any extent, for the purposes of collective bargaining' (s. 11(1)). Not complying with a recommendation was defined (EPA, 1975, s. 15(2)) as when the employer 'is not taking such action by way of or with a view to carrying on negotiations as might reasonably be expected to be taken by an employer ready and

---

[2] See Mortimer (1998), pp. 318–322, Rogaly (1977) and Wood (1998) for accounts of the Grunwick dispute.

willing to carry on such negotiations as are envisaged by the recommendation'. No legally mandated items were defined and, in practice, the scope of bargaining was not defined in specific cases. Collective bargaining was defined in the EPA (s. 126) as negotiations relating to or connected with one or more of the matters specified in the Trade Union and Labour Relations Act 1974 (s. 29 (1)) that could be the subject of a trade dispute; it thus covered a wide range of issues including terms and conditions of employment, the duties of employment, termination and suspension of employment, disciplinary matters, membership and non-membership of a trade union, facilities for officials of the union and the machinery of negotiations.

There was some discussion at the time (see Bercusson, 1976, p. 71/11) about whether the 'any extent' before the purposes of bargaining in the definition of recognition implied an expansive definition of the scope of bargaining. So, for example, could it include bargaining about corporate restructuring? It was argued that the broader definition that the 'to any extent' may have permitted was consistent with the duty imposed in the EPA on ACAS that it should encourage the extension of collective bargaining. In addition, the lack of a clear specification of mandatory items was seen by some commentators (e.g. Bercusson, 1976, p. 71/11) as a virtue in the light of the US experience where, since a Supreme Court decision (*NLRB* v *Borg-Warner*) in 1960 differentiated mandatory from permissive issues, employers had been able to limit the range of their bargaining. This interpretation of the EPA also allowed for changes in what might be seen as standard bargaining issues in the light of technological, organisational and social innovations such as the introduction of new technology and equal opportunities into the bargaining arena.

Nonetheless, ACAS never had to determine the mandated subjects for bargaining. For, though unions already recognised for bargaining could have used the EPA procedure to secure 'further recognition' (s. 11(3)) that is, to expand the scope of bargaining, the number of such instances was small and all were eventually withdrawn. No analysis has been made of how the scope of bargaining in those cases where recognition was achieved compared with the norm in other cases or whether closed shops were achieved.

Failure to recognise a union

If the employer failed to comply with a recommendation for recognition and further conciliation by ACAS failed, the union could refer the issue to the Central Arbitration Committee (CAC). This was also established under the EPA (1975 s.10) replacing the previous Industrial Arbitration Board. It was given responsibility to deal with complaints arising from a failure to comply with an ACAS recommendation for trade union recognition. (It was also responsible for the arbitration of trade disputes referred by ACAS (s. 3(1)), the determination of claims for the extension of a collective agreement, and dealing with complaints about the failure of employers to disclose information to unions for collective bargaining in accordance with the

EPA (ss. 19–21).) CAC's major powers were that it had to determine whether the employer was 'taking such action that was indicative of a willingness to bargain', and could award terms and conditions of employment that would form part of employees' contracts of employment. This amounted to the imposition of compulsory arbitration. But it covered only a narrow range of substantive issues such as pay and hours. Beaumont (1981, pp. 26–27) gives an example where the Association of Scientific, Technical and Managerial Staffs complained to the CAC that a company was not complying with ACAS's recommendation and sought to incorporate procedural elements, as well as substantive items, into the employees' terms and conditions of employment (e.g. a technology agreement, a check-off agreement and paid release for training for union representatives). These were rejected by the CAC as 'not matters on which the Committee can award'. This demonstrates that the CAC was only prepared to make individual matters a part of its awards and was making no attempt to provide 'the day to day control trade unionism can exert on the business' (McIlroy, 1979, p.14). It interpreted its powers as permitting it to award only improved substantive terms and conditions relevant to workers' individual contracts, and not to award procedures or to oblige an employer to recognise a union. It was ultimately never clear what recognition for negotiation actually meant (Wedderburn, 1986, p. 282). Although the affinity between the phrase the employer 'having to be ready and willing to bargain' and the US's 'duty to bargain in good faith' was apparent, how this was to be operationalised was never clarified.

Some legal experts (e.g. Davies, 1979, pp. 57–58) concluded that the CAC could have legally taken a different approach, but the CAC argued that Parliament had not intended to introduce an enforceable right for unions to be recognised by employers. Rather, it was simply attempting to provide a substitute for the 'hard bargaining which recognition, had it been granted, would have provided' (Award, 78/808). The conclusion many (see especially Doyle, 1980) have drawn was that it provided a weak substitute for bargaining.

Enforcement

A survey by IDS (reported in Beaumont, 1981) in 1979 found that in only 17.9% of cases where recognition was recommended had it been unequivocally achieved and in 54.3% of cases there was definite non-compliance. In 1981, ACAS (1981, p. 92) estimated that in only 55 of the 158 cases where it had recommended union recognition was the employer complying with it. A document within ACAS that contains a brief statement of subsequent developments in the first 135 cases shows that in some of these the union membership had fallen and the union was not planning any further action, but in most instances the management was simply refusing to talk to the union or accord them full recognition. Beaumont (1981, pp. 28–29) found that there was no relationship between compliance with an ACAS recommendation and the level of support expressed for collective bargaining during the inquiry. Fifty complaints of non-compliance were made, and after conciliation, eight of these led to recognition agreements. The CAC found that the employer was in breach of the ACAS recommendation in only 18 of the 29 cases with which it dealt. The legal redress against employers who did not comply with the terms and conditions imposed by the CAC was through an individual taking a case to an industrial tribunal. No case was taken.

The EPA (s. 53) introduced statutory protection against dismissal for employees who were victimised because of their union membership or activities, and also for refusing to join a non-independent (company) union. Nevertheless it remained the case following the introduction of unfair dismissal legislation in 1974 that workers on strike could *en masse* be legally dismissed. This weakened the capacity of workers to force the employer to comply with an ACAS recommendation of recognition or to substantially gain from any procedural agreement. It was, however, deemed that people who were fired or locked-out by an employer subject to a Section 11 case should be included in ACAS's enquiries into the level of potential support for collective bargaining.

Union security and the right to strike

The 1970s ACAS procedures did not contain any specific regulations as to either union security or the right to strike. Closed shops were legal at the time and workers could strike at any time, though the recognition procedure did not have the effect of extending the closed shop beyond the areas of the economy where it was traditionally found. In effect, the procedures were concerned primarily with the recognition process, not with the nature and quality of the representation that followed from that process.

The effect of the 1970s ACAS procedure

Overall, the 1970s EPA system operated relatively smoothly or, as ACAS phrased it, (1981, p. 99) made a 'positive contribution' where the employer was not resistant in principle to recognition. These cases were most likely in medium and large employers of manual workers or white-collar organisations where the employer was not wedded to a distinctive pre-existing form of personnel management. Employer resistance, however, increased over time. Even though the methods used by ACAS in statutory union recognition cases were probably becoming increasingly less vulnerable to legal challenge, it would appear that cases like Grunwick, coupled with the weak sanctions under the procedure, led employers to conclude that they could, if they wished, successfully resist recognition.

Faced with problems of complying with its statutory obligation, as highlighted in the extreme by the Grunwick case, the tripartite Council of ACAS wrote to the Secretary of State for Employment in 1979, saying that, given the way the law was being interpreted by the Courts, ACAS could 'not satisfactorily operate the statutory procedures' (Letter from the Chairman of ACAS to the Secretary of State, ACAS, 1981, p. 138). It was especially concerned that the statutory process would harm its reputation for independence and providing independent expertise, which was critical to the fulfilment of its other roles. There was seen to be a tension between ACAS's obligations under Section 2 and those under Section 11. In 1980, with the advent of a new Conservative Government, the statutory procedure was abandoned.

Many of the problems associated with the 1970s EPA system reflected its design, particularly the paradox of giving ACAS wide discretion but limited powers. Giving a reasonably free rein to ACAS signified that it was to be more than just a balloting agency that existed simply to count the votes for and against recognition claims. The aim was to enable ACAS to build on its (and others') professional expertise, as well as on the experience it could be expected to accumulate during its operation of the recognition procedures. The intention was that ACAS should be able to broker decisions based on a consensus between employers and employees, particularly through building on the legitimacy that it derived from its tripartite constitution and officers' expertise. Yet the limited powers given to ACAS meant it was relatively powerless in the face of employer resistance. The failure to develop consensus-based criteria appears to have contributed to this problem and Dickens and Bain (1982, p. 102) surmised that ACAS might have fared better in the courts had it been able to achieve this. Part of the problem in the courts, though, arose from a seeming lack of appreciation by the majority of judges of the nature of industrial relations or the policy underlying the procedure. One Lord, Lord Browne-Wilkinson, likened the statutory union recognition procedure to the compulsory purchase of private property by the state (*Powley* v *ACAS* 1977. ICR 123).

Mortimer (1998, p. 313), the first Chairman of ACAS, has noted that the ACAS Council originally assumed that the system would allow for the swift resolution of conflicts and that its members never 'anticipated at the outset that so many legal problems would arise from disputes about their procedures'. Yet some commentators have implied that the design weaknesses were in-built from the outset, since they reflected a 'tentativeness [on the part of policy-makers, trade unionists and employers] about the use of law to promote collective bargaining' (Davies and Freedland, 1993, p. 387). Dickens (1987, p. 124) has put a more positive gloss on this by viewing the EPA as an attempt to maintain voluntarism—in the sense defined by Flanders (1974) as a desire to keep the courts out of industrial relations matters and not a total rejection of the law. Wedderburn (1976, p. 183) judged the weak sanctions in this context, as 'not too high a price to be paid for the maintenance of ... a voluntary system of collective labour relations'. Yet some of the very features intended to foster voluntarism may have created the conditions in which the disagreements and conflicts implicated in the system's collapse could develop.

In process terms, the recognition procedure could be judged to have some success in reducing the number of strikes over recognition. ACAS (1980, p. 101) reported that this was below 20 in the years in which it operated, while they had been averaging around 35 in the years before this. They did, however, increase in the late 1970s, this seemingly reflecting the fact that the strike had become an action of last resort when the employer held particularly entrenched views and/or relationships were especially bitter.

The effects of the procedure in substantive terms are less clear. The period 1975–1980 was a relatively successful period for union recruitment. Membership increased by 11% overall, and by over 3% in each of 1976 and 1977, making these the only two years in this century to experience such gains. Since the repeal of the procedures in 1980, trade union membership and density have been in steady decline. The direct impact of the statutory provisions has, nevertheless, been judged to be limited. ACAS (1981, p. 100) itself argued that they 'had no more than a marginal impact' and clearly 'failed to achieve the major breakthrough [in union recognition] that had been envisaged by their early advocates'. By 1980, 16,000 employees were subject to collective bargaining arrangements established through the full EPA statutory procedure (ACAS, 1981, p. 32), though 9000 of these were from a single organisation (General Accident, Fire and Life Assurance Corporation Ltd). Collective bargaining was extended to an additional 49,000 of employees as a result of cases referred to ACAS under Section 11 and settled on a voluntary basis. Of these, some form of recognition for the employees was recommended in 35% of cases. As many as 21% of Section 11 applications were withdrawn because of low membership and support for the union.

The 65,000 employees directly affected by the procedure in fact represented only 0.27% of the total workforce and only 0.35% of those whose terms and conditions were determined by collective bargaining arrangements. Analysis by Bain and Price (1983, pp. 19–22) and by Beaumont (1981) showed that the effect was disproportionately in well-organised sectors where unions were sufficiently well established to take advantage of the benefits offered by pubic policy. 60% of cases were in manufacturing, and even when white-collar occupations achieved recognition a high proportion of these cases was in manufacturing. Beaumont (1981, p. 93) shows that seven unions out of a total of 73 which used the Section 11 procedure accounted for 64% of the references and two of these—TGWU and ASTMS—accounted for 35%. Although ACAS did imply that it might have had more than such a marginal impact in one or two sectors of the industry, key unorganised sectors (agriculture, construction and private service) remained largely unaffected.

It appears then the direct effect of the statutory procedure was limited. The *modus operandi* developed by ACAS may have not limited its effect on union membership and collective bargaining coverage, but the design underlying the procedure did.[3]

---

[3] When the statutory procedure was repealed, ACAS offered voluntary conciliation to the parties in the cases that were still under investigation, though this is reported to be only in appropriate cases (ACAS, 1980: 65). The number of those that took advantage is not known.

ACAS's voluntary conciliation of recognition disputes

ACAS's basic approach to conciliation in union recognition cases has not changed since its inception. In order to carry out its statutory duty to provide a general conciliation service, ACAS has always been concerned to adopt a neutral stance towards the parties to a dispute, an impartiality that is underscored by the fact that it does not charge for its services. ACAS's role is to help resolve disputes, not to achieve recognition for trade unions. To quote all the ACAS officials that I interviewed in the research for this paper, they have never seen themselves as recruiting officers for the unions. In general, conciliators do not favour any particular outcome in a dispute. The conciliation process is designed to help the parties reach an agreement, and not in order for the conciliator to impose a settlement. As such the conciliation process is flexible and is not standardised.

In the case of union recognition disputes, there is, as officers again stress, no one template for handling them. None the less, it is possible from interviews that I did with regional officers to detect some principles that underlie the way ACAS conducts its conciliation of union recognition disputes. Cases are always initiated by the parties themselves and never by ACAS; the process of conciliation is aimed at getting an honest dialogue between the parties; and there is no model recognition agreement that the process is striving to reach. Any assessment of the support for the union, if required, is based on potential support for the union, and the process by which this is measured can be the responsibility of one or both of the parties, or ACAS; ACAS can also carry out membership checks at any stage of the process. But before any evaluation of support for recognition (e.g. through a membership check or ballot) both parties should agree, in writing, the actions that depend on the outcome, for example that the union will be recognised given a certain level of support amongst an agreed sample of the bargaining unit and, if there is not this level of support, the union will not seek recognition for a specified period of years. The employer or the union has the right to withdraw from the conciliation process at any stage up to the point when the evaluation of the level of support for the union commences.

The cases handled by ACAS consequently have a lot in common. They are predominately initiated by the union so that the ACAS official typically reacts by contacting the management to ascertain the possibility of a meeting of the three parties. If the response is favourable, a meeting with both parties is held, during which the ACAS official endeavours to get them to be open about their position. In the case of the union this would involve their perception of current practices and grievances in the firm, of current membership figures and support, and what it will bring to the company; and in the case of the management, its views about unions, past experience of unions, and vision of what might happen were a union to be recognised. It is left to the parties to decide whether or not a ballot is necessary or if they require ACAS to do a membership check, as a tacit indication of a level of support. When used the ballot asks about support for collective bargaining and with which union, in cases of multiple unionism. Ballots are rare when more than 50% of the workforce is in union membership, but if one or other of the parties requests one, ACAS will not seek to persuade them against it. There is no attempt to impose a model agreement as the emphasis is on getting the parties to decide the issue of recognition for themselves and on leaving them to reach a procedural agreement and to bargain over the scope of the substantive bargaining, though the involvement of ACAS in this is possible as part of its advisory and mediation work. Partial recognition (e.g. for individual representation) is sometimes agreed—perhaps with a review date to consider full or consultation rights—as a compromise in particularly difficult cases. ACAS does not monitor or follow up cases to ascertain the scope of bargaining or whether the management is recognising the union in any meaningful way.

During the life of the statutory procedure, ACAS's voluntary conciliation procedures were well used. The number of cases, the proportion won by unions and the number of employees affected were all higher under the voluntary route than they were under the compulsory (Section 11) route. Between February 1976 and August 1980, 2,292 recognition cases were completed through the voluntary system, compared with the 1,613 cases which were referred under the statutory route. Full recognition was granted in 726 of the voluntary cases, with limited recognition being given in 255 other cases. The proportion of cases that led to some form of recognition under the voluntary route was thus 43%, compared with 35% under the statutory route and 77,500 employees were affected by these cases (ACAS, 1981, p. 65). In a further 857 cases the conciliation did not succeed in resolving the dispute and recognition was not granted by the employer. In the remaining 454 cases the dispute was resolved through conciliation but recognition was not part of the settlement, for example the union withdrew its claim or the employer offered improved terms and conditions. In a few of these instances the union decided to pursue the issue through the statutory procedure.

ACAS (1976, p. 10) reported on the basis of its first year of operation that there were 'no obvious differences between the type of recognition issues referred under Section 11 and those, which came to the Service in the form of requests for conciliation'. Yet, the average size of both the groups of workers and the size of the organisation covered by the voluntary settlements in which ACAS was involved was smaller than that for the statutory cases. Manual workers were disproportionally covered in the voluntary cases, a reflection, at least partly, of a growing preference amongst the manual unions for voluntary conciliation as it became disillusioned with the statutory procedure (ACAS, 1980, p. 65).

Both the results of ACAS's conciliation cases, and the details of the process of conciliation, may have been affected by the shadow of the law in the 1970s. Indeed ACAS (1980, pp. 101–102) saw the effect of the law more generally when it concluded that:

the issue of recognition has maintained over this (1976-80) period and has almost certainly increased awareness among employees of the feasibility of collective representation and has had an educative effect on some employers. It has encouraged employers to develop domestic recognition strategies and focused their minds on orderly bargaining.

There is no available data on the cases where recognition was achieved without the aid of either ACAS or the statutory procedure; but in view of the rise of union membership, especially in the white-collar area, it is safe to assume that the number exceeded those which involved either of these. Insofar as the outcomes of recognition disputes, with or without conciliation by ACAS, were affected by the shadow of the statutory provisions it may well be that the indirect effects of the legal provisions, outweighed their direct ones.

This conjecture that the shadow of the statutory provision increased the use of ACAS, as employers sought to avoid the legal route, is borne out by the subsequent decline in both the number of union recognition cases going through the section 2 procedure and the proportion of those won by the union (Dickens and Bain, 1982, p. 94). These figures will, though, have also been affected by the change in government policy and the incremental programme of union legislation that particularly constrained the ability of employees to strike. The trend for the number of ACAS cases to decline continued from 1980 to the mid-1980s; in 1985 they fell below the 200 level and in 1993 below 100 for the first time ever. The lowest proportion of successes for the union was in 1992. The success rate has subsequently begun to increase (see Table 2). By the mid-1980s ACAS (1986, p. 45) was reporting that a higher percentage of cases were pursued by the unions where the membership base was weak and/or support was difficult to sustain and there was 'little hope of success'. This was, though, being countered to some extent by the unions' unwillingness to press claims in cases where management was adopting an uncompromisingly negative approach to recognition. No figures exist on the proportion of all recognition disputes in which ACAS is involved or which result in union recognition, but the cases of recognition recorded by the Labour Research Department during the period 1995 to early 1999 represent just over double the number of successful recognition cases that involved ACAS conciliation.

The changing political climate in the late 1990s has seemingly reversed the downward trends in the number of cases and the success rates for unions, though there is no sign of the cases approaching anything like the level of the 1970s, or even the level of the 1980s. However, there have been indications, from ACAS case reports, that in the period leading up to the statutory procedure the unions were making reference to it in their communications with management and that its existence was being acknowledged in the conciliation process. The change that officers have particularly observed is in the origins of the cases. Where typically in the past cases came from active union organisations in a workplace, for example because a union member had moved to a non-union location, now cases are increasingly the result of targeted campaigning by the union. None the less, throughout the history of

TABLE 2

ACAS voluntary conciliation claims concerning union recognition

Year	Number of Claims (i.e. completed cases)	% of conciliation workload	% where recognition achieved (if reported)
1975	416	21.0	
1976	697	24.4	
1977	635	22.0	43 (32. full, 11 partial)
1978	451	16.7	
1979	392	17.1	
1980	329	17.2	
1981	247	14.4	40
1982	232	14.1	40
1983	216	13.3	
1984	221	15.3	
1985	211	15.8	33
1986	179	13.5	33
1987	140	12.2	25
1988	165	15.6	33 (18 full, 15 partial)
1989	136	12.7	23 (16 full, 7 partial)
1990	159	14.0	
1991	174	14.2	33
1992	148	13.0	21
1993	94	8.5	38
1994	93	8.0	37
1995	107	9.0	47
1996	112	9.0	58 (33 full, 25 partial
1997	102	9.0	49 (29 full, 20 partial)
1998	131	11.0	48 (33 full recognition, 15 partial)
1999	148	14.0	49 (33 full recognition, 16 partial)

Source: ACAS Annual Reports.

ACAS no union at either the national or local level has explicitly favoured using ACAS in union recognition as an automatic course of action, any pattern to its usage thus reflecting individual officers' preferences: some resort to it frequently or contingently, while others eschew it on all occasions.

So, while the way ACAS has approached its conciliation work has not changed since its conception, the existence of a statutory route may have affected the details of the conciliation. It was precisely because ACAS approached conciliation in an impartial way that its role in the voluntary system clashed with its role in the statutory procedure of the 1970s. The inclusion of the promotion of collective bargaining amongst its duties reflected its role in the Section 11 procedure. When this was abandoned, ACAS no longer had a mechanism through which it could achieve such an objective. Its *de facto* role thus was to improve industrial relations, and to try to enhance the workings of collective bargaining where this was the prevalent form of conducting industrial relations. In 1994, when its duty was altered to the more general promotion of good industrial relations, the change simply reflected the way in which ACAS had over the intervening period had come to interpret its original duty. As such, as ACAS officers confirmed, the change in the objective of ACAS did not alter the way it handled recognition disputes. ACAS's concern to preserve its existing role is reflected in its public admission that it did not want to be given responsibility for any statutory union recognition procedure that the Labour government, elected in 1997, proposed to introduce. The second part of this paper will examine the statutory procedure introduced under the Employment Relations Act 1999, particularly focusing on the extent to which the lessons of the 1970s ACAS procedure have been learnt and the extent to which it will, if at all, affect ACAS's conciliation activity.

THE EMPLOYMENT RELATIONS ACT, UNION RECOGNITION AND THE ADVISORY AND CONCILIATION AND ARBITRATION SERVICE

Under the Employment Relations Act 1999 a statutory procedure for union recognition was reintroduced. The White Paper *Fairness at Work* (Department of Trade and Industry, 1998) made it clear, however, that the government was designing a framework for the handling of recognition disputes 'not just about the application of employment law' (Department of Trade and Industry, 1998, p. 8). Moreover the overall aim of the policy of the Labour government elected in 1997—of which the Employment Relations Act 1999 (ERA) would be its main legislative expression in this government—was to promote a form of partnership which reconciled fairness with competitiveness. The promotion of collective bargaining as a policy objective has not been restored, though support for a co-operative style of collective bargaining in appropriate circumstances (largely defined as whether the parties want it) is subsumed under the partnership objective. The statutory mechanism is only one element of its union recognition procedure, as it consists of three routes—the voluntary, automatic and balloting routes. The last two involve statutory rights. Primacy is given to voluntary agreements, with the expectation that the legal route can be a long stop—the law in general is meant to provide basic minimum standards and to offer protection against the worse excesses of employers. This is in keeping with the joint statement of the CBI and TUC in 1997 (TUC–CBI, 1997).

How do the 1999 statutory procedures match up with the lessons learned from the ACAS procedures?

There are five basic features of the ERA system which appear to reflect learning from the 1970s procedure. First, an agency (CAC) other than ACAS is given responsibility for the procedures and will have responsibility for operating the procedure for resolving union recognition disputes. There is also a tighter specification of its powers than there was of ACAS's under the EPA. A mediating and conciliating role is still envisioned for ACAS in recognition disputes. Second, there are independently defined and universally acceptable criteria for deciding bargaining units and the required level of support for collective bargaining, with an automatic route to recognition available for those with 50% union membership, providing the CAC deems certain other conditions have been met. Third, employers are compelled to co-operate with enquiries concerned to gauge the level of union support and not to intimidate employees during a recognition dispute. Fourth, a provision for a mandated procedural agreement addresses the problem of ensuring that employers recognise and bargain with a union. Finally, enforcement mechanisms exist to ensure that the rights laid out in the legislation are not violated and awards are complied with. The Act thus appears to overcome some of the key procedural and operational problems associated with the 1970s ACAS system, and there is evidence of learning from the experience of the 1970s ACAS system. Evaluating how its key features fare can in fact be viewed as an important way of gauging whether the problems of the 1970s ACAS system were indeed ones of design, for if these reflected specific design flaws rather than issues inherent to statutory procedures, we would expect a system without these to be more sustainable and effective. Addressing the problem areas of the 1970s ACAS system does not, however, guarantee success. Much would appear to depend on the details of the ERA system. The key differences between the EPA and ERA systems are displayed Table 3.

Recognition criteria

The criteria for union recognition are more clearly laid out and transparent than they were under the legislation in the 1970s, while those for defining bargaining units are virtually identical to those used by ACAS in the 1970s. The tradition of allowing potential support for bargaining and not simply union membership, actual or potential, to determine recognition is maintained in the balloting route, but there is a majority requirement for union recognition. The threshold requirement of the ERA, according to which 40% of the bargaining unit must have voted in favour of union recognition, did not exist in the 1970s, and the treatment of non-respondents in the ACAS's inquiries would have to be a matter for their discretion, and may have varied from case to case; but we know that the turnouts in the ballots and responses to their questionnaires were normally high. Unions are not permitted to make claims for applications for recognition in companies or organisations with less than 21 employees.

Recognition processes

The provision for an automatic route whereby recognition is guaranteed once the union has demonstrated that a majority of the workforce belongs to it will reduce the opportunity for the kind of employer interference and procrastination that plagued the 1970s system. There is, however, a facility whereby the CAC can compel the use

TABLE 3
Comparing the EPA and ERA systems

	1970s EPA system	Employment Relations Act 1999
Recognition criteria	No fixed criteria in law, in practice potential support for collective bargaining and union *exclusions*: none *threshold:* none	Majority support required *exclusions*: employees in small firms (under 21 employees); *threshold*: 10% membership for CAC to consider and 40% of those in bargaining unit must vote for union in any ballot
Recognition processes	ACAS inquiry based on employee questionnaire or interview	Automatic (card) recognition, but subject to conditions or ballot of workforce with time restrictions of up to 110 days if a ballot is required
Employer rights and obligations	Employees protected against discrimination on grounds of union activities; no duty on employers to co-operate with ACAS	Employees protected against discrimination for union activities; employers must co-operate in the balloting process, give the union access to pre-ballot process and give CAC details of employees
Scope of bargaining	ACAS discretion to fix scope of bargaining, but no mandated scope of bargaining defined for employers who are unwilling to bargain	Mandatory duty limited to wages, holidays, and hours; parties can agree a more extensive agenda
Failure to reach a procedural agreement	No specific provisions, but failure to agree might constitute failure to bargain	Failure to agree method of bargaining leads to CAC imposition of a method of bargaining over mandated issues
Failure to bargain and enforcement	Failure to bargain leads to CAC determination of individual terms and conditions, which are then enforceable by individual action in the ordinary courts	Order to bargain from ordinary courts enforceable by contempt of court sanctions

of the ballot route even when over 50% of employees are union members if certain conditions are fulfilled. These, and especially the inclusion of 'in the interests of good industrial relations' as one of these conditions, may, however, create a situation in which the CAC feels it has to accede to employer claims that one or more of these conditions applies and hence to not sanction the automatic route. Where the employer has deep concerns about the legitimacy of the union, this could, however, increase the chances of the bargaining relationship being established on a secure footing if recognition is achieved. Otherwise it could undermine the automatic route, especially in those very cases where there is high employer resistance and hence the automatic route is likely to matter most.

Unlike the 1970s ACAS procedure, the ERA imposes time limits to ensure a more expeditious process. As much as 30 days may, however, elapse before the CAC becomes involved, and another 40 days before the CAC even rules on the bargaining unit, and there is at present no provision for the CAC to hold a ballot early in the process. Judged in comparison with the other time periods in the ERA, the ten days allowed for the CAC to resolve disputed bargaining units may appear as rather short, especially if it needs to do some investigation in order to reach a decision. This can, however, be extended by the CAC. The timings envisaged for the various stages appear to reflect the primacy of voluntarism over legalism, the aim being to give the parties as much scope as possible to reach agreement on recognition while at the same time specifying times to ensure the process has some momentum. But the timetable could result in undue delays which frustrate the ability of employees to gain ready access to collective representation. More tellingly, they could provide employers with a substantial opportunity to undermine support for a union where a ballot is required, and could enable employers to prolong the process even where a ballot is not required, as part of the kind of concerted campaign to undermine a union that occurs in the USA. The timings of the stages may not affect the likelihood of recognition where a majority has already joined the union, but the attachment of qualifying conditions to the automatic route may provide an opportunity for employers to challenge the nature of this majority.

Employer rights and obligations

The CAC has a clear responsibility for ensuring that the ballot is conducted correctly and for appointing a 'qualified person' to oversee the ballot. The requirement that employers provide access to the union and the independent person, and provide names and addresses of all members of the bargaining unit, represents an advance over the 1970s ACAS system. The CAC is given powers to impose recognition as a sanction if these duties are not fulfilled and this is especially significant given the difficulties that ACAS experienced in the 1970s. Employees are protected against dismissal or actions short of dismissal and cannot be discriminated against on the basis of union membership or activities. A code of practice (in draft form at the time of going to press) will also be available to regulate union access to workers during the ballots. This, to some extent, will circumscribe employer behaviour as well as giving detailed guidance on the access that the union can have to employees during working time. The parties are encouraged to establish an agreement about access for the union, and the underlying assumption is that, since this access is to allow the union to influence the employees to vote for recognition, the employer should have an equal right to put his/her case. Moreover it is assumed 'for access arrangements to work satisfactorily, the employer and the union should behave responsibly, and give due consideration to the requirements of the other party throughout the period' (Department of Trade and Industry, 2000, section D, paragraph 14). The lack of access prior to the balloting stage and the limited constraints on employers' campaigning could affect the capacity of unions to sign up sufficient employees for automatic recognition as well as their ability to organise where a vote is required. The intention is that the requirement for employers to grant reasonable access to the union will offset this. Whether this will be sufficient is uncertain given that employees have a relation of dependence with their employer.

The scope of bargaining

Employers are under no requirement to agree to an expansive range of issues and any procedural agreements in which they do so will have no legal standing. The *Fairness at Work* White Paper (Department of Trade and Industry, 1998) confined the scope of bargaining to pay, hours and holidays. The consultation document (Department of Trade and Industry, 2000) confirmed this restriction which the CAC must take into account when using its powers in stage one of the procedure.

This restricted mandate will be partly offset by the provision for union representation in the case of grievance and disciplinary hearings, the requirement that the employer consults with a recognised union over training, and the EU requirement that employers consult with unions in the event of redundancies. Unions also already play an important role with respect to health and safety, and consultation over working time and the transfer of undertakings mandated by other government legislation. Thus unions should be ensured some presence in the workplace once recognised. Moreover, if pay and hours are defined broadly, to include job classification systems, performance-related pay schemes and aspects of work organisation that affect pay, then this restricted mandated scope will be less limiting. The role of the union may also be substantially expanded depending on the employer's willingness to adopt a partnership orientation and, failing this, on the union's bargaining power.

Failure to recognise a union

The Act allows for a lengthy period from the time of recognition to the commencement of negotiations over substantive issues, including a 30-day period in which the parties are to negotiate a procedural agreement and a further 20 days elapsing before the CAC can impose a procedural agreement. The intention is to ensure that procedural agreements are observed, since there is a provision for the parties to apply to the CAC if this is not the case and it would be pointless to have procedural agreements which are simply statements of a method for something that never happens. But there is no provision for the imposition of terms and conditions as there was in the 1970s and much will depend on the willingness of the employer to reach an agreement. Consequently there is no ultimate guarantee that the employees will benefit substantively from the recognition order. However, the DTI's consultative document on the CAC's imposed method of conducting collective bargaining does set out the stages by which a claim from the union has be dealt with by the employer and does not permit the employer, once having recognised a union, to vary pay, hours or holidays without discussing this with the union. The specified method has six stages that the parties will need to go through to establish a bargaining relationship, the completion of which appear verifiable. The consultative document makes it clear that the CAC must take this method into account when it imposes a method of collective bargaining on an employer and a union, though it may depart from it if the circumstances of particular cases are deemed to warrant it. Yet, the involvement of the CAC in the attainment of a procedural agreement may lengthen the process by which procedural agreements are reached and have substantive outcomes for employees. This could lead employees with immediate grievances to view unionisation as an ineffective option and to seek other ways of addressing their problems (e.g. by leaving the organisation).

Enforcement

Though the CAC will be able to impose recognition where an employer refuses to co-operate with the balloting process, it will not be able to impose recognition where an employer has succeeded in undermining support for recognition. Specific performance is the remedy for breaching a CAC-imposed procedural agreement. This would amount to an order to observe the method in the CAC's original specification. If the employer fails to comply, then sanctions for contempt of court may be applied and the most likely sanction is a fine rather than imprisonment. Yet normally, the courts will issue specific performance only if it is 'appropriate to do justice in the case'. So it may be that the courts refuse to do so.

The remedy of imposing a method on employers has been heralded as a way of avoiding imposing an explicit duty on employers to bargain in good faith. The avoidance was seen as desirable on the grounds that such a duty would only lead to 'complicated legal wrangles over a highly subjective concept' (letter to the Guardian, 12/2/98, Ian McCartney, Minister of State, Department of Trade and Industry). Nevertheless the effect of specifying the methods of bargaining in detail—as the DTI will once the consultation process has been completed—will in effect amount to a duty to bargain. The consultative document implies the employer is granting the right to negotiate pay, hours and holidays when recognising a union and can not vary pay, hours and holidays unless it has involved the union. The intention is clearly that the execution of specific performance must amount to more than talks between the union and the employer. The remedy of imposing a method and the sanction of a fine are potentially strong. There may none the less remain questions about how the courts will interpret the specific performance sanction.

There will be no basis for appealing against the CAC's decisions. This is critical, because had appeals been permitted, the attempt in the Act to more tightly specify the powers of the CAC may have proved ineffective. CAC decisions may, however, be subject to judicial review on grounds such as abuse of discretion, lack of natural justice or excess of jurisdiction.

Overall, it appears that the ERA has addressed some of the major difficulties with the 1970s ACAS system. But whether it will be as effective in ensuring ready access to representation cannot be certain. On the one hand, the Act gives trade unions legal access to employees during the recognition process, and establishes remedies against employers who do not comply with the procedure. Both of these, along with the duty to co-operate with the balloting process, are improvements on the EPA procedures. Specifying unequivocally that majority support for collective bargaining is the criteria for recognition and that ballots are to be held where that support is in doubt will eliminate some of the opportunities for employers to resist the union claim and challenge the CAC decisions that were exploited in the 1970s. Provision for automatic recognition where the union can establish that this majority is not in doubt may be especially important, providing that the CAC does not deny access to the automatic route by its requiring a ballot in too many of the cases where a majority of the workforce is a union member.

On the other hand, by designing the process so as to maximise the scope for employer involvement and choice in the recognition process and for the parties to voluntarily agree to either recognition or on particular decisions such as the bargaining unit, the ERA may provide employers with substantial scope for interference and opportunity for them to undermine the union's claim. Although the code of practice on union access to workers circumscribes employer behaviour, it will only apply once the CAC's intention to ballot employees has been declared and not to the activities of the employer or union prior to the ballot being announced or during any voluntary activity. Finally, the small-firm exclusion is a significant one and may mean that access to collective representation is more restricted than it was in the 1970s—as many as 20% of the references which went to ACAS in the 1970s involved less than 21 employees, though not all these involved firms which employed less than 21 people.

Even less certain is whether the ERA's system will be effective at ensuring meaningful representation once a union is recognised. The inability to enforce substantive terms, or use of arbitration, and the possible unwillingness of the courts to impose the specific performance sanction may mean that in some recognition cases a substantive agreement is never reached. While the limited bargaining requirement which appears to be envisaged could help to ensure greater flexibility for employers, at the same time it could frustrate the ability of unions to provide significant representation and could even enable employers to marginalize a union, a problem that the 1998 Workplace Employee Relations Survey (Cully *et al.*, 1998, pp. 17–18) and Brown *et al.*'s (1999) research suggest unions are already facing. The ability of employers to use personal contracts and temporary replacement workers and to dismiss striking workers after eight weeks, coupled with the limitations on closed shops, may further limit the prospects for bargaining.

We have to exercise some caution when drawing conclusions on the basis of a comparison of the ERA with past British experience. First, we have to be mindful of the differing historical and legal contexts and particularly the changes in UK industrial relations which underlie the Government's intentions. Management has become increasingly convinced of the superiority of non-union forms of employee involvement and its commitment to these has heightened its opposition to measures that could rejuvenate the trade union movement. The transformation in public policy in the UK since the early 1980s has both reflected and fuelled this change in managerial orientations. Second, the objective of the ERA system is different: it is to foster a fresh partnership model rather than to promote collective bargaining *per se*. The ERA is premised on an expectation that industrial relations can be redirected away from antagonistic relationships towards partnerships, in which bargaining is co-operative, integrative and long term in orientation and has a reduced role relative to other mechanisms of employee relations. It is then an invitation to the unions to participate in a new employee relations, with their eventual participation depending, in the words of the White Paper (Department of Trade and Industry, 1998), on their being 'able to demonstrate value to employers' (p. 23 s4.11). The features of the ERA that our comparison with the 1970s highlighted as deficiencies—the long time periods attached to certain stages and the limited mandated scope of bargaining— could then be viewed as a means of enhancing the chances of employers accepting unions as partners, albeit perhaps on their own terms.

The question then is whether the statutory procedure can act as an incentive for the parties to take the voluntary route. The various stages and time scales attached appear to provide as many opportunities as possible for the parties to opt for the voluntary route. It may also help to add to the credibility of the union if its support is seen not to have waned during any protracted period of negotiation. Finally, the restricted mandated scope of bargaining may provide an incentive for the union to adopt a co-operative approach on the assumption that, if it can demonstrate to management that it adds value, it will be able to have a broader role than that implied in the CAC-imposed procedure. Management also has an incentive not to go right through the procedure since, by doing this, it may end up with a bargaining relationship that has been soured by a long protracted recognition dispute. Even if management does not envisage this happening, it may accept the inevitability of union recognition and prefer to get on with bedding down a union-based industrial relations on its own terms rather than to lose the initiative to the union or an outside third party.

None the less, even if such voluntarism is encouraged, this may not result in partnerships since, if employers go down the voluntary route primarily to avoid the statutory route, they may have signed an agreement out of duress. At best they will have recognised the union out of a sense of pragmatism, at worst in a state of antagonism. Although partnership may grow out of such arrangements, the chances of this in the absence of the give-and-take, co-operative mentality seem low. More-over, the employers' desire for voluntarism may not be in order to promote part-nerships with unions. The evidence of Guest and Peccei's (1998) research on partnership—albeit based on a non-representative sample of managers—is in fact that it is not readily associated, in their minds, with trade unions. Only 35% of Guest and Peccei's sample of managers viewed an independent trade union as the best means of representing employers' interests, while only 39% seeing that a trade union is necessary to make partnership successful (p. 21). Nor does it seem likely that the employers' aversion to statutory union recognition methods will be weakened by the attempt to connect them to the partnership notion. If employers could be expected to work co-operatively in partnerships with unions one would expect them to be already doing so and there would be little need for the Act's provisions. Since this is not the case, and they do not necessarily associate partnership with unionism, we are left with the issue of whether the law can really effect a change in their orientation. The emphasis on partnership puts the onus on the successful pursuit of voluntary methods.

ACAS's role in the future, in the more legalistic context and can the statutory procedure remain a long stop?

The Government's objective of partnership and the priority given to the voluntary route in the recognition framework have direct implications for ACAS. First, if the statutory procedure gives employers an incentive to deal with the recognition matter on a voluntary basis, they may well turn to ACAS for information and advice and they along with the unions may call for conciliation. ACAS Council (ACAS, 1999, p. 108) supported the separation of the voluntary procedure from the statutory procedure with the CAC responsible for the latter. Second, the partnership notion overlaps with the joint problem solving approach that ACAS has increasingly been adopting and encouraging (ACAS unpublished objectives 1992, quoted in Kessler and Purcell, nd., p. 13) and indeed the Council has stated (ACAS, 1999, p. 107) that it welcomes the initiatives designed to foster partnership, including the establishment of a partnership fund.

The way the statutory procedure has been designed means that ACAS could be involved at any stage, both post- and pre-entry to the statutory procedure. The spirit of the Act is that going through the whole procedure is to be avoided. There is flexibility built into it to encourage opting out at any stage or for the case to be transformed from a CAC case to a self-determined case, which may or may not in- volve ACAS. Moreover, in the procedure, a union can not bring a case to the CAC if the employer requests ACAS involvement. At various stages of the procedure the CAC may be involved in brokering an agreement between the two parties and it may decide to point the parties in the direction of an ACAS conciliator. It is possible then that a large number of cases not settled by the parties themselves will involve ACAS either alone or as an adjunct to the CAC. The availability of ACAS facilities can also be seen as an important way of countering the small-firm exclusion, though whether the unions have the resources to work with small workforces is questionable.

Since the procedures allow for employer involvement, scenarios of likely events could be based on differentiating between the reaction of employers. Three may be identified: the reaction that, given the level of existing membership or assumed support for the union, recognition is almost inevitable at some stage in the future; a genuine uncertainty about either the level of support for the union and/or value of union recognition, but acceptance (of the government's position) that union recognition is valid where there is majority support and the union can demonstrate that its presence adds value; and a resistance to union recognition based on either dogma or a judgement that union representation is inferior relative to other methods. ACAS could be involved in cases where management reacts in any one of these ways, but its role may vary depending on the employer's reaction. In the first case it may be largely involved in advice and mediation; in the second with conciliation and running membership checks; and in the third, as an adjunct to the CAC.

The way in which ACAS conducts its voluntary conciliation need not change because this is once again in the shadow of the law. First, its current *modus operandi* is not dissimilar to the statutory route. Although the criteria for deciding bargaining units and union recognition are ostensibly decided by the two parties themselves, it is very unlikely that these have been substantially out of line with the ERA's procedures. ACAS has always conducted membership checks and ballots in its voluntary conciliation, though it has not traditionally charged the parties for this, whereas under the ERA procedure the parties share the costs and thus ACAS may decide to reconsider its policy on not charging. Second, it is unlikely that ACAS cases will mirror the Act's timetable, and indeed it may be that employers opt for ACAS conciliation to avoid the imposition of deadlines. Third, the main threat that ACAS currently has (and uses) is that the dispute will 'go public' (e.g. it appears in local newspapers). This remains and the additional threat that the dispute will become a legal matter should not alter the way ACAS conducts its conciliation. This may not even alter the 'game' between the parties. It would indeed be a measure of the success of ACAS if it did not—a not implausible result.

CONCLUSION

This chapter has shown that there were clear lessons to be drawn from ACAS's involvement in a statutory procedure in the 1970s and that it appears that the drafters of the ERA procedure have heeded the most important ones. From ACAS's point of view the most fundamental of these is presumably that it should not be responsible for such statutory procedures. I have suggested that what appear (when judged against the 1970's experience) to be weaknesses in the procedures (e.g. long time delays) may, from the perspective of the Government's aim of fostering partnership, be strengths that facilitate co-operative labour relations and encourage employers to make voluntary agreements. Thus the Act's proposed system might engender a distinctive new approach which takes the UK beyond the 1970s and the North American models. An important role for ACAS is implied by the Employment Relations Act's procedure. There are indeed already signs that the caseload of ACAS will increase, as there were 205 new requests for collective conciliation in recognition cases in 1999, compared with 154 in 1998. The implication of the analysis that I have presented, however, goes beyond this: it is that the government's objective of partnership is only achievable if ACAS is heavily involved.

ACKNOWLEDGEMENTS

The part of this chapter that summarises the 1970s ACAS procedure is an extension of a section of my paper with John Godard (Wood and Godard, 1999) for which I did the research, while the section comparing the Employment Relations Act's provisions with the 1970s system also draws on that paper. I am grateful for John Godard's permission to build on our joint work and acknowledge the great benefit that this has had on this chapter and my ideas in general. I would also like to acknowledge the contribution of the ACAS officers I have interviewed during the research for this chapter. Finally, I am very grateful to Peter Syson and Andrew Wareing for their help and encouragement throughout this project; to Jim Mortimer, the first Chairman of ACAS; to John Goodman and Linda Dickens for their comments on an earlier draft of the account of the EPA procedure; to Paul Davies and Sian Moore for their comments on drafts of this chapter; and to Brian Towers and William Brown for fulfilling their editorial role.

REFERENCES

ACAS (1976–1981; 1986; 1999), Annual Reports. London: ACAS.

Bain, G. (1970), *The Growth of White-Collar Unionism*, Oxford: Clarendon Press.

Bain, G. and R. Price (1983), 'Union Growth—Dimensions, Determinants, and Destiny', in G. S. Bain (ed.), *Industrial Relations in Britain*, Oxford: Basil Blackwell), pp. 3-33.

Beaumont, P. B. (1981), 'Trade Union Recognition: The British Experience 1976–80', *Employee Relations*, 3(6), pp. 1–39.

Bercusson, B. (1976), *The Employment Protection Act 1975 with annotations by Brian Bercusson*. London: Sweet & Maxwell.

Bercusson, B., M. Clancy, K. Ewing, J. Foster, S. Fredman, A. McColgan, R. Robertson and S. Wood (1998), *Need to be heard at work? Recognition Laws—lessons from Abroad*. London: Institute of Employment Rights.

Brown, W., S. Deakin, M. Hudson, C. Pratten and P. Ryan (1999), *The individualisation of employment contracts in Britain*, Department of Trade and Industry, Employment Relations Research Series. London: Department of Trade and Industry.

Commission for Industrial Relations (1974), *Trade Union Recognition: CIR Experience, Commission for Industrial Relations, Study 5*. London: HMSO.

Cully, M., S. Woodland, A. O'Reilly, G. Dix, N. Millward, A. Bryson and J. Forth (1998), *The 1998 Workplace Employee Relations Survey*. London: DTI, ESRC, ACAS, PSI.

Davies, P. (1979), 'Failure to Comply with Recognition Recommendation', *Industrial Law Journal*, **8**(2), pp. 55-60.

Davies, P. and M. Freedland (1993), *Labour Legislation and Public Policy*, Oxford: Clarendon Press.

Department of Trade and Industry (1998), *Fairness at Work*, Cm 3968. London: HMSO.

Department of Trade and Industry (2000), *Public Consultation on A Code of Practice on Access to Workers During Recognition and Derecognition Ballots and A Method of Conducting Collective Bargaining.* London: Department of Trade and Industry.

Dickens, L. (1978), 'A.C.A.S. and the Union Recognition Procedure', *Industrial Law Journal*, **7**(3), pp. 160–77.

Dickens, L. (1987), 'The Advisory Conciliation and Arbitration Service: Regulation and Voluntarism in Industrial Relations', in R. Baldwin and C. McCrudden, *Regulation and Public Law.* London: Weidenfeld and Nicolson), pp. 107–131.

Dickens, L. and G. Bain (1982), 'A Duty to Bargain? Union Recognition and Information Disclosure', in R. Lewis (ed.), *Labour Law in Britain*, Oxford: Basil Blackwell), pp. 80–108.

Donovan Commission (1968), *Royal Commission on Trade Unions and Employers' Associations 1965–1968*, Donovan Report. London: HMSO.

Doyle, B. (1980), 'A substitute for Collective Bargaining? The Central Arbitration Committee's Approach to Section 16 of the Employment Protection Act 1975', *Industrial Law Journal*, **9**(3), pp. 154–166.

Employment Protection Act (1975). London: HMSO.

Flanders, A. (1974), 'The Tradition of Voluntarism', *British Journal of Industrial Relations*, **12**(3), pp. 352–370.

Gould, W. B. IV (1993), *Agenda for Reform; The Future of Employment Relations and the Law.* Cambridge MA, MIT Press.

Guest, D. and R. Peccei (1998), *The Partnership Company, Benchmarks for the future.* London: IPA.

Kessler, I. and J. Purcell (nd), *Joint Problem Solving, ACAS Occasional Paper Number 55.* London: ACAS.

McIlroy, J. (1979), *Trade Union Recognition: The Limits of Law.* Studies for Trade Unionists. London: Workers Education Association.

Mortimer, J. (1998), *A Life on the Left.* East Sussex, The Book Guild.

Rogaly, J. (1977), *Grunwick.* Harmondsworth, Penguin.

Simpson, R. (1979), 'Judicial Control of A.C.A.S.', *Industrial Law Journal*, **8**(2), pp. 69–84.

Simpson, R. (1991), *Trade Union Recognition and the Law.* London: Institute of Employment Rights.

TUC (1995), *Your Voice at Work.* London: Trade Union Congress.

TUC–CBI (1997), *Joint Statement on Union Recognition.* London: TUC and CBI.

Wedderburn, Lord (1976), 'The Employment Protection Act 1975: Collective Aspects', *Modern Law Review*, **39**(1), pp. 169–183.

Wedderburn, Lord (1986), *The Worker and the Law.* Harmondsworth, Penguin.

Wood, S. (1978), 'A Question of Recognition: Review of *Grunwick* by J. Rogaly', *Journal of Management Studies*, **15**(2), 77-84.

Wood, S. and J. Godard (1999), 'The Statutory Union Recognition Procedure in the Employment Relations Bill: A Comparative Analysis, *British Journal of Industrial Relations*, **37**(2), pp. 203–243.

6

Supporting collective bargaining: some comparative reflections

Bob Hepple QC

INTRODUCTION: THE OBJECTIVES OF CONCILIATION AND ARBITRATION

We are celebrating ACAS's 25th anniversary, so it is appropriate to ask whether our current and projected institutions for the resolution of collective disputes are capable of dealing with the new social, economic and legal circumstances at the beginning of ACAS's second quarter-century. When ACAS was established in 1974, the extension, development, and where necessary, reform of collective bargaining machinery was one of its express functions. The removal of this objective in 1993[1] was of symbolic importance as part of the removal of state support for collective bargaining in Britain, although the view within ACAS is that this has made little practical difference to the way in which it handles disputes. The Employment Relations Act 1999 (ERA) has not reinstated the pre-1993 function,[2] but ACAS and the Central Arbitration Committee (CAC) have been given an important new role in trade union recognition disputes. The general duty, 'to promote the improvement of industrial relations', is ambiguous, although broad enough to encompass the extension, reform and development of collective bargaining.

So we are left with the question which fascinated Jean de Givry, late Head of Department at the International Labour Office (ILO), author of the ILO's 1980 comparative study of Conciliation and Arbitration (International Labour Office, 1980), and of the chapter on Prevention and Settlement of Labour Disputes in volume XV of the *International Encyclopedia of Comparative Law* (De Givry, 1978). This is whether collective bargaining is to be considered as only one of the methods of settling disputes, or as a distinct process of a fundamentally different character 'of paramount importance to the development of an integrated labour relations policy' (De Givry, 1978, para. 14–80; International Labour Office, 1980, p. 25). 'If it is to be considered only as a method of settling disputes' he wrote, 'it will be dealt with as a

---

[1] By the Trade Union Reform and Employment Rights Act 1993 (TURERA), s.43,sched.10, amending s.209 of the Trade Union and Labour Relations (Consolidation) Act 1992 (TULRCA).
[2] S.16 ERA, amending s.209 TULRCA.

procedure on the same level as conciliation and arbitration; but if the intention is to foster and promote collective bargaining as an institution for rule-making and policy-making which has its own *raison d'etre*, a different approach will be necessary' (International Labour Office, 1980, p. 25). He showed that in countries where the objectives of disputes settlement are to foster collective bargaining as an institution, as well as to settle disputes and avoid work stoppages, the tendency was to emphasise procedures for voluntary settlement and to limit recourse to compulsory procedures.[3]

De Givry's question has to be answered in the context of the new ways in which enterprises are organising work and changing the nature of collective organisation and representation. In Europe these include: the fragmentation of production and the workforce, the reduced scope of collective bargaining, the trend to plant/company bargaining and the weakening of national bargaining frameworks; the use of collective bargaining to introduce flexibilisation and derogation from legal standards; the trend from substantive to procedural rules in which unions help in the organisation of work; the growing importance of transnational corporations, but the absence of countervailing workers' power, leading to an emphasis on legal frameworks for information and consultation with workers' representatives but not collective bargaining; and the lack of organisation at plant or company level so holding back collective bargaining at that level.

Faced with these developments, two models have emerged as a means of establishing some kind of countervailing workers' power in the European context. The first is an attempt to recreate workers' organisations at plant or company level. This is the British trade union recognition model, embodied in the ERA 1999 (the Schedule A1 procedure). The second is the shift towards statutory representatives elected by the workforce. This is exemplified in the German co-determination model, and also in measures adopted or proposed at European Union (EU) level. I want to make some observations about the role of conciliation and arbitration in the emerging British model from a comparative perspective. I shall do so by maintaining the importance of a distinction between disputes of rights and disputes of interests. I shall suggest that the new model fails to draw a proper distinction and so may undermine the roles of ACAS and the CAC.

DISPUTES OF RIGHTS AND OF INTERESTS

The distinction between disputes of rights and disputes of interests was developed in the Nordic countries, from the time of the September Agreement 1899, and later in

---

[3] De Givry acknowledged that occasionally compulsory arbitration could be used as a method of promoting collective bargaining, and he cited as an example the provisions of sections 11–16 of the British Employment Protection Act 1975 (EPA) which allowed a trade union to invoke unilateral arbitration where an employer had not complied with an ACAS recommendation for trade union recognition.

Weimar Germany, under the influence of the French *conseils d'prudhommes*. The negotiation of the collective agreement and its application were seen as distinct processes. The collective agreement creates legal rights and disputes over those rights can be resolved only by Labour Courts in Denmark, Sweden and Norway. In the Federal Republic of Germany the Labour Courts deal not only with collective agreements but also with disputes arising from the contract of employment and certain statutory rights. On the other hand disputes over the negotiation of a collective agreement are ones in which an adjustment of conflicting interests is required. These disputes are therefore considered to be non-justiciable and outside the scope of judicial decision-making.

Conciliation and mediation are the principal methods for the settlement of disputes of interests. The only contribution which the law can make is to persuade and encourage parties to reach a compromise by way of mutual concessions. This may be by advice or conciliation, mediation, or voluntary arbitration before they reach the stage of open conflict, or by making an objective assessment of all elements involved in the conflict by appropriate fact-finding procedures. I am using 'conciliation' here in the British sense, which is derived from the Latin *conciliare*— 'to bring together' or 'unite in thought', while 'mediation', derived from the Late Latin *mediare* means 'to occupy a middle position'. The comparatist has to beware that these terms have different connotations even in the same language, so what is usually understood as 'mediation' in the USA would be called 'conciliation' in the UK. In the USA and Canada, conciliation and mediation are seen as the main methods of settling what are usually called 'economic' disputes, while grievance arbitration is the primary means for dealing with rights or legal disputes over the interpretation and application of the agreement. This distinction is followed in most countries in which collective bargaining exists.

Three decades ago, Britain stood in splendid isolation from this almost universal trend. The Donovan Commission considered that the distinction was unrealistic in the British context, mainly because of the prevalence of custom and practice and the dynamic nature of collective agreements, especially if made by joint industrial councils, evidenced by their (usual) lack of legal enforceability and their vague and indefinite nature. The unitary nature of British disputes resolution procedures was being transformed even before the foundation of ACAS 25 years ago. An ever-increasing number of disputes are now regarded as being best settled on the basis of legal rules. The employment tribunals, courts and arbitrators are daily involved in the interpretation and application not only of statutory rights but also of company or plant agreements which are expressly or impliedly incorporated into contracts of employment.

However, this neat distinction between rights and interests, justiciable and non-justiciable disputes, should not blind us to the limitations of the distinction. Behind the language of 'rights' usually lies a question of equity, not only from the point of view of the parties to the dispute but also from the public interest. Managers and unions are right to maintain their mistrust of lawyers, tribunals, courts and arbitrators in dealing with many disputes which lie in the borderland between rights and interests.

UNION RECOGNITION DISPUTES

Let me illustrate this by the case of the so-called 'right' of a trade union to recognition for purposes of collective bargaining. The new British system introduced under the ERA (the Schedule A1 procedure) has been analysed earlier in this volume by Stephen Wood. He and John Godard have also drawn some important lessons from US and Canadian experience in a recent article (Wood and Godard, 1999), as has Brian Towers (Towers, 1999). Their analyses need not be repeated here. The comparative point which I want to make is that the new British approach is schizophrenic. On the one hand, it treats the process of achieving recognition as a dispute of interests with an appropriate emphasis on conciliation by ACAS, 'assistance' by the CAC, and ultimately arbitration by the CAC in which the focus is not on rights but rather than on 'encouraging fair and efficient practices and arrangements in the workplace'[4] or, in the designation of the bargaining unit, compatibility with 'effective management'.[5] On the other hand, where the employer fails to agree with a recognised union on a 'method by which collective bargaining should take place', and the CAC imposes such a 'method', the dispute is turned into one of rights. The imposed 'method' is, to have effect 'as if it were contained in a legally enforceable contract made by the parties',[6] and specific performance 'shall be the only remedy available for breach of anything which is a legally enforceable contract.'[7] Failure to comply with an order for specific performance could (in theory) lead to quasi-criminal sanctions for contempt of court.

The language of contract is, of course, pure fiction. As Bill McCarthy has pointed out, if there is any precedent it is the 'remedial action' under section 37 of the Industrial Relations Act 1971, where a procedure agreement was alleged to be non-existent or defective (McCarthy, 1999, pp. 18, 54). Bearing in mind the statutory model of a collective bargaining method which the Secretary of State is to specify,[8] this is in effect a legislative default procedure. The consequence of using the fiction of contract is that the remedies for breach are posited in terms of the law of obligations, not the law of industrial arbitration such as the award of improved terms and conditions by the Industrial Arbitration Board (IAB) under the 1971 Act, or by the

---

[4] Schedule A1, para. 171.
[5] Schedule A1, para. 19(3)(a).
[6] Schedule A1, para. 31(4).
[7] Schedule A1, para. 31(6).
[8] Schedule A1, para. 168.

CAC for failure to recognise under the EPA 1975. Moreover, the contractual remedy is limited to an order of specific performance by the ordinary courts (not even the specialist Employment Appeal Tribunal (EAT)), i.e. a decree of the court which compels the defendant personally to do what s/he promised to do. This will import into disputes about recognition the whole of the 'ancient and discretionary law' on the remedy of specific performance—regarded by lawyers as exceptional in the case of contracts, since damages are the normal remedy for breach. Employers and unions will have to learn all sorts of things about equitable remedies—the leading textbook by Jones and Goodhart (1996) is nearly 300 pages long and cites over 2,000 cases. For example, there is the doctrine of 'clean hands' (e.g. a union cannot obtain specific performance if itself in breach of procedure), and the remedy will be denied in a variety of typical circumstances (e.g. because the default procedure requires continuous or successive acts which the court cannot supervise, or because it imposes unacceptable restraints on the employer's or worker's personal freedom). What is sauce for the goose is sauce for the gander so far as equitable remedies of this kind are concerned, so employers will be able to seek specific enforcement of the peace obligation if this is included in the agreement.[9] Ironically, the legally enforceable procedures which the common law,[10] and the Industrial Relations Act 1971 (IRA) failed to deliver will become part of the new law of industrial relations.

Bill McCarthy (1999, pp. 44–51) and others have made the point that the ERA could have avoided this legalism by restoring, as the sanction for non-recognition, the system of arbitration by the CAC of improved terms and conditions, incorporated as mandatory terms of individual contracts utilised in the EPA 1975—a remedy which still exists for failure to disclose information for purposes of collective bargaining.[11] From a comparative viewpoint this is analogous in most Canadian jurisdictions to 'first contract' arbitration. Under this if either the union or employer believes that an impasse has arisen in attempts to negotiate a 'first agreement' following an award of recognition, they can bring a claim before the Labour Relations Board or equivalent body. The Board (in one jurisdiction, the Minister) will decide whether there is an 'immediate prospect of settlement'. If not, an arbitrator is appointed to award a legally binding one-year contract covering substantive terms of employment. This is based on settlements of comparable employers in the local area. It seems that the threat of such arbitration is usually sufficient to lead to a change in management's reluctance to negotiate. Wood and Godard (1999, p. 219) report that, in contrast with the USA where agreement is never reached in

---

[9] During the parliamentary debates Lord McIntosh, speaking for the Government, said that the default procedure would not contain a peace obligation, but the precise legal effects of the 'base procedure' remain to be seen: H. L. Deb, 7 June 1999, col.1159.

[10] *Ford Motor Co v AUEFW* [1969] 2 Queens Bench 303, upholding Kahn-Freund's view that collective agreements are not intended to operate as contracts, unless the parties expressly agree otherwise. This is now codified in Trade Union and Labour Relations (Consultation) Act 1992 (TULRCA), s.179.

[11] TULRCA, ss.181–185.

one-third of all first contract negotiations, failure to achieve a first agreement is relatively infrequent in Canada. The Canadian procedures, like the old Industrial Arbitration Board/Central Arbitration Committee arbitration awards, keep the dispute firmly within the ambit of a dispute of interests.

This may be contrasted with the American National Labor Relations Act (NLRA) model which converted recognition into a question of justiciable rights. Once a union is certified as bargaining agent by the National Labor Relations Board (NLRB), the employer is placed under a legal obligation to bargain with it in good faith. In those rare instances where the NLRB finds that an employer has not bargained in good faith (an unfair labour practice which is very difficult to prove) all the NLRB can do is to make an order requiring the respondent to 'cease and desist' from that unfair practice. Disobedience does not result in the imposition of any penalties. It is necessary to obtain a court order and only then will there be a punishable contempt of court. There are endless possibilities to challenge NLRB decisions by way of judicial review, with appeals which can lead to years of delay. The median period of delay including appeals in 1994 was three years.

The authors of the British Schedule A1 procedure have tried to avoid many of the defects in the American system. The comparatist can only express surprise that the NLRA model was used at all given the fact that, notwithstanding the NLRA, private-sector union density in the USA has fallen to 9.5%, lower than before the Great Depression and the Wagner Act. This is due to many causes, but the legalistic 'rights' model, enforced ultimately through the courts is certainly perceived, not only by critical legal theorists, but also by many American union leaders as a straitjacket which has contributed to the decline of unionism.

Even the Canadian-type model of 'first contract' arbitration does not avoid legal disputes. For example, the Canadian Charter of Rights has engendered litigation about statutory collective bargaining systems, and in Britain we can expect the Human Rights Act (which comes into force in October 2000) to lead to legal arguments on subjects such as the employer's and union's freedom of speech during ballot campaigns. Moreover, despite the list of protections against 'detriment' and dismissal in connection with acts relating to the statutory recognition procedure (much wider than in the USA), and the eight-week freeze on dismissal of official strikers (compare the USA, where the striker is entitled to his or her job back only if the strike was in protest against a substantial employer unfair labour practice), there are bound to be legitimate legal controversies about the scope of these protections.

The point is that while the new British model has done much to avoid the legalism of American-style rights disputes—in particular by focusing on conciliation by ACAS, 'assistance' by the CAC within defined (possibly over-rigid) time limits, and by granting structured discretions to the CAC when deciding upon recognition, instead of imposing a legal obligation to bargain in good faith—it has undermined this by introducing a system of rights enforcement through fictional contracts and the full panoply of judicial power which may lead to new Grunwicks or worse.

INDIVIDUALISATION AND DEROGABILITY

There is another aspect of the new British model that may undermine its success. This is the possibility which exists for the employer and employee to agree on an individual contract which differs from the terms of the collective agreement. It is true that section 17 of the ERA enables the Secretary of State to make regulations about cases where a worker is subjected to a detriment by his employer or dismissed on grounds that he refuses to enter into such a contract. But section 17(4) provides that there is no detriment if other workers receive higher pay or other monetary benefits, so long as those other workers are not inhibited in their contracts from becoming union members, and the higher payments are in accordance with the terms of a contract of employment and reasonably relate to services under that contract. It appears that workers may be induced to forego collective bargaining in return for more advantageous individual monetary rewards (Ewing, 1999, p. 288). This is a powerful weapon in the hands of an employer keen to resist collective bargaining.

This possibility exists because of a structural weakness of the law in Britain. In virtually all other legal systems no derogation to the detriment of the employee is permitted in individual contracts from the norms in an applicable collective agreement. Derogation downwards (less favourable terms in the individual contract than in the collective agreement) is never allowed. In some countries, such as the USA and South Africa, derogation upwards (more favourable terms in the individual contract than in the collective agreement) is prohibited being treated as an unfair labour practice which undermines the collective labour contract. Even the individualistic New Zealand Employment Contracts Act 1991, s.19(2) provides that when a 'collective employment contract' applies, the employee may negotiate with the employer on an individual basis but only for terms and conditions which are consistent with the collective contract.

In strong versions of what Bill Wedderburn (1992, p. 245), following the Italian concept, calls 'inderogability' (e.g. France, Sweden), the normative part of the collective agreement attaches at once to the employment relationship—this is not, in the British sense, 'incorporation' but rather automatic, immediate and imperative regulation. In weaker versions (e.g. Germany, Italy, the Netherlands, Sweden) the union is the agent of members of the union, so that non-members are not covered in law, although in practice employers apply the same terms to non-members. In Germany and France, and probably Italy, bargaining for the benefit of members only is illegal (as it has been in Britain since 1988). One must also remember that in France, Belgium, Spain, Germany and the Netherlands procedures exist for the extension of collective agreements *erga omnes*. This is a device which both protects those employers who bargain with unions from unfair competition and also avoids incentives for recruiting workers not covered by the agreement.

Wedderburn has pointed out (1992, p. 245) that until Britain resolves this structural weakness, we cannot properly safeguard the collective bargaining system within the framework of the new European legal culture of directives on information and consultation rights. This would require first some kind of procedure for the extension of collective agreements. This could not be a replica of the old EPA Schedule 11 because of the virtual disappearance of multi-employer bargaining in most sectors, but some formula such as the 'general level' among comparable employers in the same trade and district might be appropriate. Second, specific legislation (as in s.185(5) TULRCA) is needed to allow incorporated terms to be superseded or varied to the employee's detriment, only by a subsequent collective agreement or arbitration award.

CONCLUSION

My answer to De Givry's question is that the emerging British model falls distinctly into the category which views collective bargaining as no more than one method of disputes resolution. Collective bargaining is one choice for employees where a substantial majority of them favour this method. This is what I understand to lie behind the rhetoric of 'partnership' and 'greater understanding and co-operation' (Department for Trade and Industry, 1998, p. 32). The new British model is distinctly not intended as a means of transforming the fortunes of collective bargaining back into the centre of labour-relations policy. Nor does it resolve another dilemma, that of reconciling collective bargaining with the institutionalisation—through EU law—of channels of communication and influence on decision-making.

The reluctance of the Government to accept the European Commission's proposals for a directive to grant a right to employee representatives in national enterprises (as distinct from transnational ones covered by the European Works Councils directive) to information and consultation is said to be based on the fear that this will 'cut across' national arrangements. But experience in other countries is that institutional arrangements can actually strengthen the role of unions at the workplace. For example, the Report from the German Commission on Co-determination concluded that 'collective bargaining and co-determination are mutually supportive' (Bertelsman Foundation, 1998, para. 39).

Whether the new legislation can achieve its limited objective is, however, open to question because of the failure to maintain a consistent view of recognition disputes as ones of interests rather than of rights. A critical comparative lesson is that the attitudes and behaviour of employers are significant determinants of the success or failure of a recognition procedure, and that a more favourable climate can be created where there is active conciliation or mediation, as exemplified by the National Mediation Board in the rail and air transporation industries in the USA (Towers, 1999, pp. 19–20). The only way to avoid legalism may be to rely on voluntary methods whenever possible; indeed, there are recent examples of a return to voluntarism in the USA, and greater involvement by the Federal Mediation and Conciliation Service (FMCS).

The new British scheme will depend heavily for its success on the ability of the CAC and ACAS to promote voluntary settlements. If this fails, the only avenue open under Schedule A1 is a legalistic system of specific enforcement of contractual rights. Moreover, even where there is a collective agreement this may be undermined by individual derogations. Paradoxically, regulatory theory, based on international experience, teaches that for voluntary procedures to work effectively, there needs to be the possibility, even if rarely used, of imposing tough sanctions against non-compliance (Baldwin and Cave, 1999, pp. 133–136). In the context of union recognition, specific performance is likely to be unwieldy and difficult to impose. A non-derogable system of unilateral arbitration, coupled with conciliation and mediation, is the missing element in the new dispensation. In its absence ACAS will have a difficult, but indispensable role in promoting voluntary recognition agreements under the shadow of the law.

REFERENCES

Baldwin, R. and M. Cave (1999), *Understanding Regulation: Theory, Strategy and Practice*, Oxford: Oxford University Press.
Bertelsman Foundations and Hans Bockler Foundation (eds) (1998), *The German Model of Codetermination and Cooperative Governance*. Guttersloh: Bertelsmann Foundation Publishers.
Department for Trade and Industry (1998), *Fairness at Work*, Cm.398. London: HMSO.
De Givry, J. (1978), 'Prevention and Settlement of Labour Disputes Other than Conflicts of Rights', O. Kahn-Freund (ed.), *International Encyclopedia of Comparative Law, vol. XV, Labour Law*. Tubingen: J.C.B. Mohr.
Ewing, K. (1999), 'Freedom of Association and the Employment Rights Act 1999', *Industrial Law Journal*, **28**, pp. 283–298.
International Labour Office (1980), *Conciliation and Arbitration Procedures in Labour Disputes*. Geneva: ILO.
Jones, G. and Goodhart, W. (1996) *Specific Performance*. London: Butterworth, 2nd. edition.
McCarthy, Lord (1999), *Fairness at Work and Trade Union Recognition: Past Comparisons and Future Problems*. London: Institute of Employment Rights.
Towers, B. (1999), *Developing Recognition and Representation in the U.K.: How Useful is the U.S.Model?*. London: Institute of Employment Rights.
Wedderburn, Lord (1992), 'Inderogability, Collective Agreements and Community Law', *Industrial Law Journal*, **20**, pp. 245–264.
Wood, S. and J. Godard (1999), 'The Statutory Union Recognition Procedure in the Employment Relations Bill: a comparative analysis', *Brtish Journal of Industrial Relations*, **37**, pp. 203–244.

7

After collective bargaining? ACAS in the age of human resource management

John Purcell

INTRODUCTION

From its foundation in 1974 up until 1993 the statutory duty of ACAS was to 'promote the improvement of industrial relations and in particular to encourage the extension of collective bargaining and the development and, where necessary, reform of collective bargaining machinery'. At the time of the Citizen's Charter in 1991, and preceding the 1993 legislation which removed the focus on collective bargaining, ACAS was already subtly changing its pronounced role, if only, perhaps, to stave off closure in the face of a hostile paymaster. The 'ACAS Commitment', as it was called, made no mention of collective bargaining but referred to improving industrial relations, fostering employee involvement, promoting employment policies for organisational effectiveness and seeking the avoidance and resolution of disputes through impartial and well-informed advice and assistance. By 1993 ACAS had adopted a mission statement which remains prominent on the first page of successive annual reports:

> The ACAS mission is to improve the performance and effectiveness of organisations by providing an independent and impartial service to prevent and resolve disputes and to build harmonious relationships at work.

Even industrial relations has gone, to be replaced by an explicit focus on organisational effectiveness, neatly pre-dating the human resource management fixation with the bottom line, and harmonious relationships at work, whatever they mean. All that is left of the old language of institutional industrial relations is 'to prevent and resolve disputes'. This carries with it the flavour of the inevitable conflict of interest between labour and capital which will break out at any time unless channelled and expressed by trade unions through appropriate and agreed 'machinery'.

In 1975 the inevitable conflict of interest in industry was widely accepted as axiomatic by industrial relations experts, and the primacy of collective bargaining and the institutionalisation of conflict thesis seen as an appropriate, if incomplete response, to the plurality of interest. The task, following Donovan, was to extend the number of people covered by collective bargaining, and widen the scope of issues covered by bargaining, or at least joint discussions, as seen in the Bullock Report on Industrial Democracy published at the same time as ACAS was established.

This focus on collective bargaining was reflected in the way ACAS approached its advisory role, a role where it has much more choice on how to develop its work, compared with arbitration, collective and individual conciliation. At the time of the first annual report the purpose of the advisory role was 'to help management and unions create a constructive relationship in which change can take place smoothly and differences resolved before they become disputes' (quoted in Kessler and Purcell, 1995, p. 12). Reference was often made to 'the parties' implying a collectivised relationship was the norm and that ACAS's job was 'to encourage joint management/trade union approaches to problem solving' (*ibid.*, p. 13).

All this was understandable and highly appropriate. After all, with nearly 3,000 strikes recorded in 1974, industrial relations remained unsettled in both the public and private sectors, trade union membership was growing quite rapidly especially among white-collar workers and managers, collective bargaining was devolving to the workplace in manufacturing at least, and incomes policy was still a favoured tool of economic policy with all the potential for disputes that could bring. The vital role of the 'third party' in dealing with the causes as well as the consequences of conflict had been evolving throughout the century. This included the public provision of advice first started by the Wartime Ministry of Aircraft Production. And in the six years immediately before ACAS, the Commission on Industrial Relations had sought to reform industrial relations by dealing with the underlying relationships at the place of work. The problems, and the way for the third party to deal with them were familiar. ACAS's role was unambiguous and un-controversial.

By 1994, as ACAS noted to mark its 20th anniversary, massive changes had occurred in the structure of industry, and in particular, the primacy of collective bargaining had passed. Union membership had fallen every year since 1980 and the collectivist agenda seemed outmoded in management and government circles. Articles were written on the 'end of institutional industrial relations' and the root metaphor, as Dunn (1990) put it, had changed. The ideological underpinnings of state and employer support for collective bargaining, which Clegg (1994) had seen to be so vital in extending bargaining in the 1930s, were removed. In its place came a highly individualist view:

> She [Mrs Thatcher] did not accept collective social categories based on mutually hostile relations to the means of production. Instead, and more positively and predictable, she talked about individuals and consumers ...The market economy was not about collective groups of producers: instead, it devolved 'the power of consumer choice to consumers'. Here were her childhood memories of Grantham elevated into social taxonomies for the nation as a whole. (Cannadine, 1998, pp. 175–176)

Some saw this new rhetoric applied in industry and commerce as human resource management (HRM). Some welcomed it, others abhorred it. ACAS had to live with it.

To survive as a state-funded, independent body, managed by a Council drawn from trade unions, employers bodies and academics, so typical of the 'post-war settlement', in a period when all other such bodies were abolished, and when the emasculation of trade unions was in full swing, is good enough. To carve out a new role in tune with the rhetoric of human resource management and now with 'partnership' is remarkable. This has been done through the adoption and refining of a distinctive method of strategic mediation or what ACAS call Advisory Mediation. Although starved of resources as the juridification of industrial relations grew apace and the demand for individual conciliation and advice expanded, regional offices have continued with in-depth advisory work, another term for Advisory Mediation, and undertake around 500 assignments a year. By now virtually all such work is based on 'process consultancy' (Schein, 1969) where managers and employee representatives, or groups of employees work together in a joint problem-solving mode facilitated by an ACAS advisor. This can equally well be a unionised workplace or a non-union establishment and can cover a wide range of topics. There are no charges for this service, so ACAS has to be careful to show that it is not undercutting the growing number of private employment and HRM consultancies. The task has to be, 'in all circumstances ... wholly appropriate to ACAS and not one which could be undertaken acceptably by other agencies, including management consultancies' (ACAS operating criteria quoted in Kessler and Purcell, 1995, p. 12). No reports are published and ACAS does not tout for this type of work, at least not openly. If the shift from an avowed collectivist, institutional mission to one much more open ended was one means to survival, the ability to carve out a distinctive niche that could be justified as uniquely appropriate to a state-funded third party was another:

> In the context of these changes in employment relations, the shift from a single, structural model of industrial relations towards an emphasis on process can be seen as a crucial ingredient in ensuring ACAS's continuing viability as a source of third party advice. It was not enough for ACAS to loosen its link to a particular and perhaps fading institutional model. There was a perceived need to develop a way of providing advice which was distinctive and which set ACAS apart from consultancy and accounting firms—many of which set up specialist departments on human resource management and compensation in the 1980s. Central to this search for a distinctive approach was the concept of 'jointness' as a means of encouraging problem solving (Kessler and Purcell, 1995, p. 12).

In the next section it is appropriate to set out in more detail how ACAS is distinctive in its advisory work based around joint problem solving. This will then allow for a discussion of how this role may be developed both at a time of neo-institutionalisation and when the HRM agenda is becoming much clearer, especially the link with organisational effectiveness. It will be necessary to ask whether ACAS remains conditioned by an industrial relations agenda of procedural and substantive 'agreements'. Is it unable or unwilling, unlike its sometime adopted sister organisation, the Work Research Unit (WRU), to tackle the issues that enhance the quality of working life and are linked directly to organisational effectiveness? This is not easy to answer, since it raises the perennial question of how far can ACAS go in allocating resources to this type of work while maintaining a credible defence to the charge that they are competing unfairly with fee-earning consultancies. Part of the answer will be seen as a focus on small and medium-sized organisations which are less likely to use consultants and where the distinctive focus on process can have a more immediate effect.

THE DISTINCTIVE CHARACTER OF ADVISORY MEDIATION

In 1990 Ian Kessler and I were commissioned by ACAS to conduct an evaluation of the Advisory Mediation work. We did so over a three-year period by sending postal questionnaires to every organisation covered by an in-depth advisory exercise in the previous year. The respondents were the named managers on the ACAS file and named employee representatives where there were some. With a response rate of around 60% from managers and just over 50% from employee representatives we were confident that we had achieved a representative sample. Some 689 management and 299 employee-representative usable replies were collected. In brief, since the results of the research have been published quite widely (Kessler and Purcell, 1994; 1995; 1996), the key survey findings were as follows.

- During the period 1990–1993 ACAS increasingly concentrated on participative methods of enquiry and scaled-down the use of diagnostic work where an adviser investigates and reports back. Participative methods are mainly Joint Working Parties (JWPs), where representatives from management and the workforce jointly explore the issue or problem, find and implement their own recommendations for change facilitated by an ACAS officer usually in the chair. Another type of participative enquiry, the workshop, was developed in the early 1990s and was included in the final year of the research. Workshops are more often used in non-union settings and are where members of the workforce at large meet with management to generate and discuss issues of joint concern under the guidance of an ACAS officer. In 1993 90% of the cases covered in the research were JWPs (58%) and workshops (33%). In 1990, before workshops were used, 38% of advisory work used JWPs.
- The decision to come to ACAS for an advisory project was taken by the manager in most cases, but in a quarter of cases it was, according to the management respondent, a joint decision with employee representatives. More interesting, perhaps, was that in half of the cases the management respondents said they had heard about ACAS advisory work from an employee representative or a trade union official. If employee representatives had been involved in the decision to come to ACAS it was more likely that a joint problem-solving approach would be used in the project. We have no way of telling from this research how far HRM consultancies use participative methods, nor whether the decision to employ them is taken jointly or is discussed before hand. Our proposition, which should be tested, of course, is that it is much less likely than in the ACAS approach.

- Two-fifths of managers had actively considered using other bodies, such as consultants, before they chose to come to ACAS for assistance on the particular problem that faced them, and half had used consultants before. The overwhelming reason for coming to ACAS, chosen from a list of eight reasons, was 'independent/impartial service' and this was deemed 'essential' in over half of the cases. The other main reasons for choosing ACAS were 'technical competence', and acceptability to employees and to managers. A free service was essential in only 5% of the cases, and was the least important reason apart from 'little knowledge of alternatives'. Where participative methods were used there was some evidence to show that acceptability to employees became more important and the issue of charging became yet more marginal.
- The involvement of employee representatives (but not full-time union officials) *and* mangers was high in gathering information, analysing the issues, formulating recommendations and implementing the change where a JWP was used, as might be expected. Employees were directly involved in one-third of cases in gathering information, and direct employee involvement was much higher where a union was recognised.
- The more participative the ACAS method the better were the outcomes. Where a JWP was used the management respondent reported in 88% of cases that the issue was fully or mainly resolved compared with 68% of cases where traditional methods like diagnostic surveys were used. This was also the pattern when the question asked about whether the organisation had benefited from the ACAS advisory mediation. In JWP cases 52% said 'a lot' (the top item on a five-point scale) compared with 43% on non-JWP cases. Where employees and managers were involved in all stages of the project outcome measures were even higher. This improvement was evident when we measured changes in the level of trust. The movement in trust levels was so marked that we were confident we were picking up real changes despite the methodological problems of measuring trust changes in a postal survey (see Kessler and Purcell, 1994). Managers reported that the level of trust between management and employees *before the JWP* was high or very high in 24% of cases whereas afterwards it had jumped to 49%. Employee representatives were more sceptical both before and after but even so marked changes took place. Nineteen percent said trust was high or very high before while 36% reported these levels of trust afterwards. Meanwhile at the other end of the scale 37% had said that trust was low or very low before, but only 16% thought so afterwards. In short, high trust levels doubled according to both sets of respondents and low trust was more than halved.

It was hard not to conclude that these outcome results were impressive and endorsed ACAS's approach to advisory mediation, and in particular the use of JWPs and Workshops. Of course, we could not say from the survey that ACAS was the only organisation prepared and able to use these participative methods, nor were we able to quantify in terms of profit or performance data the extent to which organisations had benefited. But if the managers who filled in the questionnaire reported that their organisation had benefited a lot then we were inclined to believe them. We believed them, too, when they said they came to ACAS because of the Service's independence/impartiality, technical competence and acceptability, and not because it was a service free at the point of delivery.

The number of advisory mediation projects completed each year appears to be determined more by the resources that ACAS devotes to the work than to demand. Harsh economies were needed in 1993, including the closure of the WRU, and the number of advisory mediation cases fell after the cuts from a peak of 1,144 in 1989 to around 500 in recent years. The average cost recorded each year is astoundingly low at £4,772 in 1996/97 and £5,234 in 1997/8 although there is a wide variation in the length, complexity and therefore cost of projects. This resource constraint probably leads to pressure to reduce the amount of time that can be spent on each assignment.

If the impression of the annual reports in the 1990s was of ACAS trying hard to justify and continue to resource advisory mediation work then the question now is how it could develop when the political and institutional climate is more favourable. In particular, given the growing evidence of the connection between types of HRM and organisational performance will it be sensible to focus advisory work not just in terms of a process but also in content by concentrating on HRM or Quality of Working Life (QWL) agendas?

HUMAN RESOURCE MANAGEMENT, THE QUALITY OF WORKING LIFE AND ACAS

Although the first reference to HRM appeared a decade before ACAS was founded (Miles, 1965) it was not until the mid-1980s that HRM gained much recognition, even in the USA. In Britain the most often-quoted paper, by Guest, was published in 1987. He argued that HRM constituted a 'particular approach' to labour management and 'comprises a set of policies designed to maximise organisational integration, employee commitment, flexibility and the quality of work' (Guest, 1987, p. 503). Storey, in his survey of large companies in the early 1990s, defined HRM in much the same way:

> Human resource management is a *distinctive* approach to employment management which seeks to achieve competitive advantage through the strategic deployment of a highly committed and capable workforce, using an integrated array of cultural, structural and personnel techniques. (Storey, 1992, p. 5 emphasis added).

He went on to show how many of the companies he studied were developing systems of HRM alongside, but separate, from the traditional approach of collective bargaining and joint consultation. The machinery of industrial relations was being bypassed. What was emerging was a 'dualist approach' and the implication was that industrial relations, defined as unions and collective bargaining, was less central if not almost irrelevant to the process of change and the introduction of performance management and HRM. Many argued that this and the absence of references to unions and bargaining in the key texts showed that HRM was anti-union. Or to put it another way, the swing had moved away from collectivism to individualism, much in line with the beliefs of the Prime Minister of the day, as though these concepts were antonyms. Others argued that the type of policies typical of HRM were more often, or equally likely, to be found in union settings (Sisson, 1993; Guest and Hoque, 1996) and that collectivism and individualism were not opposites but separate dimensions to the employment relationship (Purcell, 1987).

The 'particular approach' of Guest, echoing the famous list of Walton (1985), allowed HRM to be referred to in the singular as 'it'. This has become known as the 'best practice' approach with the assumption that it can be applied beneficially to all organisations. A different line of argument, known as 'best fit', argues that the system of HRM will vary according to contingent circumstances. This implies, for example, that the type of best practice HRM for a knowledge-based consultancy company will be very different from that appropriate for an component assembly plant making products at the commodity end of the market (see Purcell, 1999a, for a debate on these two approaches). One may use 'high commitment management (HCM)' while the other may stick to more traditional approaches of control and cost minimisation. The search is for appropriateness and fit with contingent circumstances. A third approach, while recognising the need for generic types of HRM policies, argues that successful firms have distinctive, rare characteristics that make it hard for others to copy. This 'resource-based view' is concerned to achieve 'unique fit' or 'exclusive practice'. 'Notions of "causal ambiguity", "social complexity" and "path dependency" are used by strategy theorists to identify ways in which firms can build valuable resources which defy attempts by rivals at imitation or substitution' (Boxall and Purcell, 2000, p. 194). The resources that the firm has available are of two sorts, 'human capital advantage' and 'organisational process advantage'. The latter includes highly evolved processes within a firm such as cross-functional learning, labour-management co-operation and a dedication to service quality. It can also, more controversially, be linked to the core-periphery employment model where emphasis on core resource strengths is matched with the growth of contingent labour. Here firms surround an exclusive core of élite employees, managed by high commitment management, with outsourced functions and/or people working under precarious or insecure short-term contracts (Purcell, 1999b).

There is much that is common in these three approaches. All are concerned with strategy and start from the premise that HRM is critical to business performance. All, therefore, are avowedly managerialist and take a stance that a third party would find difficult *unless* it can be shown that benefits accrue to both employees and shareholders. All, too, argue that while it can now be established that systems of HRM do contribute to organisational effectiveness (in the UK see Patterson *et al.*,

1997 and Thompson, 1998), the emerging problem is one of diffusion. Why do relatively few organisations adopt the principles of high commitment management when to do so would be likely to improve performance?

This is relevant to ACAS in three ways. First, how far do, and should, the type of issues covered in advisory mediation match the key features of high commitment management? Second, is the technical competence of ACAS, so valued by the respondents to our survey, locked into particular industrial relations agendas or is it really a process competence which is highly relevant to the problem of diffusion? And third, does the Quality of Working Life Agenda, admirably, if little messianically, described in the ACAS booklet *effective organisations: the people factor,* mean that the approach of the Work Research Unit of ACAS should be re-evaluated, if not revived?

To answer the first question we need to define the component characteristics of high commitment management. This is still fairly controversial, as various authors use different lists in their research (see Dyer and Reeves, 1995). In the widely-read book of Pfeffer (1994) he initially proposed a list of 16 policies, but more recently (1998) has reduced these to seven:

- employment security;
- selective hiring;
- self-managed teams or teamworking;
- high pay contingent on company performance;
- extensive training;
- reduction of status differences;
- sharing information.

These lists are rather arid and trivialise the HRM agenda. Behind them are two important principles. The first is that the evidence we have supports the contention that it is the combination of these policies, taken together—what is called internal fit—which generates performance outcomes. One policy initiative by itself is unlikely to achieve this, and may indeed lead to negative outcomes, or 'deadly combinations'. Thus HRM has to seen as an holistic system or a 'bundle' (MacDuffie, 1995), not some ragbag of policies which are added to from time to time. Second, the integrated architecture of the *system* of HRM is best seen as a set of processes which individual companies translate into policy and practice to suit their circumstances.[1] Following the resource-based view, the need is to tailor the policies to the particular behaviour patterns, history and culture of the organisation. The processes given in most lists of

---

[1] The ACAS Annual Report 1996 follows a very similar line in referring to research by the IPD on the psychological contract. 'One of the key findings of the survey was that the use of management processes which were seen to reflect the interests of employees was the single most important factor contributing to a positive psychological contract. The processes were ... well designed jobs, the avoidance of compulsory redundancies, internal promotions and the provision of information on company performance and prospects' (ACAS 1996, p. 13).

HR policies and practices that are linked to better organisational performance usually include:

- particular care taken with recruitment, for example involving team members in selection and job previews;
- use of extensive means of communication both downwards and upwards, informing people of business performance, improving economic literacy and enhancing accountability to employees as stakeholders;
- employee training and development, especially in the broadening of skills and competencies, future oriented work activities or learning new things;
- devolved responsibility to individuals and teams for operational work decisions, problem solving and employee involvement;
- multi-skilling or cross-skilling usually achieved through team working giving more job autonomy and making greater use of skills and competence; and
- performance appraisal and feedback—some argue this should be linked to reward in some way.

Various authors note how this 'bundle' of processes is especially relevant when employees have relatively high levels of discretion, implying longer job-cycle times, and some element of job autonomy provided by the manufacturing or operation systems. Thus, Youndt et al. (1996) refer to 'scope flexibility', while MacDuffie (1995) talks about 'discretionary behaviour' in his study of car-workers in many countries. Thus job design and teamworking is at the heart of much of high commitment management (or what the Americans call 'high performance work systems') and this is in turn linked to changes in operational management systems and technology. As Wood puts it: 'serious innovations in personnel management will accompany only new production concepts ... we ought not to expect innovations in management on humanistic grounds' (Wood, 1999, p. 410).

It is difficult to know how far ACAS advisory mediation covers these topics in high commitment management. The classification list used in each annual report is oddly dated reflecting an earlier era. In 1998, not an untypical year, the annual report lists, in the order given here, the topics areas and proportion of cases as shown in Table 1.

TABLE 1
Topics areas and proportion of cases

Topic area	Proportion of cases
individual employment rights	15%
collective bargaining arrangements	17%
pay and reward systems	18%
communication, consultation, employee involvement	25%
organisational effectiveness and change	25%

Source: ACAS (1998) Annual Report

Kessler and Purcell noted that the use of JWPs was especially beneficial when complex issues were handled such as pay and reward systems. This would apply to the introduction of forms of high commitment management and this would presumably come under the heading of 'organisational effectiveness and change' which accounted for (only?) a quarter of the work.

One implication is that ACAS could be more proactive in choosing its advisory mediation work, giving preference to cases allowing for integrated HRM interventions where possible. This would be justified on the grounds of ACAS's mission to improve the performance of organisations. But what about the objectives to 'prevent disputes' and 'build harmonious relationships at work'? Much early research in HRM ignored employees, since the focus was on management strategy and policy. In recent years, however, attention has increasingly turned to employee views. In part this is because the underlying assumption in HRM that there is an ongoing need to align management and worker interests in the firm has been made more explicit following an over-emphasis on downsizing and 'positive insecurity' (see ACAS, 1996, p. 13). More particularly, attention has been given to the 'psychological contract' which covers areas of job satisfaction, organisational commitment, organisational citizenship behaviour and links these to employee expectations and beliefs about the type of policies and behaviour they think management is obliged to deliver. In one sense this can be seen as a sophisticated approach to testing 'harmony' at work. Put another way, the use of the 'balanced score card' combining a variety of performance measures from various stakeholders is, at last, being given more attention and recognition.

If it can be shown that the HR bundle, or HCM, is linked to both an improvement in organisational performance *and* helps build harmony at work, then it should be central to ACAS's work, given the mission statement, especially if it can apply equally well to unionised and non-union firms. Evidence of this sort is beginning to emerge. For example, Guest and Conway use the results of a telephone survey of 1,000 employees to show that the use of seven or more out of ten HRM practices is strongly associated with higher levels of job satisfaction, greater organisational commitment, reduced intention to quit and better perceptions of management–worker relationships (Guest and Conway 1999). Employees working in organisations where unions were recognised but where there were few high commitment-type policies were much less satisfied; and non-union employees were much more positive than union members about the extent to which fairness of treatment and the meeting of their expectations had been achieved. The authors conclude 'that if they [trade unions] are to promote fairness in the workplace, then, among other things, they should overcome their understandable scepticism and place more pressure on management to adopt progressive HRM practices' (Guest and Conway, 1999, p. 387). The 'theys' in the quote could just as easily be ACAS.

If this answer to the first question on the relevance of high commitment management to the work of ACAS is accepted, then the second question on diffusion and the third on the relevance of Quality of Working Life initiatives are easier to answer. The puzzle to some, especially those who make assumptions about economic rationality as a guide to management decision-taking, is why relatively few firms adopt high commitment management if it has such manifest benefits. We know that high commitment practices are 'most popular in those sectors where the firm competes through quality and service and can only remain viable through exploiting advanced technology (as in complex manufacturing) or through a highly skilled interaction with clients (as in professional circumstances)' (Boxall and Purcell, 2000, p. 187). But there remain a lot of firms that would benefit from their introduction. Many explanations (but not much of it informed by research) have been provided to explain this (Pfeffer, 1998; Ichniowski et al., 1996). Quite a number of factors internal to the firm have been identified, including the usual suspects of middle-management resistance, communication blocks between functions, lack of support from top management and lack of trust between management and labour. Using the language of the resource-based view we can say the problems are ones of 'organisational process disadvantage' leading to a situation where the economic and psychological cost of implementing new ways of working and destroying old competencies (Pil and MacDuffie, 1996) overwhelms the uncertain benefits that are hoped to flow in the future. In the car industry it is greenfield-site plants and factories in crisis, facing closure, that have been at the forefront of implementing new working methods (MacDuffie and Pil, 1997).

This problem of diffusion will not be a surprise to any informed observer of the management of change since the issues are essentially the ones of bringing about organisational renewal or realignment. The relevance for ACAS is obvious since the Service's unique skill, developed especially in the 1990s in JWPs, is of getting people and the 'parties' to find their own solutions to organisational process problems. ACAS's strength in 'technical competence' as identified in the Templeton Survey of ACAS advisory work could relate to the ACAS officer's detailed knowledge of a policy matter, but it is likely to refer equally to the competence in helping people with different values and interests come to terms with a change agenda and find ways of gaining mutually satisfactory outcomes.

It was particularly interesting to find in the Templeton survey that the involvement of managers in all stages of investigation, prescription and implementation was strongly associated with positive outcomes be it 'use to the organisation' or 'levels of trust'. As we commented at the time, 'we take this to mean that managers, other than the respondent (usually a personnel manager) were involved in the change process—for example line managers. This is a useful reminder that successful joint working involves both a wide range of managers and employees and their representatives' (Kessler and Purcell, 1995, p. 25). This is even more important when issues of organisational effectiveness and change are closely tied to technical and operational management involving inter-functional co-operation, as is most often the case. ACAS's particular strength can be redefined as a unique expertise in the process of managing change, and this, more than any other single competence is what is needed to help introduce the processes of high commitment management or maximise resource strengths. Since the problems of change are much to do with vested interests and fears about the future, an independent and impartial service, acceptable to all, has a peculiar advantage.

This focus on the management of change is interesting for another reason. It can be argued that the performance outcome effects of systems of HRM should not be tested only by financial results (because of the black-box problem) but should include more behavioural measures such as the way HRM helps an organisation become agile or cope with exogenous shocks (Dyer and Shafer, 1999). This is sometimes referred to as 'fitness for purpose'. The expectation is that many organisations will need to manage change on a continuous, rather than discontinuous basis, and that systems of HRM are important in achieving this. This is likely to be especially important in matching employer and employee needs as far as possible in the pursuit of 'flexibility'. Many organisations need help to manage change and build this type of competence. Why should ACAS not concentrate on this type of work?

Part of it once did. The Work Research Unit had been established in the mid-1970s within the then Department of Employment but was transferred to ACAS in 1985. It fell victim to budget cuts in 1993. 'The role of the Unit', wrote the Director:

> was modified over the years as the needs of industry and commerce changed and knowledge developed about what have become known as Quality of Working Life (QWL) issues including, for example, job design, work structure, quality management, organisation development and the management of change. In particular the emphasis of the Unit's work changed from being what might be described as an investigation and research orientation to the application through 'action research' field work of knowledge gained about QWL (Grayson, 1993, p. 2).

This action research closely resembles the work of regional ACAS staff in JWPs, and indeed ACAS were anxious to exploit the experience of the WRU in terms of participative methods. However, the subject matter of WRU inquiries was very different in profile from those of advisory mediation. In 1991, for example, the Unit provided long-term assistance through in-depth assignments in 31 cases, 17 of which were completed in the year and thus covered by the annual statistics. The main subjects covered, in rank order are shown in Table 2.

This list is much more aligned to HRM issues, but came under the more acceptable rubric of QWL. The problem for the WRU was that, in the main, its clients were very large organisations (a third had over 1,500 employees in 1991) and assignments were significantly longer. Conceivably this crossed the line into consultancy and thus became dressed up as 'action research'. But the type of issues covered and the methods WRU used do help establish the case not only for a more HRM (or QWL if preferred) focus to ACAS advisory mediation work, but also for asserting that it is possible.

A particularly interesting example of this is the WRU role in Blue Circle. The 1997 ACAS Annual Report records Blue Circle as one of the more notable 'partnership

TABLE 2
Subjects covered by the WRU in 1991

Subject	%
Organisational strategy	58.8%
Management of Change	52.9%
Job structure/work organisation	47.1%
Motivation/morale/stress	41.2%
Work methods and productivity	17.6%
Direct employee involvement	17.6%
Payment systems and related	17.6%

approaches' currently in vogue but does not mention that ACAS, through the WRU, was involved with Blue Circle in the mid-1980s and again in the early 1990s for a three-year period. The action occurred at the Cauldron plant and is summarised in an ACAS occasional paper, charting the move from an adversarial 'them and us', 'win–lose' culture in the early 1980s to an alternative strategy:

> An essential element of such an alternative strategy is the improvement of organisational effectiveness, and hence competitive edge, by maximising the contribution of everyone in the organisation. In Cauldron's case the challenge was to build a high performance business unit to compete with the best in the world, based on capital investment, a new commitment rather than control work culture and advanced working practices. This was to occur in a highly unionised, blue collar, heavy engineering environment in rural Staffordshire ... [Maximising the effectiveness of employees] was done by developing broader and more challenging jobs and work environments which both satisfied individuals, by allowing them to contribute more and be better rewarded, and greatly increased the performance and effectiveness of the business unit. This took the active involvement and participation of people throughout the organisation (Dunn, Syme and Toombs, 1994, p. 30).

The term HRM is not mentioned, yet what is described is central to high commitment management and the HR Bundle. 'Partnership' gets a small mention ('the full support and involvement of the trade unions is vital ...') but does not get the profile it would if published now. It is an excellent example of a partnership approach, which takes a long time to develop, with the improved union–management relationships facilitating partnership at the level of the individual employee, the team and operational management. Marketing and distribution staff were included after the initial concentration on production areas, nicely illustrating the holistic requirement of HR systems. Two other implications can be drawn. First, the restructuring involved redundancies on at least two occasions but it was the way these were handled which was important for the process of change. Second, the WRU/ACAS staff worked alongside consultants brought in to provide extensive training. In a sense this was another type of partnership between the public and the private sector which may be a model to follow if this type of work is to be rejuvenated.

NEO-INSTITUTIONALISM IN INDUSTRIAL RELATIONS?

The Blue Circle experience is a good example of a case where human resource management agendas, Quality of Working Life issues and industrial relations approaches combine. This no doubt made it an attractive case for the WRU. An increasing number of cases of advisory mediation, however, take place in non-union firms. Here the work of ACAS is much more difficult. Non-union work accounted for 36% of the cases covered by our research in 1990–1993. We noted how ACAS went to great lengths to try to establish some form of representative body or committee which could form the employee 'side' of a JWP. This included posting notices and asking for volunteers. Where this was not possible a workshop format may have been used to allow employees to meet directly with management in the hope, sometimes, that this would lead to some form of representative structure. It was clear, however, that this was precarious, and our research revealed cases where the representative committee or structure was abandoned or allowed to fade away after the 'problem' was solved and after ACAS had withdrawn from the case.

The obvious conclusion was that there are limits to 'jointness' and to 'partnership' when there is no form of institutional security. 'Institution' in this context can mean a statutory form of representative structure, an agreement on procedural rules, or even little more than a pattern of behaviour established over many years, leading to a sense that employees have always been represented by one or more of their number in discussion with management. We can argue which is the better, or more stable system, but the point here is that in each some form of security—an expectation that this is how things will be done—has been established for joint working or partnership to continue.

Interestingly, in those cases where there was no union recognition or pre-existing staff representative structure, the outcome of ACAS advisory mediation work using participative methods was even higher. For example in the cases where a JWP was used in a unionised setting, 54% of management respondents said that their understanding of the issue or problem had increased a lot. But in non-union cases 61% said this was the case. Where ACAS directly interviewed a large proportion of the staff this level of understanding shot up to 77% of the non-union cases (47% in union cases), and workshops were similarly very successful in non-union cases (79% compared with 54% in unionised firms). We commented later that:

> the impression painted by these data is of [non-union] firms facing a problem in the management of human resources and, with the help of a third party, finding, almost to their surprise, that employees have interesting and useful perspectives on the problem at hand (Kessler and Purcell, 1995, p. 677).

It might be hoped that this positive experience of joint working for the first time would lead most firms to establish regular means of representation and interchange whether through trade unions or staff bodies. But these processes have always been ephemeral, and, like union membership where there is no active management–employee forum, tend to wither away.

There are, then, limits to how far ACAS can take joint working in non-union firms unless or until there is a significant change in the institutional framework of employment relations. This, of course, may be happening at least on a piecemeal basis with the advent of European Works Councils, the requirement for collective consultation in cases of redundancy and ownership transfer, and the opportunity for workplace agreements under the Working Time Directive. Union recognition cases will presumably grow after the Employment Relations Act is applied and must imply some institutional framework once recognition is granted. The biggest advance would be if the government backed the current European Commission proposals for national works councils.[2] Meanwhile, in a letter to the Minister of State, ACAS has welcomed initiatives designed to develop partnership[3] and modernise employment practices and would wish that the 'joint problem solving approach' could be extended more widely and include action research on the development of partnership (ACAS Annual Report 1998, p. 108). A lot more resources would be needed if the opportunities to develop the joint working approach are to be taken.

CONCLUSION: THE SEARCH FOR FOCUS

The developing role of ACAS in advisory mediation work designed to prevent disputes, increase organisational effectiveness and develop harmony at work, to paraphrase the ACAS Mission, has been charted and assessed in this paper. The adoption of a particular method of inquiry based on process consultancy and the pursuit of 'jointness' became formal policy in 1993. Over the years, in a generally hostile environment, ACAS had learnt from the mistakes of the CIR, helped redefine the role of third parties in advisory work, and moved from a focus on the 'parties' in industrial relations to a concern with management–employee relationships in union and non-union settings. In so doing it had preserved its independence and impartiality to such an extent that this became the prime reason for managers to ask for help in resolving difficult employment issues. And it was this that led ACAS to claim that it was offering something that private consultancy companies could not and that advisory mediation was an appropriate role for a state sponsored third party in employment matters. Increasing interest is shown in this work by employment services in other countries, for example in South Africa. The advent

---

[2] But they are reported to be unlikely to do that despite all the evidence that joint working works.

[3] It is interesting to see how broadly ACAS define partnership. 'Advisory mediation is regarded by ACAS as a practical expression of partnership in the workplace. Employers, employees and their representatives can derive a number of benefits by using this co-operative and joint problem solving approach to tackling the issues that confront them. These benefits may include: preventing disputes occurring; addressing underlying issues; constructing better solutions to problems; gaining a greater acceptance of change; and an overall improvement in working relationships' (ACAS Annual Report, 1998, p. 52).

of the Labour Government in 1997 has been associated with renewed emphasis on the value of 'jointness', 'partnership' and 'community' but without a return to the central role of collective bargaining in achieving these worthy values. ACAS, as the leading state agency promoting 'working together' should be a beneficiary of this change of approach.

The problem with this is that it begs the question, working together to achieve what? The rise of human resource management in the 1990s either as a particular approach to labour management, or as a variety of initiatives modified to suit the unique circumstances of every organisation, it is argued, provides some type of answer. In particular the evidence is now emerging that a 'bundle' of HR processes is associated with improved organisational performance in some firms, and that employees report more job satisfaction, trust and commitment in these cases. This is strongly confirmed by the results of the 1998 Workplace Employee Relations Survey (WERS98):

> High commitment management practices are associated with better economic performance, better workplace well-being and a better climate of employment relations but just 14 per cent of all workplaces have a majority of them in place (Cully *et al.*, 1999, p. 291).

This resonates remarkably strongly with the ACAS mission statement. For 'economic performance' read 'performance and effectiveness of organisations'; for 'workplace well-being' read 'prevent and avoid disputes' (since this was one of the measures used) and for 'climate of employment relations' read 'harmonious relationships at work'. The assertion of this paper that ACAS should be much more active in helping organisations implement forms of high commitment management through joint problem solving is inescapable given this evidence and the low rates of diffusion. The particular strength of ACAS in joint problem solving is ideally suited for this purpose and no other agency, public or private could do it. Joint problem solving could provide a means to tackle the intra-organisational problems in the management of change which are often identified as a prime reason for the lack of diffusion of HCM especially when this is adapted to fit organisational needs rather implemented as a blanket solution.

The task, as revealed by WERS98, is enormous, even taking account of organisations where the adoption of HCM would be inappropriate or impossible. ACAS must also be wary of the accusation that it is taking work away from fee charging consultancy companies. The need is for focus. Much of ACAS advisory work is undertaken in small and medium-sized organisations, many of which are owner-managed. Just under 60% of the respondents to the Templeton survey had less than 200 employees, and 40% of the sample were independent companies.

This population of small and medium owner-managed firms has less developed systems of HRM than larger units or establishments that are part of bigger organisations. Guest and Hoque (1996) used the term 'black hole' while Sisson (1993) called firms without either collective bargaining or sophisticated systems of HRM, 'bleak house'. The ACAS survey of the South West (Tailby *et al.*, 1997) confirmed how widespread was the existence of firms with under-developed systems of employment relations or HRM. These are the sort of firms which tend not to use consultants and are unlikely to have professional personnel or HRM staff. Their importance to the economy is frequently asserted, and the UK 'tail' problem of low productivity firms is often found here. These firms tend not to perform well in the usual measures of labour management (Millward *et al.*, 1992, pp. 363–365). The public policy case for providing help in human resource management free at the point of delivery to these firms is strong, since this can help improve organisational effectiveness and make a material difference to the quality of working life. If ACAS need to focus their mission in regard to advisory mediation work, this is where it lies.

REFERENCES

ACAS (1996) *Annual Report*. London: ACAS.

ACAS (1998) *Annual Report*. London: ACAS.

Boxall, P. and J. Purcell (2000), 'Strategic human resource management: where have we come from and where should we be going?', *International Journal of Management Reviews*, 2(2), pp. 183–203.

Cannadine, D. (1998), *Class in Britain*. New Haven and London: Yale University Press.

Clegg, H.A. (1994), *The history of British trade unions since 1889, Vol 111*. Oxford: Oxford University Press.

Cully, M., S. Woodland, A. O'Reilly and G. Dix (1999), *Britain at Work*. London: Routledge.

Dunn, R., F. Syme and F. Toombs (1994), *A Change of Culture* ACAS Occasional Paper No 53. London: ACAS.

Dunn, S. (1990), 'Root metaphor in the old and the new industrial relations', *British Journal of Industrial Relations*, 28(1), 1–31.

Dyer, L. and T. Reeves (1995), 'Human resource strategies and firm performance: what we know and where do we need to go?' *International Journal of Human Resource Management*, 6(3), pp. 656–670.

Dyer, L. and R. Shafer (1999), 'Creating organizational agility: implications for strategic human resource management'. In P. Wright, L. Dyer, J. Boudreau and G. Milkovich (eds), *Research in Personnel and Human Resources Management (Supplement 4: Strategic Human Resources Management in the Twenty-First Century)* (Stamford, CT, and London, JAI Press), pp. 145–174.

Grayson, D. (1993), 'The Work Research Unit', *QWL News and Abstracts* No 113. London: ACAS.

Guest, D. (1987), 'Human resource management and industrial relations', *Journal of Management Studies*, 24(5), pp. 503–521.

Guest, D. and N. Conway (1999), 'Peering into the black hole: The downside of the new employment relations in the UK', *British Journal of Industrial Relations*, 37(3), pp. 367–390.

Guest, D. and K. Hoque (1996), 'Human resource management and the new industrial relations', in I. Beardwell (ed.), *Contemporary Industrial Relations: A Critical Analysis*. Oxford: Oxford University Press.

Ichinowski, C., T. Kochan, D. Levine, C. Olson and G. Strauss (1996), 'What works at work: overview and assessment', *Industrial Relations*, 35(3), pp. 299–333.

Kessler, I. and J. Purcell (1994), 'Joint problem solving and the role of third parties: An evaluation of ACAS advisory work', *Human Resource Management Journal*, 2(3), pp. 34–55.

Kessler, I. and J. Purcell (1995), 'Joint Problem Solving: Does it work? An evaluation of ACAS in-depth advisory mediation', *Occasional Paper No 55*. London: ACAS.

Kessler, I. and J. Purcell (1996), 'The value of joint working parties', *Work, Employment and Society*, 10(4), pp. 663–682.

Miles, R. E. (1965), 'Human relations or human resources?' *Harvard Business Review*, July–August, pp. 148–63.

MacDuffie, J. P. (1995), 'Human resource bundles and manufacturing performance: Organizational logic and flexible production systems in the world auto industry', *Industrial and Labor Relations Review*, **48**(2), pp. 197–221.

MacDuffie, J. P. and F. T. Pil (1997), 'Changes in auto industry employment practices: An international overview', in T. A. Kochan, R. D. Lansbury and J. P. MacDuffie (eds), *After lean production: Evolving employment practices in the world auto industry*. Ithaca: ILR Press.

Millward, N., M. Stevens, D. Smart and W. Hawes (1992), *Workplace industrial relations in transition*. Aldershot, Dartmouth.

Patterson, M., M. West, R. Lawthorn and S. Nickell (1997), *The impact of people management practices on business performance*. London: Institute of Personnel and Development.

Pfeffer, J. (1994), *Competitive advantage through people: Unleashing the power of the workforce*. Boston MA: Harvard Business School Press.

Pfeffer, J. (1998), *The human equation: Building profits by putting people first*. Boston MA: Harvard Business School Press.

Pil, F. T. and J. P. MacDuffie (1996), 'The adoption of high involvement work practices', *Industrial Relations*, **35**(3), pp. 423–455.

Purcell, J. (1987), 'Mapping management styles in employee relations', *Journal of Management Studies*, **24**(5), pp. 533–548.

Purcell, J. (1999a), 'Best fit and best practice: Chimera or cul-de-sac?', *Human Resource Management Journal*, **9**(3), pp. 26–41.

Purcell, J. (1999b), 'High commitment management and the link with contingent workers: implications for strategic human resource management', in P. Wright, L. Dyer, J. Boudreau and G. Milkovich (eds), *Research in personnel and human resources management. Supplement 4. Strategic human resources management in the twenty-first century*. Stamford, CT and London: JAI Press.

Schein, E. (1969), *Process Consultation: Its role in organization development*. New York: Addison-Wesley.

Storey, J. (1992), *Developments in the Management of Human Resources*. Oxford: Blackwell.

Sisson, K. (1993), 'In search of HRM', *British Journal of Industrial Relations*, **31**(2), pp. 201–211.

Tailby, S., E. Pearson and J. Sinclair (1997), *Industrial relations in the South West*. London: ACAS.

Thompson, M. (1998), 'What works at work in aerospace?', *Further analysis from the DTI/SBAC survey*. London: Society of British Aerospace Companies.

Walton, R. (1985), 'From "control" to "commitment" in the workplace', *Harvard Business Review*, **632**, pp. 77–84.

Wood, S. (1999), 'Getting the measure of the transformed high-performance organization', *British Journal of Industrial Relations*, **37**(3), pp. 391–417.

Youndt, M., S. Snell, J. Dean and D. Lepak (1996), 'Human resource management, manufacturing strategy and firm performance', *Academy of Management Journal*, **39**(4), pp. 836–866.

Conclusions
The best and the worst of times: ACAS's survival and progress, 1974–2000 and beyond

Brian Towers

INTRODUCTION

ACAS has been in continuous existence over a period which can claim to have been among the most turbulent and transforming in modern British industrial relations history, comparable with the two decades before the Great War and the period after it culminating in the General Strike. Perhaps this long survival is its most remarkable achievement, equal at least to that claimed by the Abbé Siéyès in revolutionary France.

The history of post-war British public policy is littered with the remains of once prominent, but short-lived, agencies such as the National Incomes Commission, the National Board for Prices and Incomes, the Pay Board and the Comparability Commission. These primarily economic agencies arose and fell with changes of policy and government and were intended to stem what the policy-makers saw as the inflationary excesses of collective bargaining. The industrial relations agencies[1] have, however, had a better survival rate. The Commission on Industrial Relations (CIR) lasted only five years, from 1969 to 1974, but it owed its origins to the Donovan Commission and straddled both the Wilson and Heath governments, first as a Royal Commission and later as a statutory agency under the Industrial Relations Act 1971. Though it was abolished in 1974, its experience has remained important in the design of the recognition procedures of the Employment Relations Act 1999 (Kessler and Palmer, 1996; Adams, 1999; Towers, 1999a; Wood and Godard, 1999).

The longevity prizes must, however, go to the Central Arbitration Committee (CAC) and ACAS. The CAC can trace its arbitration and judicial functions—if not

---

[1] The distinction between economic and industrial relations agencies is not always clear. The Commission on Industrial Relations could, and did, handle references on pay structures and low pay. The Central Arbitration Committee also had a role in minimum-wage setting and collective bargaining itself is centrally concerned with pay determination. Additionally, it was (and still is) widely believed by policy-makers that conflict-free, orderly industrial relations contributes to economic success.

its name—back to the Industrial Court of 1919. It quietly survived under its more limited role after 1979, arising from the final demise of formal incomes policy, to re-emerge 20 years later as the agency charged with the central role of regulating and adjudicating the new statutory recognition procedure. It will, however, have the advantage of ACAS's collective conciliation role in attempts to influence the parties to opt for voluntary, negotiated, recognition agreements—the preferred route of policy.

ACAS can claim similar longevity in its conciliation role, although not as an independent agency. Conciliation in industrial disputes was an important function of the old Ministry of Labour. The 'Ministry for Free Collective Bargaining' (Freedland, 1992, p. 276) survived changes of name and functions but retained its conciliators until the emergence of ACAS. But there was some concern, at the time, that the Department of Employment's loss of its conciliation role would seriously limit its value as the '... eyes ... ears and even its nose as to exactly what is going on in industry'.[2] The benefit was that conciliation gained the advantage of visible, political independence under a statutory agency. The Department did, however, lose prestige. Within twenty years it had lost its separate identity and was absorbed into the new Department for Education and Employment.

ACAS has however had its own pilgrim's progress. It survived the strains of a quasi-judicial role under the recognition procedure of the late 1970s and was happy to revert to its traditional voluntary, conciliation role when the statutory procedure was abolished in 1980. This was then followed by the tensions with government over the revised Disciplinary Code of Practice which seemed to pose a threat to ACAS's independent statutory status, and later in the decade there was also a real possibility of privatisation, especially of its advisory services. But these were minor matters compared to the violent shaking of the industrial relations system's norms and understandings by the confrontations in the steel, water, coal-mining and printing industries which were largely seen by influential figures in the Government and unions as struggles to be won and not disputes to be settled.[3]

These disputes and their outcomes had profound implications for the trade unions and the industrial relations system. These have been extensively analysed and discussed elsewhere. But there were also longer-term changes taking place which were transforming the culture of traditional industrial relations and the organisation and management of work, which were only marginally related to the big industrial disputes of the 1980s. These changes inevitably had an impact upon ACAS. It was obliged to adapt the balance and emphases of its functions to the changing workplace environment. It also needed to react to the changes imposed upon the agency

---

[2] James Prior in 1975 (quoted in Freedland, 1992, p. 276).
[3] For example, Norman Tebbit's comment on ACAS's conciliation in the water-industry dispute of 1982: '... the intervention of ACAS I found generally unhelpful ... having not adjusted to the idea that unions which overplayed their hands should be forced to face up to the consequences' (quoted in Wood, 1992, p. 268).

by government, i.e. the changes in its purposes away from those given to it in 1974. These dimensions of change and ACAS's response to them are the themes of this chapter. We begin with an outline of these changes from 1979 but, where appropriate, taking the story back a little further.[4]

THE DIMENSIONS OF CHANGE

The changes of the last quarter of a century can be conveniently discussed under three dimensions although, in practice they were not discrete: the rapid weakening and erosion of collective bargaining which had become especially apparent by the middle of the 1980s; increasing managerial pressure, towards the improvement of workplace performance which was made easier by, and accelerated, the decline of union membership and collective bargaining; and the growth of individual statutory employment rights.

The weakening of collective bargaining

In 1960, Kahn Freund described the British system as a framework of auxiliary, regulatory and restrictive laws within which, wherever possible, there would be scope for the 'two sides' to establish a collective relationship without legal compulsion. It was a system long in the making. Between 1867 and 1903, four Royal Commissions concerned themselves with finding a sustainable, and especially, peaceable, system which allowed trade unions to advance their purposes within the laws and institutions of capitalist liberal democracy. Each Royal Commission led to significant legislation including the landmark Trade Disputes Act 1906 which was followed, after the Great War, by J. H. Whitley's Committee on Relations between Employers and Employees. The Committee did not need to be 'Royal' to produce five influential reports which confirmed in place the 'Whitleyism' triad of voluntary collective bargaining, arbitration and minimum-wage setting.

This policy of collective *laissez-faire* was, by 1944, the source of great pride, even hubris, at the Ministry of Labour:

> ... the method best adapted to the needs of industry and to the demands of the national character ... [it] involved the Ministry in the negative commitment of keeping the law out of a coercive role in industrial relations and the positive one of maintaining a smooth-running triangular relationship between the Ministry, the employers and the trade union movement (Freedland, 1992, p. 276).[5]

---

[4] The political context is discussed in the concluding sections of the chapter.

[5] This hubris reached even greater heights in the USA at the end of the War: '... its primary practitioners and theoreticians in the realm of industrial relations declared the American system near perfect, a thing of wonder in which bargaining and decision-making could be ceded to ... unions and corporations unimpeded by an intrusive state or the demands of political parties' (Dubofsky, 1994, p. 198).

Given this degree of self-satisfaction and the long period of its growth and consolidation, the policy was not seriously challenged until the middle of the 1960s. It was even roundly endorsed by the Donovan Commission, and the Industrial Relations Act of 1971 retained much of the voluntarist spirit, if not its form. By 1974, the 'single channel' of collective bargaining, with minimal regulation, returned and, with the collaboration of unions and employers, attempts to add on new 'channels', such as worker directors on supervisory boards, were rejected.

The real inroads into the old system came after 1979. The Conservative Government, through legislation and policy initiatives, restricted the influence and autonomy of the trade unions thus withdrawing the official support within the system which they had enjoyed—albeit with some serious tensions and frequent confrontations—since 1906. But it now seems probable that the long decline of trade union membership after 1979 was far more to do with longer-term changes in the structure of the economy and employment than anti-union public policy. It is also of some note that the annual rate of membership decline accelerated in the 1990s, at a time when anti-union public policy and legislation was much less in evidence. But however trade union decline is explained, the outcome has been clear. The fall in membership has seriously weakened collective bargaining as the central institution of the old system. This decline has been monitored in official data as well as the Workplace Industrial Relations Surveys (WIRS) and the most recent Workplace Employee Relations Survey (WERS).[6]

The 1998 WERS survey reports a decline in collective bargaining coverage, between 1984 and 1998, from 70% of all employees to 46%. At the same time, reflecting the growth of employer bargaining power, national, industry-wide, multi-employer collective agreements have become a rarity. Single employers have also preferred to shift bargaining to the lower levels of their organisations. The outcome is that collective bargaining is now almost entirely a workplace activity, further weakening its authority and influence. Furthermore, the non-union or minority union workplace without collective bargaining is now the norm rather than the exception, especially in the new high-tech industries, the service sector and in small businesses. A sizeable 'representation gap' exists in terms of the decline in union presence and representation of employee interests. Over half of all workplaces have no union presence, and such workplaces are much less likely to have any alternative means of representation, including consultation. There is an 'enormous gap' between workplace managers who said they consulted their employees (70%) and those employees who agreed with them (30%). (Cully et al., 1999, p. 297).[7] Employees,

---

[6] WERS, in 1998, surveyed 30,000 managers, workplace representatives and employees in 3,000 workplaces. The survey was sponsored by the Department of Trade and Industry, the Economic and Social Research Council, the Policy Studies Institute and ACAS. See Cully et al. (1999) and Millward et al. (2000). For earlier commentaries on the surveys, in this volume, see Brown and Towers (p. ix) and, especially, Hawes (pp. 13–16).

[7] Such wide disparities are also revealed in US surveys of the perceptions of managers and their employees (Towers, 1997, pp. 196–198).

however, whether members of unions or not, did not markedly differ in wanting to handle their own efforts to improve pay and conditions. Managers also over-whelmingly seem to prefer not to work with trade unions. The 1998 WERS Survey found that managers in 72% of workplaces preferred to consult directly with their employees rather than through unions (Cully *et al.*, 1998, pp. 87–88). Hence a 'voice' at work is not simply equated with union representation.

This picture does, however, require some caveats. The coverage of collective bargaining, though much reduced from its 1980 peak, is still substantial and on current official data the TUC is beginning to be optimistic that the long decline in trade union membership has drawn to a close and some recovery should now be expected (TUC, 1999; Kelly, 2000). The Government is also a strong advocate of partnership alongside the major TUC affiliates, and is providing funding to encourage its development under the provisions of the Employment Relations Act 1999. The Act also specifically favours voluntarism over the law as the preferred route in the processing of claims for recognition. Moreover, in comparative terms, UK collectivism as measured by trade union density, is in the medium group among EU countries and is still more than twice that of the USA.[8]

Yet despite the still relatively widespread survival of the institutions, customs and practices slowly developed and consolidated over a very long period, the system which attracted such praise from its protagonists and participants in 1944 has been, at least, severely challenged by the developments of the last 20 years. The 1998 WERS has even described the changes over that time as a 'metamorphosis' or 'sea change':

> There has been a metamorphosis in the discourse and practice of industrial relations in Britain since that time. The term 'industrial relations' has been replaced in common parlance by 'employee relations', 'employment relations' and a range of other terms, none of which carry the collectivist overtones of the phrase that came so naturally to mind when we were designing the 1980 survey. Our renaming of the survey in 1998 and, more fundamentally our redesigning of it, acknowledged the sea change that took place in relations between employers and employees over the previous 18 years (Cully *et al.*, 1999, p. 246).

Performance and commitment in the workplace

Associated with the decline in trade unions and the contraction in collective bargaining have been attempts by management, especially since the early 1980s, to improve workplace performance through 'high commitment management practices'.

---

[8] Within the EU, the UK in 1997 exceeded Germany (33% against 29%) but was much below Sweden, Denmark, Finland, Belgium and Ireland (ranging from 91%–49%) (ILO, 1997). The USA recorded an increase in membership in 1998 but a further fall in density to 13.9% (Towers 1999, p. 7) although 1999 data is now indicating that the long decline in both membership and density may now be beginning to be reversed, albeit at low levels of increase. The US record is, however, still of some relevance to current official policy on statutory recognition. US labour laws and agencies, with a history dating back more than six decades, were designed to provide an equitable legal framework for trade unions seeking recognition. In the event, the outcome has been the opposite of the original intentions. The principal explanatory factor is the influence of strong employer opposition (Friedman *et al.*, 1994; Gould, 1994; Towers, 1997).

The WERS 1998 survey, which complements earlier studies of the depth and diffusion of these practices (Oliver and Wilkinson, 1992), lists the most common as procedures for dispute resolution, briefing meetings, performance appraisal, single status and family-friendly working arrangements. Less common are employee share-ownership schemes, psychometric tests, profit-related pay and guaranteed job security. Whilst only a small minority of workplaces (14%) have a majority of these practices in place, there is a strong association between their presence and economic perform-ance (Cully et al., 1999, pp. 291–292).

Workplaces with high commitment management practices are also associated with a number of characteristics. First, they are more likely to have a personnel specialist and strategic focus on employee development, providing evidence that ' ... a human resource management approach [is] well entrenched in many British workplaces' (Cully et al., 1999, pp. 81–82). Second, these workplaces tend to be those with an 'active union presence' and this, along with recognition, is more likely to be present where managers favour unions and less likely where they do not.[9] Third, there is a strong association between high commitment management practices, committed employees and a better employment relations climate.[10] Fourth, about half of all employees were satisfied, or very satisfied, with their jobs; and their level of satisfaction was strongly associated with workplaces where ' ... management showed understanding about balancing work and family responsibilities, encouraged skill development, involved them and treated them fairly ... ' (p. 185).

The strong link revealed between good management practices, committed and satisfied employees and a better employment relations climate is not surprising. Such associations are also likely to be stronger, as noted earlier, when an active union presence is favoured by management. Management though, which suggests another conundrum, rarely favour dealing with unions: WERS reports that 72% ' ... would rather consult directly with employees than with unions' (p. 88).

The high commitment movement, despite its manifest advantages to employers and their employees, is clearly limited in its extent. Nor is employee satisfaction universal. The 50% satisfaction rate reported by WERS also indicates that half were *not satisfied* with their jobs. This is supported by evidence from other authoritative sources. Workplace grievances rose rapidly through the 1980s and 1990s (Abbott, 1998; Kelly, 1998, 2000) and ACAS's own data on employment tribunal conciliation cases confirms this trend. Such workplaces are also more likely to be in small businesses with higher rates of formal workplace sanctions, voluntary resignations and dis-missals than larger workplaces and with lower levels of union membership and

---

[9] However, the association between recognition and high commitment is at least partly explained by recognition being more likely in large workplaces.

[10] The strength of this evidence produced a wry comment from the WERS Survey authors: 'As ever, a conundrum remains: why if this is the case, are such practices not more widespread?' (Cully et al., 1999, p. 295).

recognition.[11] Unions will also be unable to apply for statutory recognition under the Employment Relations Act 1999 in businesses employing fewer than 21 employees. This will exclude some 30% of the total workforce.

Statutory employment rights

The number of individual employees seeking potential redress at employment tribunals is a useful indicator of workplace dissatisfaction. In 1975, in ACAS's first full year, the total number of individual conciliation cases handled by the agency was 24,367—all unfair dismissal claims (ACAS, 1976, p. 41). The total had reached 100,399 in 1996 and by 1998 was 113,636 (ACAS, 1999, p. 72). The number of jurisdictions expanded over the period from 3 in 1975[12] to 16 in 1980, 23 in 1991 and is currently 30. These jurisdictions are not, however, related exclusively to claims by employees against employers and some have arisen from the obligation to comply with EU legislation, such as equal pay for work of equal value, transfer of undertakings' rights and the rights in the Trade Union Reform and Employment Rights Act 1993.[13]

The increase in jurisdictions has clearly widened the opportunities for individual employees to pursue claims. But this has not been the whole story. High levels of unemployment in the 1980s and the shift in employment towards the more dismissal-prone service sector, especially in small businesses, has had an impact upon the figures. The decline in collective bargaining and trade union representation may also have been important. Individual, union-supported, claims against employers have provided an alternative for unions rather than through the diminishing, and increasingly legally-constrained, route of collective bargaining (Brown *et al.*, 1998).[14]

The new representation opportunities for trade unions provide potential for them to regain influence and members and could limit the pressures towards increasing juridification of disputes over the employment relationship. But these pressures are strong. High commitment workplaces are still only a small minority, job dissatis-faction is widespread and, possibly, growing. Employees have wider opportunities for claims against employers, and further EU legislation extending individual employment rights remains important. Many employees, for whatever reasons of omission or commission, also lack representation in the workplace. The traditional protections of

---

[11] The WERS sample of small businesses was those with 10–99 employees—60% of these were businesses employing 10–24.

[12] Unfair dismissal was the first jurisdiction followed by equal pay and sex discrimination at the end of 1975.

[13] See Dickens, Chapter 3 in this volume for further discussion of the growth in individual conciliation.

[14] Another alternative arises from the employee's statutory right under the Employment Relations Act 1999 to be accompanied at disciplinary and grievance hearings by a 'companion' who can be a full-time union official, trade union representative or fellow worker. A further route, for unfair dismissal claims, is the arbitration alternative to employment tribunal. This has yet to be implemented. The arbitration alternative is discussed by Dickens.

union membership and collective bargaining, even consultation, are absent in about half of all workplaces. The trade unions now believe that they can recover some of this lost ground. But even quite remarkable union successes will still leave many unrepresented employees with no other option than trying for legal redress of their grievances.

ACAS AND CHANGE

It is legitimate to argue that 'industrial relations' is no longer appropriate to describe a condition in which less than one-third of the workforce are union members and less than half are covered by collective agreements. But it may be premature to suggest that this evidence marks an irreversible unravelling of collectivism (Kelly, 1998; Kelly and Waddington, 1995). There is also some evidence that trade union membership has ceased to decline and the unions themselves have put much emphasis upon the stimulus to recruitment and retention from the minimum wage, the working time regulations, the recognition provisions of the Employment Relations Act 1999, the fashion for partnerships and their own efforts in initiatives such as the TUC's Organising Academy. At the least, the terms 'metamorphosis' and 'sea change' may be more attractive than real in fully assessing what has taken place during ACAS's lifetime.

Yet despite these reservations it cannot be denied that there has been significant change using the evidence of the WIRS and WERS surveys. There has also been a change in the political context which may fairly be described as a metamorphosis. Trade unions and collective bargaining became increasingly to be seen, by government, as impediments to the development of an efficient, flexible market economy. This strongly held view became legislative and policy fact between 1980 and 1993. However, this view has not entirely disappeared under the present administration. Economic and business success remain the primary goals of policy, and collective bargaining is no longer seen as the preferred route to industrial order. Union-free organisations are encouraged if that is the wish of their employees and they are efficiently managed. Where unions exist they are measured in terms of 'adding value' and are urged to enter into partnership with employers.

Reacting to political change

The long traditions and beliefs of the 'Ministry for Free Collective Bargaining' were transferred to the new statutory agency in 1975, both in its purpose set out in legislation and in the persons of the conciliators re-deployed from the Department of Employment. ACAS's first chairman has also recently strongly endorsed the Employment Protection Act 1975's duty on the agency to encourage the extension of collective bargaining on grounds of both industrial democracy and practicality

(Mortimer, 1998, pp. 299–303). Its removal in 1993 under the Trade Union Reform and Employment Rights Act[15] placed a narrow emphasis upon settling strikes and other disputes, ie:

> The Service shall be charged with the general duty of improving industrial relations, in particular, by exercising its functions in relation to the settlement of trade disputes ... (section 43).

This emphasis was removed in the Employment Relations Act 1999. What remained was '... the general duty of improving industrial relations' (section 26) without prescribing [or proscribing?] the ways of implementing that duty.

The removal of the commitment to collective bargaining as late as 1993 was perhaps surprising given the former Thatcher government's vehement opposition to trade unions and the necessary compromises of collective bargaining. However, such a commitment, in practice, was difficult to promote in the context of the government's opposition to the purposes, even existence, of trade unions. There was also the obvious constraint that collective bargaining had been contracting, without pause, since the high point of 1979 and any serious policy of promotion would have been ineffective as well as bringing ACAS into confrontation with government policy. It may therefore be that the encouragement of collective bargaining is a viable duty only when it coincides with labour market conditions in which it is already growing. These conditions were not present from 1979[16] and only recently has there been any evidence of their return (TUC 1999). Furthermore, the simple general duty of 'improving industrial relations' does not logically preclude encouraging collective bargaining where it is appropriate. For example, ACAS's early voluntary conciliation role under the new statutory recognition procedure could lead to agreements without unions pursuing the CAC route of automatic recognition and/or workplace ballot. Indeed, the statutory procedure, as a whole, is specifically designed to allow for an orderly extension of collective bargaining, by agreement or compulsion, where conditions warrant it.[17]

Promoting organisational change

One of the findings of the WERS survey, noted earlier was that high commitment management practices, if present in number, are strongly associated with economic performance. These practices commonly include procedures for dispute resolution, briefing meetings, performance appraisal, single status and family friendly working

---

[15] The Act also gave powers to the Secretary of State to require ACAS to charge for its services, subject to consultation with the agency (section 44).

[16] It is also of note that the National Labor Relations Act 1935 (Wagner Act) in the USA gave the same duty to the National Labor Relations Board. However, despite its good offices and prestige as a federal agency its duty has been effectively negated by the presence of highly unfavourable conditions—not the least hostile employers—for virtually all of the years of the Board's existence (Gould, 1994; Towers, 1997).

[17] It of course also provides for an orderly contraction through the de-recognition procedure.

arrangements. There is also a strong association between high commitment management practices, committed employees, and a better industrial relations climate as well as the likelihood of employee satisfaction. Such workplaces also tend to be those with a 'union presence'.

Purcell argues in Chapter 7 that working in this area of organisational change, but even more directly through action research, was once one of ACAS's functions through the Work Research Unit which was established in the Department of Employment in the mid-1970s and transferred to ACAS in 1985. The Unit was discontinued in 1993 under cuts in ACAS's budget. This was also the year in which the agency's duty to promote collective bargaining was formally removed by the government and a 'mission statement' first appeared in ACAS's annual report:

> The ACAS mission is to improve the performance and effectiveness of organisations by providing an independent and impartial service to prevent and resolve disputes and to build harmonious relationships at work (ACAS, 1993).

Improving the '... performance and effectiveness of organisations ...' could, as Purcell argues, include advising on the introduction of key aspects of the HRM agenda, such as '... job design, work structure, quality management, organisation development and the management of change ...' as the Work Research Unit did during the eight years of its existence.

Yet despite the demonstrated benefits to be derived from high commitment management practices and the case for their much wider diffusion across the economy, ACAS is currently involved in promoting and developing the procedures for achieving organisational change and effectiveness without becoming directly involved in promoting the techniques of change themselves. Hence the agency's advisory mediation assistance, which was developed after the abolition of the Work Research Unit, uses joint workshops and working parties of employers, employees and representatives as a '... practical expression of partnership in the workplace [a] co-operative and joint problem-solving approach to tackling the issues that confront them' (ACAS, 1999, p. 52).

But, despite Purcell's advocacy of a more proactive approach, it is difficult to see how ACAS could more directly move into the overt implementation of an HRM agenda without a change in its remit which could involve some compromising of its independence. HRM and organisational change are not neutral terms, and their implementation can evoke conflict as well as partnership and co-operation, especially when the outcome is insecurity and job loss as the price of greater organisational effectiveness.

CONCLUSIONS

How far, therefore, has ACAS changed since it was founded in what was a very different era? To a certain extent, to paraphrase Malvolio, it has had change forced upon it. It arose in a period when collective bargaining was still growing and had the overt support of Ministers and officials in the Department of Employment from which ACAS's staff and traditions were taken. After 1979 the agency found itself in a context of decline in the institution which it was officially required to promote and a decline of which the Government not only approved, but sought to hasten.

That it survived the 1980s was remarkable. It had all the hallmarks of an era which the government was at pains to discredit: it was pragmatic and pluralist; it gave equal legitimacy to the claims of business and trade unions; and it had a governing council which, in its tripartite composition, recognised that there were more ways than one of looking at important issues. Nor were the Government's views simply rhetoric. It abolished Clegg's Comparability Commission in 1981, because it persisted in upholding principles of pay determination established in the 1970s. It then proceeded systematically to dismantle all vestiges of tripartism from important government agencies by the removal of trade union representation although it curiously lingered over the last survivor of tripartite, indicative planning of the 1960s — the National Economic Development Council. It was finally abolished in 1993.

Yet survival has not required the agency to pay too high a price. That it has changed the time and resources allocated to its traditional, dispute resolution work is without doubt. But this was largely *reactive*, i.e. in response to the long-term decline in collective bargaining and, in the 1990s, the dramatic fall in industrial disputes. There was also a sharp fall in cases and disputes going to arbitration, which easily exceeded 300 in each year of the 1970s and by 1998 had fallen to 51 (ACAS, 1999, p. 131). What has remained in this area of work is ACAS's integrity, professionalism and impartiality. These qualities must largely derive from its traditions and reputation in collective and individual conciliation which have protected its high public standing through difficult times.[18] It is also far more than symbolic that ACAS's senior officer, below the Chairman, retains the job title of Chief Conciliator.

The balance of work has, over the years, shifted substantially. A large part of this has again required the agency to react to developments beyond its control, notably the growing demand for its individual conciliation services. The individual conciliation growth, as noted earlier, is partly explained by the increase in the total number of available jurisdictions. But there has also been a long-established change between jurisdictions. Unfair dismissal cases, as Dickens points out, though the most numerous, are proportionately much fewer than they were in the 1980s. The actual number is also in decline, from a five year average of 43,226 (1993–1998) to a 1998 figure of 40,153 (ACAS, 1999, p. 132). The remaining jurisdictions are consequently growing rapidly, perhaps most notably those relating to equal pay as well as sex, race and disability discrimination.

---

[18] See, especially, Chapter 4, in this volume, by Dix, for evidence of the work and reputation of its 'front-line' conciliators.

The advisory service is also under considerable pressure, having over the period 1994–1998 been required to respond to about 500,000 calls per year (ACAS, 1999, p. 38). Not surprisingly, advisory meetings have been much less numerous at just over 3,000 in 1998, with a small increase over the average of the previous five years.

These considerable pressures, exacerbated by frequent cuts in its budget, have not precluded a more *proactive* role. The agency has, as we have seen, developed its advisory mediation approach in the prevention of disputes and problems and in facilitating procedures for the parties to improve organisational effectiveness. ACAS's activity here does of course fall short of Purcell's recommendation of a commitment to promoting HRM practices but, as we have again noted earlier, such a development could pose problems for the agency. However, there is an emphasis upon 'promoting good practice' in the strong growth in the number of conferences, seminars and workshops promoted in this area. It ran 466 of these events in 1998, charging a fee for 280 of these (ACAS, 1999) under the discretionary powers made available in 1993. But even if there was a policy decision within ACAS to expand its proactive work this, under current budget constraints and the demands of its other functions, is difficult to envisage.

Where then is ACAS going? It was not intended in 1974–1975 to be a radical, reforming institution[19] and, in any case, needs to work, within the limits of its statutory duty. Though it was originally conceived as an industrial relations agency with a corresponding duty to encourage collective bargaining, by 1993, as Purcell discusses in Chapter 7, under political pressure and legislation industrial relations had disappeared from its masthead to be replaced by an HRM-style mission statement with a double emphasis on improving organisational performance and preventing and resolving disputes (ACAS, 1993, p. 6). This was extended and clarified into 'key areas of activity' which ACAS publishes in its annual reports as a new framework for its activities.[20] The new statutory duty in the Employment Relations Act 1999 restores industrial relations to its old prominence although it is not clear, through omission, how far collective bargaining has also been restored as at least one instrument of improvement. An obvious limitation is the greatly diminished scope of collective bargaining compared to the middle of the 1970s or even the beginning of the 1990s. Some of this ground may be made up over the next decade but a return to earlier levels is highly improbable. This is because of the scale of the recovery required and the broadly established, mildly negative, policy consensus towards trade unions and industrial relations which now covers the centre ground of the political spectrum. A further limitation, influencing all of ACAS's actual as well as

---

[19] One insider has even recently described its main purpose as 'counter-revolutionary'.

[20] i.e. 'preventing and resolving disputes; conciliating in actual and potential complaints to employment tribunals; providing information and advice; promoting good practice' (ACAS, 1999, p. 37). These activities, including the authority to issue Codes of Practice, are derived from statute, most recently in the Employment Relations Consolidation Act 1992.

potential areas of activity, arises from its continuing budgetary and staffing restrictions. This places clear limits to the scope for growth and experimentation but also puts pressure on the effective maintenance of existing services—notably those of advice and conciliation, as several authors in this volume have emphasised. At the same time, ACAS is also required, by the present Government, to extend its conciliation role under the statutory recognition procedure as well as administer the alternative arbitration route for those employees claiming unfair dismissal. These new functions may stretch the resources of the agency to breaking point: greater efficiency is only part of the response.

Yet despite these constraints and uncertainties, some speculation is possible in response to the question posed at the beginning of the previous paragraph.

First, ACAS's role under the recognition procedure is one which it is well-equipped to carry out by both experience and inclination. It may also keep it very busy since it is likely that union applicants for recognition will wish to exhaust the negotiated recognition possibilities before seeking the automatic and ballot routes. It may also be that more often than not employers will see advantages in voluntary outcomes. It is significant that a large number of organisations have been influenced to conclude agreements in anticipation of the implementation of the recognition procedure.[21] Furthermore, it is the clear intention of the statutory recognition procedure, and earlier policy statements, that the voluntary negotiated route should be the preferred option of unions and employers, an option which they can exercise at any stage of the procedure. Indeed, the statutory procedure may even be considered to have failed if the outcome is to take the parties primarily into CAC-imposed ballots, polarised positions and damaging litigation.

This last, doom-laden scenario may well be improbable and ACAS may be able to head it off through its early role at the negotiation stage. But though voluntarism is also available throughout it is not encouraged at the post-recognition stage. The CAC has the powers to impose a legally enforceable contract specifying the method by which collective bargaining is to be conducted[22] but this *procedural* provision does not in any way guarantee that an employer will subsequently 'bargain in good faith' on *substantive* issues towards a collective agreement. This important omission has already been discussed elsewhere by Lord McCarthy (1999) and in this volume by Hepple who sees the present provisions as introducing a potentially harmful legalism which '... may lead to new Grunwicks or worse.' (p. 158). Here the North American experience is instructive. Some 30% of successful US certifications are not

---

[21] A recent TUC Survey reports that 38% of their union sample said that the Employment Relations Act 1999 had been influential in securing new agreements (TUC, 2000).

[22] ACAS, under the Act, can also be required to consult with the Secretary of State in the specifying of a *model* method for conducting collective bargaining which the CAC must take into account although the CAC may adapt the method where it '... thinks it is appropriate to do so in the circumstances', (Employment Relations Act 1999, para. 168.)

followed by first contracts, (Friedman *et al.*, 1994). This sharply contrasts with Canada where certification is almost invariably followed by first contracts. Part of the explanation is the availability in Canada, unlike the USA, of first contract arbitration which can encourage the parties to reach post-recognition agreements or behave more reasonably to avoid prejudicing their case at arbitration (Gould, 1994, pp. 167–170). In UK conditions the improvement of the procedure through the introduction of first contract arbitration under CAC auspices is an attractive option. It could also provide an 'indispensable' opportunity for ACAS conciliation to encourage and influence a negotiated outcome (Hepple, this volume) or at least prepare the parties for a mutually acceptable arbitration award.

Second, individual conciliation has been a major area of growth since ACAS was founded. A new jurisdiction (redundancy payments) has recently been added to the list and unfair dismissal cases are likely to resume their growth following the reduction in the qualifying period for applications from two years to one. Such developments will place even more pressure on already hard-pressed conciliators in the field. The alternative, which could relieve some of the pressures on conciliators, is the voluntary arbitration procedure. But it has yet to be implemented under the Act and it is uncertain how far applicants will opt for arbitration rather than employment tribunal.[23]

Third, the Government and the Act are firmly committed to encouraging partnership at work, although in both academic and practitioner circles there is as yet no consensus as to its meaning. ACAS has some experience of promoting partnership through its advisory mediation work and this route may provide scope for ACAS to develop its proactive portfolio.

Finally, but very speculatively, the Government has firmly set its face against the EU-wide extension of national works councils. This does not necessarily exclude their future implementation given the byzantine, horse-trading machinations of the EU's decision-making procedures. The present proposals apply to workplaces of 50 or more employees which fits uneasily with the small firms' exclusion of less than 21 under the statutory recognition procedure. But such problems are resolvable. An ACAS involvement in facilitating the implementation of national works councils would not be wholly unlike its original duty to encourage collective bargaining or, at least, to provide a complement to it. That would indeed be a full turn of the wheel.

---

[23] One earlier indicator is the experience of the arbitration procedure under the national agreement in the former nationalised electricity industry. Appellants opting for arbitration following dismissal were numerous but the chair could reinstate, and often did, something which is rare at tribunal. Nor did going to arbitration preclude taking cases subsequently to tribunal. The arbitration procedure under the Act is highly unlikely to increase opportunities for reinstatement and the tribunal alternative is not subsequently available.

REFERENCES

Abbott, Brian (1998), The emergence of a new industrial relations actor: the role of the Citizens' Advice Bureaux, *Industrial Relations Journal*, **29**(4), pp. 257–269.

ACAS (1976), *First Annual Report 1975*. London: ACAS.

ACAS (1993), Annual Report.

ACAS (1999), *Annual Report 1998*. London: ACAS.

Adams, Roy J. (1999), 'Why statutory union recognition is bad labour policy: the North American experience', *Industrial Relations Journal*, **30**(2), pp. 96–100.

Brown, W., S. Deakin, M. Hudson, C. Pratten and P. Ryan (1998), *The Individualisation of Employment Contracts in Britain*. London: DTI.

Cully, Mark, Stephen Woodland, Andrew O'Reilly and Gill Dix (1999), *Britain at Work: As depicted by the 1998 Workplace Employee Relations Survey*. London and New York: Routledge.

Dubofsky, Melvyn (1994), *The State and Labor in Modern America*. Chapel Hill NC and London: University of North Carolina Press.

Employment Relations Act (1999). London: HMSO.

Freedland, M. R. (1992), 'The Role of the Department of Employment: Twenty Years of Institutional Change', in William McCarthy (ed.), *Legal Intervention in Industrial Relations: Gains and Losses*. Oxford and Cambridge, Mass: Blackwell Business.

Friedman, Sheldon, Richard W. Hurd, Rudolph A. Oswald and Ronald L. Seeber (eds.) (1994) *Restoring the Promise of American Law*. Ithaca, NY: ILR Press.

Gould, William B. (IV) (1994) *Agenda for Reform: The Future of Employment Relationships and the Law*. Cambridge, Mass: MIT Press.

Kahn Freund, Otto (1954), 'The Legal Framework', in A. D. Flanders and H. A. Clegg *The System of Industrial Relations in Great Britain*. Oxford: Blackwell.

Kelly, John (1998), *Rethinking Industrial Relations: Mobilization, Collectivism and Long Waves*. London and New York: Routledge.

Kelly, John (2000), 'Unions in the New Millennium', *Labour Research*, **89**(1), pp. 11–13.

Kelly, John and Jeremy Waddington (1995), 'New Prospects for British Labour', *Organization*, **2**(3/4), pp. 415–426.

Kessler, Sid and Gill Palmer (1996), 'The Commission on Industrial Relations in Britain, 1969–74: A Retrospective and Prospective Evaluation', *Employee Relations*, **18**(4).

McCarthy, Lord (1999), 'Fairness at Work and Trade Union Recognition: Past Comparisons and Future Problems'. London: Institute of Employment Rights.

Millward, Neil, Alex Bryson and John Forth (2000), *All Change at Work: British Employment Relations 1980–1998, as portrayed by the Workplace Industrial Relations Survey series*. London and New York: Routledge.

Mortimer, J. E. (1998), *A Life on the Left*. Sussex, The Book Guild.

Oliver, Nick and Barry Wilkinson (1992), *The Japanization of British Industry*. Oxford: Blackwell.

Towers, Brian (1997), *The Representation Gap: Change and Reform in the British and American Workplace*. Oxford: Oxford University Press.

Towers, Brian (1999a), '... the most lightly regulated labour market ...' the UK's third statutory recognition procedure, *Industrial Relations Journal*, **30**(2), pp. 82–95.

Towers, Brian (1999b), *Developing recognition and representation in the UK: how useful is the US model?* London: Institute of Employment Rights.

TUC (1999), *Trade union trends: today's trade unionists*. London: Trades Union Congress.

TUC (2000) *Trade union trends: focus on recognition*. London: Trades Union Congress.

Wood, Sir John (1992), 'Dispute Resolution: Conciliation, Mediation and Arbitration', in William McCarthy (ed.), *Legal Intervention in Industrial Relations: Gains and Losses*. Oxford and Cambridge, Mass: Blackwell Business.

Wood, S. and J. Godard (1999), 'The Statutory Union Recognition Procedure in the Employment Relations Bill: A Comparative Analysis', *British Journal of Industrial Relations*, **37**(2), pp. 203–245.

Contributors

WILLIAM BROWN is Master of Darwin College and Montague Burton Professor of Industrial Relations in the University of Cambridge. He was previously Director of the SSRC's Industrial Relations Research Unit at the University of Warwick. He has been a member of the ACAS Panel of Arbitrators for many years and is currently a member of the Council of ACAS. He is also a member of the Low Pay Commission and the Independent Chair of the Disputes Committee of the Fire Brigades National Joint Council.

LINDA DICKENS is Professor of Industrial Relations at Warwick Business School, University of Warwick and a member of its Industrial Relations Research Unit. She has been a disputes arbitrator and mediator for the Advisory Conciliation and Arbitration Committee since 1994. She was a Vice Chair of the Industrial Law Society (1992–1995) and is currently President of the British Universities Industrial Relations Association.

GILL DIX is Head of Research and Evaluation at ACAS. She has worked there since 1994, originally employed as Senior Research Officer. During 1997–1998, she was part of the research team for the 1998 Workplace Employee Relations Survey, and is a co-author of the main report from the survey. Prior to ACAS, she worked in social research at the Social Policy Research Unit at York University, at the Arts Council for England and for the National Association for the Care and Resettlement of Offenders (NACRO).

JOHN GOODMAN CBE is Frank Thomas Professor of Industrial Relations in the Manchester School of Management at UMIST, and has been head of the School for three periods. He has written extensively on industrial relations, and is an experienced arbitrator and mediator. He has been on the ACAS Panel of Arbitrators since 1979, and was an independent member of the ACAS Council (1987–1998). He was appointed a Deputy chairman of the Central Arbitration Committee in 1998.

W R HAWES headed the ACAS Secretariat and research branches between 1982 and 1998. Before that he was a Principal Research Officer in the Department of Employment responsible for industrial relations research. He was a member of the Steering Group for the three WIRS surveys as well as the recently-published WERS survey. He also co-authored the main report on the 1990 WIRS survey.

BOB HEPPLE QC is Master of Clare College and Professor of Law in the University of Cambridge. He is a barrister at Blackstone Chambers specialising in employment and discrimination law. He was formerly a Chairman of Industrial Tribunals (1974–1990) including five years in a full-time capacity, and a member of the Commission for Racial Equality. He has acted on numerous occasions as an independent expert for the ILO and the European Commission.

JOHN PURCELL is Professor of Human Resource Management at the University of Bath and Director of the Work and Employment Research Centre. He worked for the Commission on Industrial Relations (CIR) from 1969 to 1974. His first major piece of research while at Manchester Business School was an evaluation of the effectiveness of the CIR in bringing about workplace reform. Later, while at Templeton College, Oxford, he and Ian Kessler undertook a study of ACAS's advisory mediation role. His long run research interest is the link between the management of employees and organisational effectiveness. He has recently been appointed as a Deputy Chairman of the Central Arbitration Committee.

BRIAN TOWERS is a Professor of Industrial Relations at the Nottingham Business School, Nottingham Trent University and Emeritus Professor at Strathclyde University. He has long and continuing experience as an arbitrator and mediator, serving on the ACAS panel for all of its first twenty-five years. He is the Editor of the *Industrial Relations Journal* which he jointly founded with the late T.G. Whittingham in 1970 and Joint Editor, with Professor Michael Terry, of the Industrial Relations Journal European Annual Review. His research interests and publications have, for many years, been focused upon public policy towards industrial relations in Britain and the USA.

STEPHEN WOOD is Research Chair at the Institute of Work Psychology, Sheffield University, Research Associate Centre for Economic Performance, London School of Economics and Chief Editor of the *British Journal of Industrial Relations*. His current research includes human resource management practices in the UK, including their relationship to unionism; the analysis of statutory union recognition procedures in the UK and North America; a comparison of consultation across Europe in large British multinationals; and the application in US and UK organisations of family-friendly policies.

Index

ACAS (Advisory, Conciliation and Arbitration Service) ix–x, 21, 36–7, 153, 182, 194; establishment of 11–13, 34, 63; free services 12, 26; impact of change 21–8; mission statement 163, 178, 190; pressures on 81; terms of reference 26, 35
ACAS Commitment 163
acceptability of ACAS 32, 45–6, 50–1, 63, 167, 168; in arbitration 53–4
accreditation for conciliators 120
advisory booklets 24, 26
Advisory, Conciliation and Arbitration Service see ACAS
advisory mediation 23–4, 38, 165, 166–8, 177–8, 190, 192; and high commitment management 171–2, 173; in non-union firms 176
advisory role, in individual conciliation 84, 103–4, 107
advisory work 21, 22, 26–7, 164, 192
apologies, employers at employment tribunals 78
arbitration x, 5, 22, 31, 33–4, 37; as alternative to tribunals 88–9; and incomes policies 34–5, 36; and non-recognition 157–8, 161; see also voluntary arbitration
arbitration awards 53, 54, 60
arbitrators 54; qualities 53, 55; recruitment 54; for unfair dismissal claims 88–9
assisted bargaining 38, 86
ASTMS (Association of Scientific, Technical and Managerial Staffs) 133, 136
awareness and understanding of case, promotion of 100, 101, 106, 108, 117

Bain, G. 123, 135, 136
ballots: access to workers 144, 147; on industrial action 50; in union recognition cases 137–8, 142, 143, 144–5, 147
Beaumont, P.B. 61, 133, 136
Blue Circle 174–5
boards of arbitration 51, 54
breach of contract 71, 73, 156
Brown, A. 62
budget cuts xi, 22, 26, 168, 192, 193
Bullock Report on Industrial Democracy 164
Burrill, D. 47

CAC (Central Arbitration Committee) see Central Arbitration Committee
Canada 155; certification 194; Charter of Rights 158; first contract arbitration 157–8
case law, discussing 102–3, 107
CBI 127

Central Arbitration Committee (CAC) 31, 33–4, 51, 52, 181–2; and union recognition 132–3, 134, 141, 143, 144, 145, 146, 153, 156, 158, 193, 194
charging by ACAS 12, 26; for advisory mediation 165, 167; for conciliation 150
CIR (Commission on Industrial Relations) see Commission on Industrial Relations
Citizens Advice Bureaux 86
clarification of issues 101, 105
Clark, J. 88–9
Clegg, H.A. 164
closed shops 134, 147
Codes of Practice 12; on disciplinary and dismissal procedures 24, 27, 182
collective agreements 20; disclaimers 9, 10; industry-wide 3, 8, 11; voluntary dispute procedures 52
collective bargaining x, xii, 3–4, 10, 21, 145–6, 147, 153–4, 160, 189; coverage 16, 26, 136, 183–5; in Europe 154; industry-wide 4, 13, 16, 21; and pay 16–17; scope 17, 132, 145, 192; statutory duty to promote 25, 27–8, 127, 131–2, 140, 163, 164; and union recognition 16–18; and union representation 124; voluntary methods 126
collective conciliation x, xi, 11, 12, 22, 25, 26–7, 31–2, 50–1; ACAS and 22, 26, 31, 36–7, 38–9, 63–4; causes of dispute 42–4; definitions 37–8; demand and usage 39–42; failure of 47; impact of changes in law 49–50; outcome of cases 46–7; source of requests 45–6; success of 46–7
Commission for Racial Equality 25
Commission on Industrial Relations (CIR) 9, 11, 12, 124, 125, 126, 164, 181
committed conciliation 86–7
Comparability Commission 191
compulsory arbitration 133, 161, 193, 194
Concannon, H. 56
conciliation 4–5, 6, 9, 155, 160, 182; ACAS reputation 191; extending role 193; problems 10–11; in union recognition disputes 128–9, 130; see also collective conciliation; individual conciliation
Conciliation Act 1896 4–5, 33
Conciliation Managers 80
conciliators 79, 80, 89; caseloads 80–1, 84; in collective conciliation 38–9, 47; roles of 76, 77, 85, 94, 95–111, 118; types of 119–20; working styles 111–18
conferences 192
confidentiality 39; of arbitration awards 54
Conservative governments 13, 41; and arbitration 61; attitude to ACAS collective conciliation 48, 49; and trade unions 20, 184

Conway, N. 172
core-periphery employment model 169
courts 4, 9; in union recognition disputes 135, 146, 147, 156–7
Courts of Inquiry 6, 33, 52–3

Department of Employment 14, 35, 182; conciliation services 10–11; sourcebooks 15
Department of Trade and Industry 145, 146
derogability 159–60
Dickens, L. 123, 129, 130, 135
disciplinary procedures 12, 83–4
discussion of cases 75, 76, 77
dispute mediation 38, 52
disputes of interests 59, 154–6, 160
disputes of rights 59, 154–6
Donovan Commission (Royal Commission on Trade Unions and Employers' Associations) 8, 71, 94, 124, 155, 184

economic performance, high commitment management and 186, 189–90
Economic and Social Research Council (ESRC) 14
economy 7
effectiveness of ACAS 32, 46–7, 64
Ellis, W.D. 11
empathy 99
employee representation 87
employees, views of in union recognition cases 127, 129, 131, 142
employers 160; attitude to union representation 124; disclosure of information to unions 12; individual conciliation settlements 74–5, 76–7; recognition of unions 123, 129, 130–4, 146, 147, 149, 150, 160; requests from 45; resistance to third-party conciliation 32, 41, 43, 49; rights and obligations 130–1, 142, 143; visits to 24; and voluntary conciliation 149–50
employment, changing contexts 35–7
Employment Protection Act 1975 34, 35, 51, 69, 125, 126, 131, 134
Employment Relations Act 1999 xi–xii, 125, 153, 157, 185, 189; and ballots 50; and union recognition 141–50; Section 17 159
employment rights x, 69–72, 94, 187–8
Employment Rights (Dispute Resolution) Act 1998 88
employment tribunals (ETs) x, 36, 67, 68, 77, 187; arbitration as alternative 88–9; awards from 72, 77, 79, 108; caseload 69, 72–5; explaining system 77, 100, 103, 107; outcomes 78, 108–9; stopping cases going to 79; talking through perspectives of 107–8, 114; unrealistic expectations of 108–9
Employment Tribunals Act 1996 68
enforcement of union recognition 133–4, 142, 143, 146
equal opportunities 24–5
Equal Opportunities Commission 25
Equal Pay Act 1970 69

equal pay cases 74, 87
equitable remedies 157
Europe: collective agreements in 155, 159; derogability in 159; union recognition in 123; worker representation in 154
European Union, legislation of 20, 71, 72, 187
European Works Councils xii, 177
evaluation research 27, 166
expectations of parties in conciliation 108–9
explanations of the law 75, 76, 77

face saving intervention 110–11
face-to-face contact 81, 97, 101
failure to recognise unions 132–3, 145–6
Fairness at Work (White Paper) 141, 145
first contract arbitration 157, 158, 194
fitness for purpose 174
Flanders, Allan 124, 135
flexibility 98–9, 119, 120
foreign ownership, and employee relations 17

Givry, Jean de 153–4
Godard, J. 157
Goodhart, W. 157
Graham, C. 77
grievances 186; applicants wanting to express 108–9
Grunwick dispute 131, 134
Guest, D. 148–9, 168, 169, 172, 178

Head Office (ACAS) 40, 44, 49; arbitration unit 53
high commitment management (HCM) 169, 170, 172, 173, 178, 185–6; component characteristics 170; and economic performance 186, 189–90
Hilltrop, J. 47
Hoque, K. 178
HRM (Human Resource Management) 28, 36, 164, 168–70, 178, 186, 190; bundle of processes 170–1, 175, 178; and management of change 174
human capital advantage 169
Human Rights Act 158
Hunter, L. 33

impartiality 51, 67, 167, 168, 177; in individual conciliation 80, 97, 99–100, 102, 115, 117; in union recognition disputes 21, 137
imposition of method of bargaining, by CAC 143, 146, 156, 193
In Place of Strife (White Paper) 9
incomes policies 7–8, 10, 14; arbitration and 34–5
independence of ACAS 5, 34, 37, 51, 167, 168, 177
individual conciliation 9–10, 22, 24–5, 38, 93–4, 191, 194; ACAS and 67–90
individual employment rights 20, 36, 67; and work of conciliators 93–121
individualism 164, 169
industrial action 13, 18–20; absence of 4; effect of legislation 49–50; reduction in 18, 50; see also strikes

Industrial Arbitration Board 33
Industrial Courts Act 1919 4, 5
industrial relations 1–6, 7; change in 15–20
Industrial Relations Act 1971 9–10, 125, 126–7, 184
Industrial Relations Handbooks 13
industrial tribunals 9, 12, 24, 27; cost-saving in 88, 89, 90; increase in claims 19–20; *see also* employment tribunals
industry-wide bargaining 7, 8, 11, 13, 16, 21
inflation 7
influential style of conciliators 114, 115, 116, 117, 119
information 13–14
information provider role in conciliation 95, 96, 100–4
inquiries, in union recognition process 5, 6, 129–30
integrity of ACAS 99–100, 191

job satisfaction 186
joint problem-solving 23, 25, 165, 166, 177, 178
joint requests for conciliation 45
Joint Working Parties 32, 38, 166, 167, 172, 176, 190
Jones, M. 47
Justice Committee 86

Kahn Freund, O. 183
Kessler, I. 84, 165, 166, 172
Kresse, K. 105

Labour governments 11, 13; attitude to ACAS collective conciliation 49; and union recognition 124–5, 141
last offer/pendulum arbitration 55, 60
legal representation 83
Law Centres 86
legalism 155, 156–7, 158, 161, 193
Legard, R. 113, 114
legislation 49–50; change and 20–1
Lewis, J. 113, 114
Lewis, N. 77
Lewis, R. 88–9
listening, to parties in individual conciliation 97–8, 110
Lowry, P. 41, 42, 49

McCarthy, W.E.J. 11, 156, 157, 193
MacDuffie, J.P. 171
management: and advisory mediation 166, 167; attitude to conciliation 47; attitude to unions 148, 149, 186; in voluntary conciliation or recognition disputes 137
management of change 173–4
mediation 37–8, 52, 155, 160
message bearer style of conciliation 112, 114–16
Ministry of Labour 3, 33, 182, 183; conciliation service 6; contacts with informants 13
Mortimer, Jim 22, 41n, 135, 188
multi-jurisdiction claims 73

National Board for Prices and Incomes 7–8
National Economic Development Council (NEDC) 7, 191
National Labor Relations Board 158
National Union of Bank Employees 125
national works councils 160, 177, 194
neo-institutionalism 176–7
neo-unitarism 36
New Zealand Employment Contracts Act 1991 159
News International 74–5
non-IT1 cases 68, 73
non-union employers 184, 188; assistance for 84; joint working 176–7

options, exploration of 105
organisational change, promotion of 189–90
organisational effectiveness 63, 83, 165, 173, 190, 192; HRM and 169–70, 171, 172, 178
organisational process advantage 169
owner-managed firms 178–9
ownership changes, and employment relations 17

panel of arbitrators 53–4
partial recognition 138
partnership 28, 141, 148–9, 175, 185, 194
passive-forceful style of conciliation 112, 116–18
pay 42, 44, 59, 61, 145, 146
pay negotiations 5, 16; comparison between sectors 7; in private sector 17
Pay Review Bodies 61
Peccei, R. 148–9
personal contracts 147, 159
personnel management 20–1; use of external advisers 21; *see also* HRM (Human Resource Management)
personnel management advisory service 6, 12
Pfeffer, J. 170
Policy Studies Institute 14
political change, reacting to 188–9
positive clearance rates 84
pre-hearing assessments 72
prevention of disputes 83–4
Price, R. 136
principled resistance 48
private sector: collective bargaining 16, 17; foreign ownership 18
proactive conciliation 76, 86, 113
procedural agreements 3, 143, 145–6, 156
process consultancies 165, 177; *see also* advisory mediation
Pruitt, D. 105
psychological contracts 28, 172
public sector: and arbitration 61–2; collective bargaining 16; and collective conciliation 48–9
Purcell, J. 84, 165, 166, 172, 190

Quality of Working Life Agenda 170, 174–5
questionnaires, in inquiry stage of union recognition 129, 130

race discrimination 69, 75
rapport building, in conciliation 97–9, 106
reactive style of conciliation 76, 113
recommendations 54
redundancies 43, 44, 145, 177
redundancy payments 194
Redundancy Payments Act 1965 68
references 78
reflexive role in conciliation 95, 96–100
regions 165; conciliation work in 80, 81
reinstatements 78, 79–80
representation at conciliation 81, 82–3, 86, 90, 94
representation gap 28, 184
Resolving Employment Rights Disputes (Green
    Paper) 87–8
resources, reduction in 64, 89–90, 165
right to strike 134
roles involved in conciliation 111–18

sanctions for non-recognition 133, 145–6, 156,
    157, 161
satisfaction with individual conciliation 85
Scotland, collective conciliation cases 46
self-employment 18
sensitivity of conciliators 97
service sector jobs 18
settlements: in individual conciliation 68, 75–80;
    promotion of 110–11, 117
sex discrimination 75, 77, 87
Sex Discrimination Act 1975 69
Sisson, K. 178
small firms 186–7; exclusion from union
    recognition process 142, 147, 149, 194
Smith, Douglas 24n
solicitors, giving information to 100–1
specific performance 146, 147, 156, 157, 161
splitting the difference 60, 61
staffing cuts 22, 80, 193
state intervention 6, 11, 33
statistics 14
statutory duties 26, 35, 36, 163; in individual
    conciliation 67–9, 79, 85, 86–7, 94, 121; in union
    recognition 125–35, 141–50, 192, 193 (removal
    of 22, 153, 189, 190)
stop-gap settlements 32
Storey, J. 168
strikes 18–19, 50; dismissal over 134, 144, 158;
    right to 134; reduction in 36, 41; over union
    recognition 135–6; unofficial 37
substantive agreements 147
substantive role in conciliation 95, 96, 104–11
Sunday Trading Act 1994 71
support for unions, as criteria for recognition 126,
    127, 129, 134, 137, 147
surveys 14–16, 47–8; see also Workplace Industrial
    Relations Surveys (WIRS)

technical competence of conciliators 51, 167, 170,
    173
telephone x, 12, 26–7; individual conciliation by
    81, 82, 83, 90

terminology, legalistic 99
terms and conditions 42, 44, 59; as sanction for
    non-recognition 133, 157
time limits in union recognition disputes 143–4
timing of ACAS intervention 39
Trade Disputes Act 1906 2, 183
Trade Union and Labour Relations Acts 11
trade union duties, time off for 12
Trade Union Reform and Employment Rights
    Act 1993 26, 153, 189
trade unions 2, 3–4, 21, 71, 187–8; Conservative
    governments and 20, 184; and reduction in
    industrial action 50; reform of 20; requests to
    ACAS 45, 46; using individual rights 74; and
    voluntary conciliation 137; see also union
    membership; union recognition
Trades Union Congress (TUC) 41, 127–185
training, consultation over 145
training materials 39
trust 97–9, 167

unemployment, and applicants to employment
    tribunals 72
unfair dismissal 68, 72, 74, 75, 76, 77, 191, 194;
    awards for 72, 77; statutory protection
    against 8, 9; for union activities 134, 144, 158
unilateral access to arbitration 51–2, 61
union membership 13, 123, 126, 127, 136, 164;
    decline 36, 184, 188
union recognition 9, 11, 12, 41, 123; ACAS
    and 124, 125–41, 141–50, 153; and collective
    bargaining 16–18; and collective
    conciliation 42, 44; criteria for 126–8, 142, 143;
    delays in process 129–30, 144; Donovan
    Commission and 124; processes 128–30, 142–4,
    193; reduced coverage 36; voluntary
    agreements 6, 141, 148–9, 189, 193–4
union recognition disputes 153, 156–8, 177; decline
    in 139; voluntary conciliation 137–9, 149–50
United Kingdom Association of Professional
    Engineers 127
United States of America: certification in 193–4;
    mediation in 155; union recognition in 123–4
unrepresented applicants: clarifying issues for 106;
    information for 100, 103–4; role of
    conciliators 97–8, 118; satisfaction of 85

views of users 47, 62, 64, 89–90
voluntarism 5, 33, 47, 52, 124, 126, 135, 144, 148,
    160, 185
voluntary agreements 6, 9; on union
    recognition 141, 148–9, 189, 193–4
voluntary arbitration 51, 53–5, 62–3, 194;
    advantages/disadvantages 59–60; as alternative
    to tribunals 88–9; definitions 51–3; loss of
    control in 59, 60, 63; public sector and 61–2;
    subjects of 59; trends in ACAS caseload 56–8;
    user surveys 62
voluntary procedure for union recognition 126,
    137–41, 148–9, 150, 193

wage drift 8
Wages Act 1986 71, 74
Wages Councils 12, 71
Wedderburn, K.W.W. 8, 135, 159
Whitley, J.H., Committee on Relations between
    Employers and Employees 183
Wilson, Sir Roy 53
winning confidence of parties 97–9
women, employment of 18
Wood, S. 157, 171

Work Research Unit 24, 165, 168, 174–5, 190
worker participation 12
Working Time Directive 177
Workplace Industrial Relations Surveys (WIRS)
    1, 18, 184; WERS 1998 147, 178, 185, 186
workplace performance 185–7
workshops, in advisory mediation 166, 176, 190

Youndt, M. 171

Printed in the United Kingdom
by Lightning Source UK Ltd.
134261UK00001B/275-322/P